**BARRON'S
BUSINESS
LIBRARY**

Human Resources

Third Edition

Richard G. Renckly, SPHR
Senior Professional in Human Resources

BARRON'S

All inquiries should be addressed to:
Barron's Educational Series, Inc.
250 Wireless Boulevard
Hauppauge, NY 11788
www.barronseduc.com

Library of Congress Catalog Card Number 2010020870

ISBN-13: 978-0-7641-4318-2
ISBN-10: 0-7641-4318-2

Library of Congress Cataloging-in-Publication Data

Renckly, Richard G.
   Human Resources/Richard G. Renckly.—3rd ed.
      p. cm.—(Barron's business library)
   Includes bibliographical references and index.
   ISBN-13: 978-0-7641-4318-2
   ISBN-10: 0-7641-4318-2
  1. Personnel management. I. Title.
   HF5549.R4594 2010
   658.3—dc22   2010020870

PRINTED IN THE UNITED STATES OF AMERICA

987654321

Contents

Preface

"The conceptions by the light of which men will judge our own ideas in a thousand years—or perhaps even in fifty years—are beyond our guess. If a library of the year 3000 came into our hands today, we could not understand its contents. How should we consciously determine a future which is, by its very nature, beyond our comprehension? Such presumption reveals only the narrowness of an outlook uninformed by humility."

Professor Friedrich Hayek quoting Michael Polanyi

New personnel managers, human resources managers, directors, or vice presidents of human resources will find no scarcity of books, magazine articles, videos, conferences, and seminars on the subject of how to be successful in human resources. They will discover that there is much in the literature regarding the organization and maintenance of a personnel/human resources operation within a corporate structure. A great deal of that information will include statistical and technical charts, graphs, matrices, and other helpful data explaining the details of operations, staffing, budgeting, compensation, employment, personnel relations, handling human capital, and practically any other management function. And I definitely urge new HR managers to take full advantage of every opportunity to read and study the data most closely related and applicable to their corporate situation.

Although you will want to keep up with new state-of-the-art developments and ideas in our chosen field, you will undoubtedly not have the time or inclination to read and check into anything but a fraction of the material written about business management in general and personnel management in particular.

So, if you begin to feel overwhelmed in terms of complex or conflicting expert recommendations, and theories of human resources management, in particular, keep in mind some of the basic thoughts and ideas offered in this book as they relate to employees, AKA *people*:

1) People always have been, are, and always will be the most important and valuable asset any corporation could ever hope to have.
2) Despite everything you may read and hear in our modern era of rights rather than responsibilities, the vast majority of people (employees, customers, vendors, suppliers, and outside agencies) will respond and react favorably to any company management that genuinely treats them with dignity and respect.

3) When employees are regularly informed by management about the status of the business relating to profits, losses, problems, new expansions, hard times—or any other matter concerning their company, they consider themselves part of the team, and communication then flows rapidly up as well as down. Also, in such companies, employee loyalty is just about assured, even in difficult economic times when reductions in the work force are unavoidable, since employees will be confident their management has done its best to keep layoffs to an absolute minimum.

4) Employees always expect equity and fairness from their employer in all aspects of business including wages, promotion, and discipline, as well as in work rules and working conditions. Companies can always gain the trust of employees when they sincerely try to *earn* it.

5) The personnel or human resources manager can and must become one of the most valuable members of the management team by doing everything possible to ensure that the above recommendations and philosophies become a basic part of company culture. If these commitments are made and kept, a company is almost always guaranteed to be successful, since its most important asset and the company now have a common cause and can merge into one unbeatable team.

The era of the employee, the customer—the "person"—is now, and promises to continue as such for many years into the future. You are privileged to deal with the challenge of people. You have a serious responsibility to make sure to the best of your ability that your top management is fully aware that *the company that handles this asset properly is the company that prospers and survives*.

With this reference to the real-life "in-the-trenches" human resources person, I would like to open this book with the words of Theodore Roosevelt in 1910, as valid today as they were then:

It is not the critic who counts, not the man who points out how the strong man stumbles, or where the doer of deeds could have done them better. The credit belongs to the man who is actually in the arena, whose face is marred by dust and sweat and blood; who strives valiantly; who errs, and comes short again and again (but)...who knows the great enthusiasms, the great devotions, who spends himself in a worthy cause; who at the best knows in the end the triumph of high achievement, and who at the worst if he fails, at least fails while daring greatly, so that his place shall never be with those cold and timid souls who know neither victory or defeat.

Acknowledgments

No man is an island. Similarly, authors cannot claim complete originality and total credit for what they think, organize, write, edit, and correct. Even when the first creative idea reveals itself to the author, selecting the ground, planting the seed, nurturing, feeding, and maintaining the embryonic idea is often (to one degree or another) the result of the efforts of others who may have an instinctive belief in the value and worth of the author's original concept.

In the case of this book, the author, having had quite a few years of experience in the personnel/human resources field, has seen a myriad of positive changes and new developments in the profession. There are probably any number of others who can claim the same length of experience, but I am convinced that not many could have had the same amount of encouragement, guidance, cooperation, and enthusiasm shown to me in the course of making this book a reality.

In all truth and fairness, I first must mention my dear wife Mary Elizabeth, whose patience and understanding in enduring many lonely hours enabled me to spend those hours in planning, researching, and writing my work. Her encouragement, praise (when merited), and candid critiquing of the book were all absolutely invaluable in bringing it to life originally, as well as in preparing this second edition.

My mentor, Alan Weinstein, a friend and business associate, was extremely instrumental and encouraging on so many occasions in recommending to me which path to take and how to stay with it once the choice was made. Alan, himself an accomplished author and editor, was my sounding board for many important aspects of the book and especially in helping to make it acceptable for publication. I have no idea of how any comments of mine may have influenced his own new book (if at all), but I cannot measure the importance of his advice and encouragement to me regarding my own.

Others who must be mentioned include my ever-supportive family, especially my son Michael as well as my son-in-law Dave Cameron, both of whom, together with another son Tom, constituted my inexhaustible pool of knowledge and information relating to electronic communication, particularly the personal computer, the Internet, and the World Wide Web. Their skills and patient cooperation would be impossible to overstress. The advice and counsel of friend and attorney Brad Gardner were especially meaningful and deeply appreciated. Friends and business associates Rich Lee, Neil Dempster, and Erv Spille graciously provided necessary support and buoyancy.

A former employer, U-Haul International, must also be recognized for its most cooperative attitude in allowing me to draw on some of its HR forms and policies for inclusion in this work. Retired U-Haul Senior Executive Vice President John M. Dodds gave unceasing encouragement and support to me as the book was being written, as well as later. U-Haul Executive Vice President, the late Harry B. DeShong, was always most helpful and cooperative. My former business associates, Marti Patton and Bob Platek, gave unselfishly of many hours of their own time in helping to prepare the original manuscript and advising on information systems. Liz Jolly, Debbie Tooker, and Connie Bartlett were also of great assistance in gathering and providing information to me. At the time, these folks were all members of the U-Haul International Human Resources department, the most capable and enthusiastic group of HR professionals it has ever been my pleasure to be associated with. I must also mention that this third edition is especially indebted to my son Drew, as well as current U-Haulers, HR Vice President James "Butch" Greer, Angie DeWinter, "Sam" Brown, Jacque Owens, and Connie Bartlett.

As with any book or work of this scope, I have probably omitted some people I should have acknowledged. If so, it is purely unintentional and my thanks for their help is extended to them with the same sincerity as for those mentioned.

Finally, although no names are mentioned in this book, I find no fault with and mean no disrespect to any former subordinate, peer, or superior whose ideas, philosophy, or management style may be referred to in the text. I learned **much** from each of these associations and would be the last to criticize them for "...always following a sensible strategy for getting along in the kind of world they think they live in."

RGR
2010

The Structure of Human Resources

INTRODUCTION AND MAIN POINTS

This chapter examines the structure of the human resources function. To demonstrate how widely the structure can vary, three examples of organizational charts from variously sized organizations are included. The rest of the chapter describes the flow of human resources operations to illustrate HR's key areas of responsibility. The description may be considered a cross-section of the principal, typical functional elements found in the modern, proactive human resources department.

After you have studied the materials in this chapter:

■ You will be aware of the different areas of responsibility that comprise the structure of a typical human resources department.

■ You will know that there can be great variety in the structure of the human resources function.

■ You will understand the internal relationships of different functions within a human resources department.

STRUCTURE IS BASED ON FUNCTION

In this chapter, we will examine the structure of a typical human resources department. We know that not every company will be large enough to have either a separate human resources department or one containing all of the personnel functions or areas of responsibility that are mentioned here and described in greater detail in following chapters. Even some of the largest corporations are not necessarily structured in the same manner as we have described below. Nevertheless, similarities exist among organizations and thus it is possible to show the essential functions in which every human resources department should be involved. For a suggested organization of three different structures of the human resources function, see Tables 1-1, 1-2, and 1-3.

TABLE 1-1
Human Resources Organizational Chart
(Example for organization with 10,000+ employees)

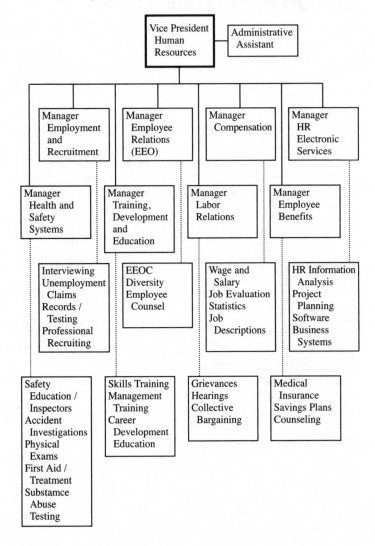

TABLE 1-2
Human Resources Organizational Chart
(Example for organization with 500–1,000 employees)

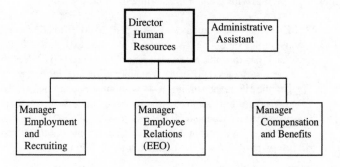

TABLE 1-3
Human Resources Organizational Chart
(Example for organization with 25–100 employees)

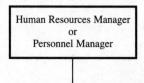

Job may include a wide variety of other duties in addition to HR, including the supervision of the bookkeeping, payroll, hiring, sales, and clerical functions, and the personnel who perform them.

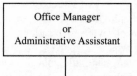

In smaller companies, the office manager may direct other office employees in the performance of HR as well as other functions mentioned above. The owner of the company may also reserve these responsiblities for himself or herself. The advantages of such flexibility often disappear, however, as companies grow in size and revenue.

HUMAN RESOURCES' TYPICAL AREAS OF RESPONSIBILITY

A brief description of the flow of human resources operations through the department might help to illustrate HR's key responsibilities and how they interact with the rest of the organization.

> **NOTE:** It must be emphasized here that the HR functions and responsibilities set out below, although intended to describe duties performed in companies having the luxury of their own HR departments, are nonetheless applicable and important in any size company. Whether the HR responsibility rests with the company owner, the office manager, administrative assistant, accounting clerk, or others (as is usually the case in small HR environments), the HR responsibility is often an extra hat that people need to wear, but they must still be aware of current HR methodology and regulations.

Compensation

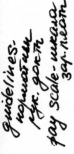

To begin with, in order to attract competent job candidates, as well as to retain current employees, it is the responsibility of the human resources compensation staff to establish proper wage and salary guidelines, pay scales, and other compensation programs, including well-designed employee benefit packages and strategies. Thus the employment department, armed with solid, competitive wage and salary scales and attractive benefits, can better fulfill its responsibility of recruiting and hiring the competent employees every company needs to succeed and survive.

Employment

The human resources employment staff begins its work by designing and developing policies, procedures, and programs to recruit the most able and qualified applicants available for the job openings the company is attempting to fill. It then begins the actual recruiting process by employing a wide variety of sources including the Internet, media advertising, private employment agencies, state employment services, schools, churches, local civic organizations, and chambers of commerce, and by using whatever sources are available in order to find and attract the most qualified individuals for the company.

Once sufficient applicants are found, employment then begins the task of screening, interviewing, and testing candidates (including coordination of preemployment drug testing programs, where applicable), and referring the best of these to appropriate line or staff managers for further interviewing prior to the final hiring decision being made.

In some organizations, the human resources department also makes the hiring decision and sends the applicant to work in the department where the job opening exists. This is especially true when production or assembly line job openings are being filled. In most cases, however, managers and supervisors usually prefer to personally select the employees who will be working in their departments. Whatever procedure applies to or works best for your company should be the preferred method.

Having found the most capable people available to fill your job openings, you must now be in a position to offer them a salary or wage commensurate with the duties and responsibilities of the position, and one that is generally competitive with comparable job openings at other companies in the local area. If the successful applicant accepts the job at the salary offered, he or she now joins the company as a bona fide employee (system member, associate, or whatever the company's nomenclature might be).

bona fide (in good faith) — good, good, instrument

Training

The human resources training section now begins its function of providing whatever training and orientation the new employees might need in order to make certain that they are well equipped to perform their new duties, and that they have some idea of the history and policies as well as the culture of the company.

The training group also performs the functions of designing and implementing management training programs in which new recruits, as well as current employees, may be involved.

Employee Relations

As some of the new system members eventually find their way into management positions, the human resources employee relations staff will undoubtedly be of assistance in providing guidance and counsel to them on discrimination matters as well as on other human relations opportunities or challenges. These concerns are ever present in today's sensitive business environment, and they promise to become even more evident in the future.

Benefits Staff

The human resources benefits staff is charged with the responsibility of administering, recommending, and monitoring all phases of the company's employee benefits program. Group insurance plans, paid time off (vacations, holidays), retirement programs, service awards, and a host of other benefit features are all within the scope of the HR benefits function.

One of the more challenging areas of this group's duties is to ensure that existing retirement programs are properly designed, developed, managed, and communicated to participants, and that they fit in with the overall objectives, strategies, and philosophy of the company.

They are also responsible for presenting and recommending tax-favored retirement programs such as 401(k)s, Individual Retirement Accounts (IRAs), and other tax-deferred and government-backed savings plans, as well as perhaps a well-designed and implemented Employee Stock Ownership Plan (ESOP). Such savings programs are designed to assist these new hires as well as all of the current, eligible employees, to be able to enjoy a comfortable retirement at the end of their career and service with the organization.

The human resources benefits group should also be committed to rendering every assistance possible by answering employee questions and providing and explaining benefit policies. This same courtesy, of course, should also be shown retired employees. By so doing, the company not only conveys its wishes for their happy and successful retirement, but also lets them know that they are still considered members of the organization family.

CHAPTER PERSPECTIVE
This chapter examined the internal structure of a typical human resources department by tracking the flow of its operations, from advertising a job and hiring a new employee to the employee's promotion, retirement, and beyond.

Three examples of organizational charts from differently structured organizations were included.

The Human Resources Function

INTRODUCTION AND MAIN POINTS

This chapter defines and then illustrates through numerous examples the function of the personnel or human resources department within an organization. When and how the HR department should become involved in employee problems or complaints is delineated.

Here we describe the tools and techniques of the HR profession in resolving employee problems or complaints, and how they are best used in specific cases. In all cases, however, an attentive and helpful manner and good listening skills on the part of the HR staff are stressed.

The conditions that give rise to a union drive are described. The rights of organized labor, as guaranteed by the National Labor Relations Act, are explained. Possible outcomes of a representation election are discussed.

This chapter stresses that the human resources focus remains a genuine concern for employee welfare and application of the People Principle, whether or not the employees are represented by a union.

After studying the material in this chapter:

■ You will learn what the function of the human resources department is.

■ You will gain an overview of the proper procedures for investigating and resolving an employee problem or complaint.

■ You will become aware of the underlying causes of a union drive.

■ You will understand the importance of human resources' role in reassuring employees that management is genuinely concerned with their welfare.

■ You will learn about the application of the People Principle in all situations.

THE HUMAN RESOURCES FUNCTION DEFINED

The primary function of the human resources (HR) department is:

■ to essentially establish, develop, maintain, and communicate personnel policies to the entire company;

■ to represent, help, advise, and consult with the employees of the organization; and

■ to add value and increase the organization's competitiveness.

At the same time, the human resources staff members must never forget that they are to represent first, last, and always, the best interests of their employer—the top management of the corporation.

While on the surface it may seem to be a conflict to claim it represents both the employee and employer equally well and at the same time, the HR staff must, nonetheless, acquire this highly complex and technical skill. It is the hallmark of the well-run and more qualified human resources department.

EMPLOYEE RELATIONS

From Personnel to Human Resources

Most companies, large or small, normally include in their table of organization a department known as "personnel." In more recent years, this department's name has evolved into "human resources." Many experienced people in this field resisted the term human resources, because they felt that human beings should not be categorized as mere resources, especially if they are a company's most important asset. Eventually, however, the term became generally accepted in the industry without really changing the primary objective of all such departments, namely, serving their most important and special clients—the employees of the organization.

Industrial Relations Department Defined

The personnel principles stated in this work generally apply equally well in a unionized as well as nonunionized corporate setting; however, in some unionized companies, the industrial relations function may either be a component part of the human resources operation or a stand-alone department. For purposes of this book, we will assume that industrial relations staffs that deal directly with union contract matters are separate and distinct from the human resources function, in which case the industrial relations department is the sole and exclusive representative of management, and not of those employees who may be union members.

THE HUMAN RESOURCES DEPARTMENT AS NEUTRAL GROUND

The employees of the company, in turn, should regard the human resources department as neutral and impartial ground where they can

■ take their problems or complaints;

■ expect help, information, and advice; and

■ certainly anticipate a fair and impartial hearing, and assume an environment of trust and confidentiality.

Successful personnel or human resources managers, through their staff, create the atmosphere in which this will happen.

THE CHAIN OF COMMAND

It is also most important to know and remember that the primary responsibility for resolving employee complaints and grievances lies with the immediate supervisor. No human resources department has the time or inclination to hear, investigate, and resolve every problem that arises in day-to-day operations, nor should it! The immediate boss—manager, supervisor, or working leader—is by far the best first line of defense in resolving personnel problems, and thereby protecting the company's best interests.

In the event, however, that the problem situation is not resolved at the immediate supervisor stage, it should then be referred to the next level of supervision, and ultimately up the chain of command to the top of the organization, if necessary. Again, depending on how company personnel policy is structured, the human resources department must be brought into the picture by management. Often, the employees involved will not wait for upper management intervention but, assuming the human resources staff has created the proper climate or environment of listening and concern, employees will ask human resources to work with them.

Assuming that the human resources department is involved, we will examine some of the tactics and strategies the HR professional should and should not use in attempting to resolve problems successfully.

DEALING WITH PROBLEMS EFFECTIVELY

Avoid the Quick Draw

If you are currently in human resources or have had experience in the HR field, you may have known staff members who could be overly influenced by an employee complaining about his or her supervisor. In their righteous indignation, and without bothering to thoroughly check out the employee's complaint or quarrel with the manager or supervisor involved, they may make snap judgments based solely on the employee's input. Thus, the supervisor is judged guilty without benefit of hearing or trial. The old expression about ". . . two sides to every story" certainly applies here.

Get Both Sides of the Story

About 99 percent—or perhaps even more—of employee complaints or problem situations are never totally one-sided. In most cases, the truth lies somewhere between the contentions of both parties in the nebulous "gray" area. For example, an employee may be upset because the manager allegedly reneged on a promised wage increase. The manager may, perhaps, claim the employee did not accomplish his or her goals, such as meeting expected performance standards as previously agreed upon, and is therefore not deserving of an increase.

The skilled professional always looks for and considers facts on both sides of the story. The most important responsibility you as a personnel professional have when employee problem situations are referred to your attention is to make sure you have absolutely *all* of the facts you can possibly get your hands on before you make any decision or recommendation to the personnel or human resources manager, or to the operating manager.

The Personnel File

Most companies, even the smallest ones, maintain what is known as a personnel file. Such a file may consist of
- an elaborate, titled folder of documents and data; or
- a manual, even handwritten, employee work history card; or
- an on-line computer listing of the person's work history and employment record with the company.
- HR must also keep in mind the special treatment of employees' medical information, including confidentiality and restricted access based on the recent Genetics Information Nondiscrimination Act (GINA), which increases employers' responsibilities in this area. (See discussion of GINA on page 192.)

No matter what your format may be, you will find that the number one, most helpful, and just about the most essential tool you can have for any and all aspects of your personnel job is the personnel files of the employees. It matters not how well you *think* you know your employees, including the department where they work, their rate of pay, date of last increase, and so forth; you must have the personnel record in front of you before you even begin your research. And, if available, the same applies to personnel files and records of employees who may no longer be employed with the company but who may in some way be involved in the case or problem at hand.

First you must satisfy yourself that you know
- *who* the person or persons are,
- *what* their jobs are,
- *where* they work, and
- *when* they were hired, transferred, promoted, rehired, and so on.

All this information is indicated in personnel files and records. Then the next questions are:
- *Why* are we having a problem?
- *How* can we resolve it?

It is hoped that the solution will be to everyone's satisfaction—or nearly so.

Given the importance of the personnel file, never let anyone talk you into letting the personnel files and records be stored, warehoused, or kept in any way outside of your HR department. You may be advised that, since they are just another type of record, they should more properly be kept in the corporate records area or department together with other company statements, accounts, contracts, or payroll logs. Not so! From the standpoint of confidentiality, convenience, and quick and after-hours accessibility, the personnel files are *not* run-of-the-mill documents or data and they belong in the human resources department! Even if you input and maintain these files in your computer database, or keep them on microfiche or microfilm, you will still find value in having hard copies available within your department, or at least stored under your immediate access and control.

Talking with People

Before you make any judgments or decisions, of course, it might be a good idea to talk with several people, such as the complaining party or parties, and all supervisors involved, as well as any witnesses, coworkers, or other persons who might possibly have some knowledge of the situation, the person(s) in question, and the events leading up to the present impasse.

The Investigation

Once you've assembled and studied all the facts, you're now finally in a position to begin the investigation. As described at the beginning of this chapter, you, as a human resources manager or specialist, represent your company or corporation first and foremost, but you must also fill the role of employee representative to assure equity to the individual. By maintaining this balance, you are truly performing your job, benefiting your company's reputation, and undoubtedly adding to its bottom line.

Resolution of the Problem

When the investigation reveals that an understandable disagreement or impasse exists, it may mean that an honest mistake was made between supervisor and employee; therefore, some kind of compromise or settlement is probably in order. In the case of legal actions involving charges of discrimination or wrongful termination, for example, the experienced human resources staff member knows that sometimes a modest financial settlement makes sense. This is especially appropriate if the company's position has some weaknesses and the administrative or legal costs of defending it in the future are anticipated to be far greater than any settlement amount that may be involved. In some situations, the company may also want to consider resorting to private or governmental arbitration or mediation services, depending on the scope of the charges and the risks involved.

It is most important to know when to settle or to comply with the employee's request and when it is wiser to fight for and to defend the company's position to the limit. In the latter event, you must really feel that the company has a strong case and that the manager or supervisor involved acted in good faith. When the company's position is valid, refusing to concede or to settle an issue for money almost always sends the right signal to other potential claimants that here is a company that will *not* give in under pressure if it feels it's on solid ground.

As a final step in "wrapping up" the case after a settlement or decision has been reached, it would be advisable for HR to follow up with the employee(s) involved to ensure that the problem has been resolved and also that no form of retaliation has occurred.

Listening Skills

Regardless of the circumstances, good listening skills are most important and should never be underrated. For instance, when employees or their spouses persist in calling every company official from the chairman of the board on down in order to right a perceived grievance, the best response may be to simply listen to what they have to say. Sometimes these complaints have merit, but other times people just want someone to listen to them and they may be satisfied to have a willing ear. Often, the payment of as little as one week's additional (severance) pay or even a neutral reference to employment inquiries from outside companies will remedy what initially sounded like a serious complaint against the company. Similarly, if complaints from customers are listened to with the same sense of helpful attention and respect, customers will often express satisfaction that a representative of the company took the time to listen to them and at least tried to help them with their problem or complaint. While employees are the company's most valuable asset, customers pay their salaries and, therefore, merit the utmost consideration and attention.

In some cases, had the employees with complaints been handled by their immediate or first-line supervision with the attention and dignity due to a company's most important asset, no further time-consuming phone calls up the chain of command or to human resources might have been necessary.

THE UNION CONNECTION

We will later discuss (in Chapter 3 and elsewhere) the value and importance of an employee to a company. Therefore, it must be stressed that it becomes one of the primary functions of the human resources department to play a major role in reassuring employees of management's concern for equity and fairness in all employee relations matters—assuming such concern does in fact really exist!

Failure to Reassure Employees of Equity

If human resources fails in this effort, it is highly likely in the nonunion company that employees will at some point turn to a union with the frequently mistaken hope that this third party will represent their best interests to their employer. More often than not, if the general attitude of a company toward its people is one of mere tolerance, or if employees are viewed by top management as simply necessary overhead, almost any union has a better-than-average chance of winning a representation election by convincing a majority of people in the bargaining unit just how much improved their wages, benefits, and job security will become when they are represented by the union.

In addition, depending on how much or how little regard was paid to the employees by management before the union arrived, union allies within employee ranks will make every effort to convince their co-workers how improved their lives will be when they are represented by Local 754 of the Amalgamated Ironworkers of America, the Machinists Union, or the Food and Commercial Workers of America.

Intimidating Managers, Supervisors, or Leaders

Allowing for the inevitable exceptions to the rule, experienced HR and labor relations managers would probably agree that the root cause of a union drive is not necessarily issues over wages or benefits. Many nonunion companies have found that the reason they have a letter or phone call from a union claiming to have sufficient authorization cards signed by company employees to represent them is in no way related to increased compensation or benefits. It is, in fact, a result of the unfeeling, intimidating management style of a particular manager, supervisor, or even working leader.

This lack of considerate and decent treatment of people is assumed to be condoned by top management or ownership of the company, inasmuch as nothing ever changes and no one up the line seems to care.

Such union drives are often instigated by one employee or a small group of employees who have found working for such an individual simply intolerable. When people find themselves working for a tyrant with no hope whatever of relief or redress, including going to higher company authority, they will inevitably go to an outside third party (such as a union), to help them. At this point, the company's battle is totally uphill, and what could have been a relatively small and inexpensive ounce of prevention relating to employee respect and consideration, now becomes a tidal wave of resistance by employees to all of management's efforts to convince them that "we're a team, and we want you to believe we really do care about you!"

It is also very interesting to predict as well as to observe how a company's "take-'em-for-granted" attitude, philosophy, or culture suddenly takes on a new dimension and reverses its field at the first hint of union presence or activity. Management professes to be aghast as well as deeply shocked and hurt to think that its work force did not first bring their complaints or problems to their supervisor or to their boss's boss, or, as a last resort, to the office of the chairman of the board whose door has been perpetually open. To make matters worse, the human resources staff, as well as any labor lawyers or consultants on the scene, will now dutifully remind the chairman that all activities must be in accordance with provisions of the National Labor Relations Act.

The National Labor Relations Act

Under the provisions of this act, the company's management
- can make no **T**hreats of retaliation against employees for union interest;
- cannot **I**nterrogate employees about their union views;
- cannot **P**romise increased wages, benefits, or better working conditions; and
- cannot undertake **S**urveillance of union activities, including watching who goes in and out of the union hall or spying on union/employee meetings.

The use of any of these unlawful practices, which comprise the familiar **TIPS** acronym, could result in the National Labor Relations Board (NLRB) charging the company with an unfair labor practice. In flagrant cases, such a charge might even mean automatic certification of the union by the board as representative of the employees without the formality of a secret-ballot election. Thus, the chairman's hands are effectively tied so that it may even now be too late to try to convince people that the corporation—and particularly the chair—has always listened to their problems, and has certainly always tried to provide them with competitive wages, generous benefits, and good working conditions.

The Representation Election

The Captive Audience Doctrine. Under the so-called Captive Audience Doctrine, employers may speak to their employees in a mass meeting on company time about the union campaign, and may require employees to attend the meeting. A union may not do the same on company time, and must limit its campaigning to employees' homes and to distributing literature and answering employee questions and inquiries.

The 24-Hour Rule. The general exception to the captive audience doctrine is known as the *24-hour rule*. The NLRB will set aside a representation election if an employer gives a speech to a mass employee audience on company time within the 24-hour period just prior to the election. The employer may *start* a meeting prior to the period but must *complete* his or her speech *before* the 24-hour period begins. Even if it runs a few minutes into the 24-hour period, the board will set aside the election and, due to precedent, will make no exceptions. (This rule does not include casual one-on-one or truly voluntary meetings with employees.)

This speech which many company CEOs will try to give as close to the restricted deadline as possible (but not beyond it), has come to be known as the 24-hour speech, and in most instances would probably sound something like the following.

My Fellow Workers:
You will very soon have the opportunity to vote on whether or not you want union representation.

Our management doesn't want a union, and we believe that a majority of you feel the same—but it's your vote that will decide this. Both you and our management will be bound by the choice you and your fellow workers make tomorrow.

In its campaign, the union has "pulled out all the stops," since it has nothing to lose and everything to gain. The union has made wild promises; the union has used false figures and untrue rumors to mislead you and to tear down our management; and the union has threatened and pressured our workers to try and prevent those who don't want this union from having their say. In short, the union has done anything to get your vote.

Our management has not made a single promise or uttered a single threat. What we have done is try to give you straightforward answers and honest facts. We believe that the facts can lead to only one decision—no union here!

The decision you make tomorrow is your decision. This is the way it must be because you are the ones who will be most affected.

The union can only gain, through your dues, if you vote it in. If the union loses, it will simply try to organize at some other company.

Our management will operate, union or no union. We are not concerned with any strike threat. We are not worried about union pressure forcing an increase in our costs. We would deal with this union, as the representative of our family members, in the same way we deal with any outsider: on a cold, hard impersonal basis. There would not be and could not be consideration for the individual. We would be buying labor through a labor broker, a union, and we would pay only competitive prices for it.

But where do you stand? You would be bound by any contract the union negotiated, whether it was for your best interest or not. You would be pressured to join the union and pay dues. You would be subject to possible strike action, and the trouble and violence that goes with strikes, not to mention your personal loss of wages and other problems. You would face the day-to-day bickering and backbiting that goes with the union and its supporters. You would have to deal with two bosses—the union and its stewards and your supervisor.

It's your job. It's your working conditions. It's your decision.

Albert B. Collins
Chairman of the Board and CEO
ABC Company

A very stirring and emotional appeal indeed, but in most cases, probably just a bit overdue, and a perfect illustration of too little, too late! In many cases, it is probably years too late.

If by some serendipitous turn of events the company does succeed in obtaining even a simple majority of votes in its favor, the union attempt is thwarted for at least another year, in accordance with the National Labor Relations Act. The chairman and company management breathe a long sigh of relief and, though some tangible improvements in employee/employer relations will usually occur for the moment, chances are good that before too long *business as usual* will prevail, memories will become faded and dim, and employees will find themselves in the same environment that created the union interest in the first place.

Now let's also consider the scenario where employees, despite all of management's pleas, veiled promises, and rosy portraits of the future, still feel they want the Amalgamated Clerks, Ironworkers, or some other labor organization to represent them and they vote them in accordingly. We now have a new ballgame, especially in the case of a previously all nonunion company. The employees have mandated the union to help change and improve real or perceived miserable working conditions, low wages, or benefits. In point of fact, however, the benefit they probably want most is to have their management pay some attention to them and to show them the care and respect they could and should have long before the day a union came on the scene. But now the opportunity is lost, and a union from here on in becomes a part of everyday corporate life. Thus, another company is unionized, and the oft-heard statement that the company that gets a union deserves one again proves to be true.

A GENUINE CONCERN FOR EMPLOYEES' WELFARE

The principle of showing respect toward employees and allowing them dignity also applies whether a company has just acquired a union, has had one for 20 years, or perhaps has no union at all. In human resources, you are still dealing with people either directly or through a third party, and they are still the company's most important asset. Even if a union is well entrenched, with apparently little or no chance of decertification, employees will still respond favorably to a management that demonstrates a genuine concern for their welfare.

Apply the People Principle

If the People Principle is really properly understood and applied, even in a unionized situation you will find there are fewer (if any) strikes, jurisdictional disputes, boycotts, work stoppages, and similar work actions. This is because the majority of employees truly believe and want to believe that "...this is a pretty good place to work...," and that their company considers them something more than a necessary evil or overhead item. Keep in mind that this principle operates the same, regardless of whether you do or do not operate in a union environment!

CHAPTER PERSPECTIVE

This chapter focused on the functions of the personnel or human resources department: The department must maintain fairness to individual employees while simultaneously representing the interests of the company's management. Also, on a day-to-day basis, the department is responsible for establishing, maintaining, and communicating personnel policies to the entire company. In addition, adding value and increasing the organization's competitiveness also becomes one of the primary responsibilities of the HR professional.

We also discussed how employee problems or complaints are properly routed though an organization, how an investigation of a problem is fairly conducted, and how problems and complaints can be resolved.

The origins and development of a union drive were described in relation to the HR function in reassuring management's concern for equity and fairness in all employee relations.

Finally, the chapter stressed the importance of the People Principle, treating employees with respect and allowing them dignity in union or nonunion situations.

An Organization's Most Important Asset

3

INTRODUCTION AND MAIN POINTS

This chapter emphasizes an organization's most important asset: its employees.

Through positive and negative examples from the American business community, the effects of respect and loyalty in human relations are explored.

The employee relations of a large, nonunionized, Fortune 1000 corporation are profiled as a model of success.

The idea of individuals within companies and of companies within society "making their own personnel records" through their performance is developed.

The chapter closes with the practical need for establishing the personnel or human resources function to represent the interests of all employees, including management.

After studying the material in this chapter:

▬ You will know why the success of a company is dependent upon its people.

▬ You will be able to recognize the values of top management that produce positive results for companies, as well as the opposite.

▬ You will understand the need for a personnel or human resources function in any size organization as a means of maintaining a company's most important asset.

THE VALUE OF PEOPLE

In newspapers, magazines, and business journals, on television, at seminars, in boardrooms, and around office water coolers, the word is out: Employee loyalty to companies is no more, and the trade-off of loyalty for job security has gone the way of the slide rule, typewriter, and adding machine. Even as layoffs, downsizing, restructuring, reengineering, and job elimination still dominate many areas of the current corporate business scene, in the typical bust/boom cycle, the country slowly emerges from a recession and profits in many companies look moderate to good as they steadily improve. So how important can loyalty to an employer really be with results like that to reinforce the opinions of so many business analysts and experts? One certainly would have an uphill battle refuting the effectiveness of these practices, especially in the short run.

The really savvy companies, large and small, recognize that people have never been more important to business success than they are today. Every business depends upon its employees for tomorrow as surely as it does for today. Getting and keeping the best will be a priority for every employer who expects to have any chance of competitive survival, and this book tells the decision makers just how to do it.

The large companies of today were once small organizations with some very good personnel. When these businesses were small, they genuinely believed in and practiced the principle of primary reliance on their employees for the success of the corporation. But as they grew larger, they published bigger and better recruiting brochures, annual reports, and operating statements, and began to forget that their people brought them to where they were and would take them to where they're going. Many of those growing businesses who forgot to practice the principle of primary reliance on their employees no longer exist. But now let's look at two examples of modern companies who do rely on their most important asset.

Lincoln Electric Company

One major and outstanding example of a company that has *always* considered employees its most valuable asset is the Lincoln Electric Company of Cleveland, Ohio. This large, progressive corporation is a nonunion manufacturing plant founded over 100 years ago. It is the world leader in the design, development, and manufacture of arc-welding products, robotic arc-welding systems, and plasma and oxyfuel cutting equipment. Good piecework rates, annual multi-million-dollar bonus programs, and a guaranteed employment policy are a few of the reasons Lincoln can boast of superb quality products, and a healthy pool of job applicants for as far back as anyone can remember. However, the genuine attention and concern of top management for its employees has to be the primary reason for Lincoln's success, including its reputation for recognizing its most important asset.

Managers from all over the country have come to visit Lincoln Electric to learn its techniques and secrets of success. The traffic was so great that the company conducted guided tours of the plant each month. After the tours were completed, these highly respected and greatly impressed executives would then return to their respective companies on Monday morning to tell their colleagues of this most moving management experience. Unfortunately, in most cases, implementation was another story. Substantial changes rarely occurred in the management style of those companies whose management visited Lincoln Electric. Their policies rarely paralleled or even vaguely mirrored Lincoln Electric's employee policies. However, Lincoln Electric's long-standing success and its openness as a role model in the HR field have triggered great interest in a number of performance-based programs such as those featured in the *Wall Street Journal*. (It should be noted that though the tours [now primarily for customers, prospective customers, and investors] still continue at Lincoln Electric, the modern-day focus is on the manufacturing transformation taking place on the shop floor, including new machinery and a lean manufacturing and Just-In-Time inventory system.)

In the interest of a balanced business approach, it should also be understood, however, that Lincoln does not "give the store away" to their employees either, as the following policy examples will attest:

■ Employees on the shop floor, called *direct production workers*, receive no base salary; their compensation is based strictly on output known as *piecework*.

■ The company observes holidays but it grants its employees *unpaid* time off.

■ The company encourages continuing education but has only recently established a tuition reimbursement program.

■ Lincoln Electric wants its employees to enjoy needed time off from their jobs, but it does not pay for personal time off, sick days, or other missed time. (However, vacation pay is given, based on years of service.)

■ And what company today does not pay at least in part for health care benefits? You guessed it—Lincoln Electric. At the end of each year, health care benefit costs are deducted from the employee's bonus, based on the individual employee's use of the medical benefits program during the course of the year.

Yet, despite all the apparently negative benefits, the waiting list of applicants still exists. With the average length of service at about 17 years, Lincoln Electric must be doing something right! And, of course, their employees do appreciate the following benefits:

■ a generous annual profit-sharing bonus, which averaged 98 percent of each employee's earnings over a 50-year period such as, from 1934 through the early 1980s; an annual bonus that for the years 1984 to 2001 hovered between 30 and 75 percent of an employee's earnings;

■■ guaranteed employment for anyone with at least three years of continuous service;

■■ an employee stock purchase plan and 401(k) match;

■■ a very competitive pension plan;

■■ stock options for the best performers;

■■ promotion from within;

■■ an open-door policy; and

■■ open lines of communication through an elected advisory board to the chief operating officer.

These features are highlighted to call attention to what one company has accomplished in the field of human relations as well as to the not-so-coincident phenomenal success it has enjoyed for more than a century. Undoubtedly, other companies both large and small offer some of these same advantages to their employees to one degree or another, but the difference lies in the almost total awareness and focus of Lincoln on its people. From the early beginnings of the company, brothers John C. and James F. Lincoln recognized the inherent advantage of treating employees as valued business partners, and the concept has flourished ever since.

Malden Mills

On December 11, 1995, Malden Mills, a textile plant in Lawrence, Massachusetts, was mostly burned to the ground, putting 3,000 people out of work. The majority of the 3,000 thought they were out of work permanently, but a few employees who were with the CEO in the parking lot during the fire heard him say, "This is not the end." And with these words began a saga that has made Aaron Feuerstein a legend among American business leaders and a hero to his employees.

The story of Malden Mills and Aaron Feuerstein is the story of leadership. Business proceeds in cycles and the most recent cycle is one in which extremely highly paid CEOs are celebrated for cutting costs, downsizing, moving plants to venues of cheap labor, and delivering maximum worth to stockholders. Leadership in these cases would appear to be synonymous with *profit maker*.

Aaron Feuerstein spent millions keeping all 3,000 employees on the payroll *with full benefits* for three months. Why? What did he get for his money? Is he a fool? Did he have some dark motive? Here is Aaron Feuerstein's answer: "The fundamental difference is that I consider our workers an asset, not an expense." Indeed, he believed his job went beyond just making money for shareholders, even though the only shareholders of Malden Mills are Feuerstein and his family. "I have a responsibility to the worker, both blue collar and white collar," Feuerstein added. "I have an equal responsibility to the community. It would have been unconscionable to put 3,000 people on the streets and deliver a death blow to the cities of Lawrence and Methuen. Maybe on paper our company is worth less to Wall Street, but I can tell you it's worth more. We're doing fine."

Feuerstein did not throw his money away. It was not largesse. It was a well-reasoned and sound *leadership* decision to invest millions in Malden Mills' most critical asset, its workers. The contrast between this CEO and the currently celebrated ones making $30 million, $60 million, or $100 million a year by eliminating jobs and moving plants is simply astounding. It probably would be a safe bet to speculate that every company that closed a plant in recent years to boost stock prices has a vision statement with words like ". . . we value and respect our employees as our most important asset." How many of the laid off employees do you suppose believe that? Aaron Feuerstein wagered his money on his employees—did it pay off? Judge for yourself from his own words: "Before the fire, that plant produced 130,000 yards a week. A few weeks after the fire, it was up to 230,000 yards. Our people became very creative. They were willing to work 25 hours a day."

Conclusion: Conviction, Communication and Courage constitute the formula for success. The message from Malden Mills is that its CEO did what any rational person might do given time to reflect and put priorities in perspective. Human resource leaders can serve their companies well by constantly encouraging and assisting top management to rethink their values; have the courage of their convictions; communicate them properly to their employees, customers, stockholders, and community; and stand by such values under any circumstances. (Above section on Malden Mills based on from "Leadership Focus, Malden Mills, A Study in Leadership," article by Art Boulay of the Organizational Productivity Institute; October 1996 *Quality Monitor Newsletter*. All quotes in this section are from *Parade Magazine*, 9/8/96, pp. 4–5.)

EMPLOYER/EMPLOYEE LOYALTY

When any company structures its employer-employee relations philosophy on the principle of genuine concern for its people, you can be sure that company has the respect of its employees, its customers, and the community it serves.

We should not and do not assume that this loyalty and attention on the part of the company to its employees is only a one-way street from company to employee. It is quite the contrary. Similar to one of the basic laws of physics, employees must demonstrate their goodwill and loyalty by their own equal and opposite reaction to the actions of their employer. Loyalty to one's company may not be too popular an idea in our modern business world, but today's employees can and always will respond in the same positive manner as their parents and grandparents did to their employers, if they perceive that respect and loyalty come from their companies in return.

Lincoln Electric and Malden Mills are real-life, present-day examples of the rewards of employer/employee interactive loyalty.

YOU MAKE YOUR OWN RECORD

From time to time, we all come across quotes or sayings in some publication that appeal to us because of their wisdom or clever expression. The following statement (author anonymous) is worthy of preserving and framing, namely:

You make your own personnel record, we just keep it!

If we think about it a bit, in the long run we're all employees and, in general, most of us do have the ability to advance in whatever field we choose. Sometimes, the opportunity may not be there; other times, sickness or injury intervenes. Occasionally, fate takes a hand. However, by and large, employees in our country, in particular, can and do control their own destinies. Sometimes they succeed only after a number of unsuccessful starts, but sooner or later hardworking, conscientious, and honest effort wins out over mediocre performance or the lackluster, unplanned approach to the work ethic. So the somewhat corny axiom, "the harder I work, the luckier I get," will probably always have application in business, as well as in life in general.

Hardworking, conscientious people with reasonable intelligence and competency usually succeed in any business field and with practically any employer they choose. However, the Lincoln Electric-type company attracts more than its fair share of this kind of employee. Its people-oriented personnel policies and its sincere concern for employee welfare practically assure a continuing supply of highly motivated and competent personnel who consider this company to be *the* place to work. In other words, it assures its own continuing success, almost without regard to the product it sells or the service it provides. Here again, we could almost say: *Each company makes its own personnel record; its customers just keep it.*

Now that we have demonstrated, through the above examples, that in any business organization people are the most important asset, how shall we guard, protect, and nurture this asset so that it continues to flourish, and may eventually be taken for granted as *the* most essential element of our U.S. corporate culture?

We have advanced the hypothesis that without question this precious resource grows and thrives in direct proportion to the genuine concern of top management and the amount of attention it pays to its employees. As we progress through this book, we will discuss the ways and means corporate managers have at their disposal to convince their employees that they are indeed appreciated, and that they are the most valuable line item on any profit and loss statement or on any company balance sheet.

One very practical means of emphasizing and maintaining this valued resource would be to establish, as most companies have, a department or function known as the personnel or human resources department to represent the best interests of their employees and thereby of management as well.

The truly effective, proactive, and functional human resources department can be the key that unlocks the doors of apathy, unconcern, or, in some cases, outright hostility toward employees that some chief executives and boards of directors seem to feel toward the people who work for them. The personnel staff must first understand and believe in its own mission and role of emphasizing the value of people. Then it must aggressively act as a catalyst in making the necessary changes in corporate attitude toward people. Pursuing this theme, we will explore in the following chapter what makes a good human resources department work and how it can be structured to operate with maximum effectiveness through people recognition.

CHAPTER PERSPECTIVE

This chapter demonstrated how important positive human relations are to any business organization. It provided a clear profile of two successful corporations as a model for good human relations. The value of mutual respect and loyalty within a business organization was observed. In addition, the chapter offered some negative insight into the reluctance of some top managers to substantially change their views on the value of their employees. Parallels were drawn concerning how individuals and companies create their own personnel records. The importance of establishing a human resources function as a means to maintain a company's most-valued asset was stressed.

The Human Resources Executive and the HR Managers

INTRODUCTION AND MAIN POINTS

This chapter focuses on the human resouces executive position, the selection of HR managers, and the relationship between HR executives and their managerial staff. The executive position is described, as is the best temperament needed to match the requirements of the job. The qualities most necessary for the HR managerial staff are clearly delineated, with people-orientation at the top of the list for the "people" department. Lastly, guidelines for the relationship between HR executives and their staff of managers are given.

After reading the material in this chapter:

■ You will understand the role of the HR manager and which personality traits best suit the job.

■ You will know which functional areas the HR management staff has responsibility for.

■ You will understand how important people-orientation is in the people department and others.

■ You will know what other personal qualities are needed to succeed in HR management.

■ You will understand the parameters of a good working relationship between the HR executive and the HR managerial staff.

THE HEAD HUMAN

The position of human resources manager, director, or vice president, also known in some circles as the *head human*, is a multifaceted job, a fact that cannot be emphasized too much. The job consists of many complex and technical aspects, as does that of lawyers, engineers, doctors, CPAs, and others, but the human resources executive must deal with the most complex of all organisms—the human being. With that in mind, it is probably true that the variety of potential problems and challenges to which the human resources manager is subject exists in almost no other profession. The personnel director must be concerned with an employee's physical and emotional well-being, as well as with other components such as competency, morale, attitude, personality, and conscientiousness. In addition, as the human resources function plays an increasingly important role in the survival and success of an organization, the HR professional must be a businessperson with strong business acumen and background to be able to understand as well as contribute to the business strategies of the corporation.

A Challenging Profession
Those in the HR profession find the job challenging because they handle so many diverse subjects at one time and rarely meet the same problem twice. In addition, human resources executives are patience personified. Their phone voice never discloses the frustration or anger they have just experienced from the preceding call when they may have learned that a new program, procedure, or special event that could not go wrong, did. If they remember to maintain their equilibrium, to use righteous indignation at the proper time and place, and especially to learn what to delegate and what to do themselves, their job should proceed well.

Quality of Persuasiveness
Human resources executives must be able to sell their programs to the top executives and managers in the organization. Sometimes the interface of long-standing relationships within a company can be helpful in obtaining approval and enthusiastic acceptance of a proposed new program. HR managers may first have to win the support of those who are in a stronger position than they are, in order that the program be accepted by key persons. At times the political process becomes just as important an ingredient in the human resources profession as it is in public life.

Metrics
One of the specific methods of selling human resources programs and gaining the support of top management is in the use of HR metrics, which is rapidly becoming an important weapon in the HR arsenal. For example, does top management really understand the actual dollars-and-cents cost of hiring and replacing its most important asset, an employee? What is the current rate of turnover in the company? Is heavy turnover and loss of people related to possible inadequacies of the compensation structure? (Yes, even in difficult economic times!) How engaged are company employees with their work, with each other, and with the company, and how well would they survive any layoffs with

associated work changes and new demands? And how about determining the dollar value of your workforce's productivity this year versus last year and factoring in related expenditures for training, technology, and so on? Such information—and much more—is readily available to the human resources department and in fact, much of it originates there! It can also be an integral part of HR planning, setting goals and objectives, and measuring progress. Caution: Such strategic HR management of human capital is not intended to use metrics for measuring literally hundreds of functions but rather just those essential—usually not more than a dozen or so—to your specific company. But HR professionals, new and veteran, are strongly urged to give metrics a try. It works!

STAFFING THE HUMAN RESOURCES DEPARTMENT
Similar to the captain of a ship, the first thing the head humans will want to do is to pick their own crew. Of course, this may be impossible under certain circumstances, for example, when HR managers are put in charge of an existing department. In such a situation, they must, at least for the moment, go with the current staff, but sooner or later, they will probably need to designate their own managers or supervisors. If, however, the task at hand is setting up a personnel/human resources operation from the ground up, the HR manager will want to staff each job in the department with the persons he or she wants and thinks will do the best job.

Human resoucies executives should not worry about mistakes they make in the selection of people. The most experienced and respected human resources vice presidents or employment managers in the world can never guarantee that they will always hire the right person for a job opening—such an employment executive does not exist. So, by having the self-confidence and courage to move people laterally, down, or even out when it is obvious that employees are not right for the job, HR managers can be of great value to a company.

If called upon to do so, HR managers can effectively set up a new human resources function or reengineer an existing department in many different ways. No one table of organization can possibly fit every situation; nevertheless, similarities exist among organizations, and thus it is possible to show the essential functions in which every human resources department should be involved. Most of these functions are often the direct responsibility of the HR department, and HR staff members should have at least a working knowledge of each of the areas listed, even if it is not their direct concern.

HR Jobs and Titles

The organization of HR duties and responsibilities into formal jobs and titles is usually determined by company size and availability of resources. If a company is relatively large and the HR department has sufficient personnel, staff members may have the luxury of specialization. On the other hand, if the personnel/human resources department consists of only one person, the personnel/human resources manager can expect to wear many different hats.

In either event, the suggested job titles listed below represent some of the aspects of personnel management with which the modern-day personnel/human resources operation should be concerned. The job titles listed are not necessarily in the order of importance, nor are they meant to be literal: When a job title of "Manager" is used, that function could also be named "Supervisor" or even "Leader." For example, especially in larger companies, it is common to have a "Manager, Benefits," a "Supervisor, Benefits," and one or more "Leader, Benefits" positions. The structure above a "Manager, Benefits" might well include a "Director, Benefits," and at the top in the largest organizations, a "Vice President, Benefits." Some companies may also combine different personnel functions while others keep them separate. For example, the "Manager, Benefits" and the "Manager, Compensation" positions in one company may be combined into a single "Manager, Compensation and Benefits" in another. In addition, practice varies regarding the use of the functional designation before the individual title on all the titles listed, such as, "Employment Manager" and "Compensation Manager."

The following job title listing stresses function rather than format:
- Manager, Employment and Recruiting
- Manager, Compensation
- Manager, Benefits
- EEO, Coordinator (or Manager, Personnel Relations)
- Manager, HR Information Systems
- Manager, Diversity
- Manager, Safety and Security
- Manager, Ethics and Sustainability
- Manager, Wage and Salary Analysis
- Manager, Training and Development
- Manager, Payroll
- Manager, Unemployment Compensation
- Manager, Executive Compensation
- Manager, Retirement Planning
- Manager, Employee Assistance Program
- Manager, Outplacement Services

- Manager, Union/Labor Relations
- Manager, Community Relations
- Manager, Quality Circles/Suggestion System
- Manager, Health and Wellness Programs
- Manager, Workers' Compensation Administration
- Manager, Organizational and Employee Development
- Manager, Medical Services Administration

In effect, at least some fifteen managerial titles are possible in a human resources operation, in addition to all the other levels of supervisor and/or leader that might be associated with each functional area. However, rarely would the HR department actually include all or even most of these managerial job titles in its organizational chart. They are spelled out here to demonstrate the extent of human resources responsibilities. Small companies, of course, might have one individual covering all fifteen bases. As the company begins to increase in size and scope, the need to divide some of the major functions becomes apparent, and the head of the department then has the duty and the challenge to convince top management to adjust the human resources budget to allow for the new position(s) within the department.

Choose Leaders on the Basis of People Orientation

HR executives should choose team captains and leaders carefully and on the basis of people orientation. Filling these key managerial slots with individuals who are first and foremost people-oriented men and women is extremely important. Technical competence, education, and job knowledge are important, of course, to the success of any job; however, individuals who relate to people easily and who are normally patient and understanding with customers are the proper choice in any business situation and especially in a retail sales operation. In addition, the person hired will inevitably hire into his or her group employees who share the manager's values and approach to handling customers and others, thus perpetuating good customer service and satisfaction, as well as success and profits. The corollary to this is that HR executives should have no hesitancy whatsoever in replacing those managers who, for whatever reason, forget their people/customer orientation.

The ability to relate to people is extremely important in every leadership or supervisory role; in fact, it is important in any job, supervisory or not. From the standpoint of the human resources function, the credo is clear and simple:

It is absolutely vital that each personnel staff member be an unabashed, all-out, proud-of-it *people* person whose primary goal is to help and to serve the people of the organization with enthusiasm, competency, and cooperation. There must be a willingness to go the extra mile, to do whatever is necessary to investigate and resolve problems, answer questions, and do everything within his or her power to assist others in the effective performance of their jobs.

This is the human resources/personnel mandate, and it has universal application whether the HR manager *directs* a department of 100 people or *is* the department.

Other Important Qualities for Success in HR

In addition to the all-important quality of relating to people, success in human resources also requires a sense of fairness and tough-mindedness with the ability to make objective decisions based on an analysis of facts rather than on appearance, assumption, or emotion. And regardless of how the organizational chart is designed, these will be the kind of people who will make for a strong, effective, and well-respected human resources operation.

It should also be noted that while human resources first and foremost represents the management of the organization—indeed, HR must always play a prominent role in aligning HR functions with overall business objectives as well as helping to achieve these objectives—it must also represent the employees of the company. This is only good business and tends to strike a balance between business needs and people needs.

The role of HR continues to evolve and take on more importance in the overall success of any business organization.

HR EXECUTIVE AND MANAGERIAL STAFF RELATIONSHIPS

Human resources managers' actions, attitudes, and motivations will essentially determine whether HR executives succeed or fail. These people are a head human's first line of defense. Although they report to the executive and the executive is their boss, things will go much more smoothly and successfully if HR executives can subtly convince them that they primarily work *with* him or her rather than *for* him or her.

The staff must respect HR executives as their leader, and the best way for HR executives to gain that respect is to earn it. In dealing with people—whether they are employees, customers, or the public in general—it is often the so-called little things that cause the biggest problems. As with most procedures that work, many are the result of trial and error, successes and failures, until the right solution is found. While the following guidelines do not apply to every company's individual circumstances they may nevertheless apply to a future situation. They concern the relationship between HR executives and the HR management staff:

1) No employee, whether manager or operative, always makes the right decision, and there is no such thing as an employee who never makes a mistake. Regardless of these truths, however, one of the first principles to be observed between HR executives and the management staff is that HR executives must back them up and support their decisions to anyone outside the department. This does not imply that they can never be wrong, nor that HR executives openly support them when they *are* wrong, but it does require that HR executives not condemn their action or concede that they were wrong until they have had the opportunity to discuss the matter with them first. If their decision was wrong or even questionable, the matter can then be corrected without embarrassment, and the human resources management staff will admire and respect the stand of the HR director and will undoubtedly make every effort to prevent a repeat situation.

2) In any human resources operation, regardless of the size of the company, a great variety of events, problems, situations, and opportunities will occur, primarily because the function of human resources is to deal with people. The challenges are literally endless; therefore, HR executives will want to keep in daily contact with their managers. To have detailed knowledge, HR executives should hold weekly or biweekly staff meetings with them, as well as require written, but brief, weekly status reports from them covering their current and anticipated projects. Many chief executives and some managers dislike meetings of any kind and characterize meetings as events where minutes are kept and hours wasted. Nevertheless, a well-conducted, stick-to-the-subject session will prove a highly effective communication tool for all participants, and especially for HR executives. Staff meetings do not have to be dull or boring; the more interesting and lively they are, the more the management staff will look forward to them and will participate and contribute productively. A bit of genial and genuine humor from time to time can further enhance staff meetings.

3) Before HR executives make any kind of substantive business decision, they should ask the management staff what they think about the matter. While executives still reserve the right to make the final decisions, the input of the managers might provide that additional bit of light to guide their thinking. The staff may even be flattered that they have been asked for their opinion. By asking for the advice of the management staff, executives give the staff recognition, and earn their respect.

4) HR executives should be careful when dealing with their staff, either privately or in a meeting environment, not to put down or harshly criticize the company for some decision or action taken by the CEO or board of directors. All employees at some time or other gripe about their company, even considering it their prerogative to do so, and directors and managers are no exception However, as the head of the human resources department, the executive must demonstrate dedication and loyalty to the organization and its top management in his or her speech and actions. It is also advisable to not let HR management staff members be overly critical or outspoken about company management policies, programs, or procedures. These people also represent the HR department and their opinions do influence other company employees and supervisors. The expression, "we ride for the brand" implies that we either support top management fully or seek employment at another ranch.

5) HR directors must at any cost maintain the harmony of the group; they must never let petty differences between staff personnel go unnoticed or unattended. They must all understand that, although HR directors may have the highest regard for them individually, they will not permit constant internal arguments and disagreements, which might easily lead to a polarization of their group and be damaging to the department, the company, and the HR director. If necessary, the HR director should hold a meeting with the managers who are not seeing eye to eye, and make it unmistakably clear to them that, regardless of how valuable they are to the department and the company, their behavior will not be tolerated. Unless they agree to work together in harmony and to cooperate with each other, they can no longer continue as members of the human resources department. By being straightforward, HR directors can usually manage to bring the dissident members together in peaceful coexistence.

6) The management staff needs to understand that each of them has his or her primary specialty within the department, and that all questions should be referred to the appropriate individual. By adhering to this practice, HR executives can eliminate or reduce the possibility of misinformation regarding HR programs, company policies, and so forth. It must be noted, however, that staff personnel should be able to handle general inquiries that overlap into other areas. In fact, managers should have at least a working knowledge of each other's areas of

responsibility because human resources functions interlock with each other. For example, the employment group relies on the compensation staff to create accurate job descriptions and establish competitive wage ranges for hiring purposes. The equal employment coordinator depends on employment interviewers and recruiters to ensure that company hiring practices are nondiscriminatory. All human resources managers trust that the HR management information systems or computer people are providing them with reliable recommendations as to which software and hardware systems will enable them to economically and effectively carry out their job responsibilities.

7) Another important procedure that the HR director should require is the dating of all letters, memos, notes, reports, or other documents generated in the human resources department for either external or internal communication. Nothing is more frustrating than to find an important note in a personnel file, for example, which is dated August 6th, without indicating the year. It is best to avoid the confusion and time wasted to reconstruct the year of the writing. A corollary to this policy is for HR executives to require authorship of various notes and memos to be made clearly, directing, for example: "Please sign your name to everything you write or, at least, initial it."

8) Finally, a brief word on some "housekeeping" matters is appropriate:

(a) The HR executives should socialize with managers as little as possible, except in the environment of company-sponsored or related events. Socializing under other circumstances can create erroneous impressions and make disciplinary situations more complex and difficult and invariably sends the wrong signals to other members of the HR staff.

(b) When dealing with managers in a staff meeting, individually, or any other time, it is important for HR executives to display a sense of humor. When used properly and discreetly, a genuine sense of humor can often ease tensions, while letting the management staff know that the HR director personally enjoys association with them in a business context.

(c) Say "Good Morning" to them when you arrive at work and "Good-bye," "Have a good evening," or similar greeting when you leave at night—you might be surprised at the goodwill this small but thoughtful action generates.

CHAPTER PERSPECTIVE

This chapter concentrated upon the key positions in the human resouces department: the executive and the management staff. What types of personal characteristics are necessary for success in these positions was discussed. The importance of people orientation for the "people" department was emphasized. The important relationship between HR executives and their managerial staff was explored using specific guidelines.

Compensation: Surveys, Wage and Salary Guidelines, and Job Descriptions

INTRODUCTION AND MAIN POINTS

This chapter focuses on the following areas of responsibility: analyzing wage and salary data and statistics, conducting surveys, analyzing and evaluating job duties and requirements, and writing and maintaining job descriptions for all jobs within the organization—all part of the compensation function of human resources.

The tools that the compensation professional uses to accomplish the above objectives are defined, and the proper sequence and use of the tools are discussed.

The chapter describes how to conduct a survey for information regarding wages of specific job descriptions. Included are useful hints and examples on how to motivate competitor companies to participate, how to maintain anonymity, and how to ask the right questions to get specific information.

An overview of how wage and salary guidelines are constructed is given.

The chapter also gives practical and detailed instructions on how to analyze jobs and how to write good job descriptions.

After studying the material in this chapter:

■■■ You will know what is involved in making job data analysis and surveys, wage and salary guidelines, and job descriptions.

■■■ You will be familiar with the tools that compensation professionals use to accomplish their objectives.

■■■ You will be acquainted with the general concepts of constructing wage and salary guidelines.

■■■ You will know how to go about analyzing jobs and how to write good job descriptions.

THE COMPENSATION FUNCTION

Compensation's primary responsibility is to study and analyze wage and salary data, surveys, and statistics. This is to insure internal pay equity and to maintain the company's competitive edge in recruiting, hiring, and retaining qualified people.

If the company has a formal wage program, this group will also have the following responsibilities:

■ Analyze and evaluate job duties, requirements, and responsibilities;
■ Write and maintain job descriptions for all jobs within the organization.

Listing the compensation function first among human resources responsibilities is not necessarily intended to indicate priority ranking; however, compensation always ranks high—and in most cases *Number One*—in importance on the wish list of the average wage earner. This is true despite the much-publicized scientific conjectures about compensation being an issue far down the list of wants and needs of employees.

Compensation Staff

The compensation group is often comprised of the following types of employees:

■ Wage and salary analysts
■ Statisticians
■ Administrative and clerical support

The Tools

The compensation group accomplishes the above objectives just as all professionals do—by employing to the fullest extent the tools of their trade. Some of these tools are

1) a wage and salary program.
2) a point-scoring plan based on job duties.
3) computers and specialized software.
4) trade publications.

A formal wage and salary program and a point-scoring plan based solely on job duties and responsibilities are of primary importance. Probably the two most popular wage plans used by companies with a formal compensation program include those of the American Association of Industrial Management (AAIM) and the Hay organization. Before choosing a plan, the compensation manager and staff should thoroughly research and analyze different plans for their applicability to the company's particular needs. There is no one best plan for all companies; the best plan is the one that will work for you.

Other tools available to compensation professionals today are personal computers and a wide variety of software programs, which are not only convenient but absolutely essential in the gathering, calculation, maintenance, and retrieval of wage and salary data. From a practical standpoint, the processing and storage of data such as wage surveys and cost-of-living and competitive salary information cannot be done without the management information and data processing hardware and software that exist today (and that will be even more helpful tomorrow). The constantly changing and improving state of the art of these tools insures greater speed, accuracy, storage, and retrieval capabilities of information so vital to compensation as well as to most other company functions.

The human resources professionals today have available to them any number of valuable HR software programs and systems. Listed below are some of the better-known HR software vendors, their products, and contact information:

GENESYS CORPORATION

An industry leader in providing comprehensive human resources, payroll, benefits, and learning management solutions, designed to handle the full spectrum of human capital management systems needs. All Genesys solutions come with a high performance Web-native architecture that enables users to conduct their day-to-day business—including complex payroll production, data entry, reporting and inquiries—via a standard Web browser interface.

For information: Genesys Software
5 Branch Street
Methuen, MA 01844

SPECTRUM'S HR VANTAGE SYSTEMS

This system handles all aspects of the human resources function while streamlining departmental and organizational processes. The system features near effortless data entry, manipulation, and access capabilities. Permits tracking and reporting on all HR-related tasks, including:

applicant activity
new hire processing.
job or position assignment.
employee status.
benefits enrollment and tracking.
training and development.
licenses and certifications.
skills assessment.
absence tracking/Family Medical Leave Act (FMLA).
emergency medical contacts.
employee history.
performance/salary review.

compensation planning.

terminations.

company-property inventory.

For information: Spectrum Human Resources Systems Corporation
707 17th Street, Suite 3800
Denver, CO 80202–3438

ACCERO (formerly Cyborg Systems)

For over 35 years, the Accero Cyborg© Human Capital Managament (HCM) solutions have been the choice for mid- and large-size companies in the United States, Canada, the United Kingdom, Australia, and New Zealand—companies that demand scalability, performance, and flexibility. Accero Cyborg (HCM) delivers an affordable, enterprise class, fully integrated HCM solution designed to meet demanding and complex corporate requirements.

For information: Accero, Inc.
17040 Pilkington Road
Suite 300
Lake Oswego, Oregon 97035

ERI (Economic Research Institute)

Founded 20 years ago as an outsource of salary survey analyses, ERI has evolved into a geographic and industry-specific salary survey, cost-of-living, and executive compensation benchmark survey firm dedicated to research and development, with a focus on data. ERI assists HR professionals and managers by collecting, compiling, and analyzing thousands of survey data points that comprise any one city's wage and salary rates as well as cost-of-living levels. Their scope extends to and includes the United States, Canada, and Europe.

For information: ERI—Economic Research Institute
8575 164th Avenue NE, Suite 100
Redmond, WA 98052

SALARY.com

A leading provider of on-demand human resources software that helps businesses and individuals manage pay and performance. This on-demand service requires no capital investment, no costly maintenance fees, and access from any location with an Internet connection. Services include:

- Full-service talent management software
- Industry-leading compensation data and software
- Integrated HR, payroll, and benefits management

- Competence and skills management software
- HCM consulting services based on best business practices
- Targeted online advertising

For information: Salary.com, Inc.
                195 West Street
                Waltham, MA 02451

HR COMPLY CORPORATION (A Ceridian Service)

HR Comply™ —Preeminent electronic human resource compliance system. Available on both CD-ROM and Internet, the components of the HR Comply Web reference system give HR professionals fast, easy access to information that will help them better manage employment policies and practices, especially to ensure compliance with changing federal labor laws. The HR Comply system enables users to obtain all needed compliance information quickly, easily, and economically.

For information: HR Comply (Ceridian)
                PO Box 534429
                St. Petersburg, FL 33747

SOCIETY FOR HUMAN RESOURCE MANAGEMENT (SHRM)—Compensation Data Center

SHRM, in collaboration with Watson Wyatt Data Services, provides SHRM members with accurate and customized salary information for an entire spectrum of jobs ranging from top executive to entry-level positions. The SHRM Compensation Data Center helps organizations formulate competitve compensation programs and provides a variety of compensation data options, whether same job level or job family, or a single position report.

Online compensation reports are available for a variety of industries, job families, and functional areas.

For information: Society for Human Resource Management
                1800 Duke Street
                Alexandria, VA 22314

Note: In addition to the above, some SHRM chapters also conduct salary studies and may be a good source of local salary information.

In addition, a number of trade publications can assist compensation managers and their wage and salary analysts in keeping aware of what goes on in this most vital and key world of compensation. These publications are sources of wage and salary survey data by occupation within different geographic areas, federal and state wage law information, and a myriad of other data relating to compensation practices, policies, and procedures. They are published by organizations such as the Bureau of National Affairs (BNA), a Washington DC-based management information service; and Commerce Clearing House (CCH), a management business/legal service headquartered in Chicago, Illinois.

Now let's turn to the practical usage and application of all these tools and data available to the human resource professional.

USING THE TOOLS

First, let's assume that you have just been appointed manager or director of compensation in a company that possibly has always had its own informal wage program, but it has perhaps never used (or even heard of) standardized or formal wage ranges, rate positions, job descriptions, job analyses, relation-to-range techniques, or similar useful items. From a practical, economic, and efficiency standpoint, you may justifiably ask, "Just where do I start?" Good question. Several possible answers will be considered below.

In order to have competitive, equitable, and reasonable wage ranges, you must first determine what these ranges should be in the environments or areas in which the company operates or is located. Since local companies all bid for employee services for their available job openings, you naturally will want to know—and indeed *have* to know—what the competition is paying for the services of its work force. If your company is a national or international one with many outlets or facilities, your scope broadens, because you must know just what it takes to attract and keep good employees at each and every company location, domestic and foreign.

SURVEYING

How do you find and develop such highly confidential and competitive information? There is only one proven and effective method: You *ask* for it, meaning you dig, you write, you call, you listen, you discuss, you do everything in your power to find out from other companies, from chambers of commerce, from local personnel associations, from any source you can, just what hourly and salary rates other employers in the area pay for generally the same kind of work or jobs you may have in your company.

The general term for this type of inquiry is *surveying*, which ranges from telephone surveys and the other informal methods mentioned above, to the more formal written survey or questionnaire forms sent out to other companies, especially those in the same community in which your company operates. Incidentally, you might be surprised at how many of these companies will accede to your survey request, even knowing that you will probably be in competition with them for employees as well as for customers. Don't be discouraged or skeptical about how much success you'll have in getting this data from other companies. It is unlikely you'll get a 100 percent return rate, but you normally can anticipate a sufficient number of responses to provide some insight into what these jobs generally pay. Some motivators are as follows:

1) If you commit to give all participants a copy of the survey results, you may have offered enough enticement to insure a reasonable response.

2) Your assurance of strict confidentiality regarding the identities of participants should also help to increase your rate of return.

If you do not use company names, no participant will be able to identify any other company. Usually, each company in the survey is assigned a symbol or letter, such as A, B, C, D, and the only company that can be identified by participants is, therefore, their own.

In the cover letter or survey form, you should

▬ ask for their cooperation and assistance in providing this information, including a request that they complete and return the survey by a specified date;

▬ briefly describe the duties and responsibilities of the job categories in which you are interested, for example, accountants, engineers, mechanics, programmers, or janitors; and

▬ ask for compensation data on these jobs, such as low, midpoint, and high *actual* salaries, as well as salary *ranges*.

You would normally request return of the survey forms within four to six weeks. Once they are returned, they, together with other research you've done on your own, should put you in a position to begin constructing a compensation range for each of your jobs. See Figure 5-1 below for sample survey cover letter and Figure 5-2 for questionnaire form below.

FIGURE 5-1
Sample Survey Cover Letter

July 1, 2010

DEF Manufacturing Company
132 East Main Street
Hartford, CT 06163
Attention: Director of Human Resources (or Compensation Manager):

Dear Sir or Madam:

ABC Company is asking you and a selected group of private and public employers in our community to participate in a wage and salary survey designed to provide wage and benefit information on the positions listed on the enclosed survey form.

Your responses to this survey will be kept in strictest confidence, and all survey participants will be assigned an identification letter (A, B, C, etc.), in order to identify their own organization when survey results are published to all participating companies.

If you are interested in participating in the survey (and we sincerely hope you are), we ask that you complete and return it (mail or fax) to us at the address given below on or before July 25. If you have any questions concerning the data requested in the survey form, please do not hesitate to contact me for clarification.

We very much appreciate the investment of your valuable time in answering the survey, and we would be more than happy to reciprocate by providing whatever wage or salary information you may need from us in the future.

Very sincerely yours,

Jennifer Rankin
Manager, Compensation
ABC Company, Inc.
2818 Asylum Avenue
Hartford, CT 06161

Voice - (203) 422-6871
Fax - (203) 422-6775

Enclosure: Survey Reply Form

Figure 5-2 below is an example of a brief but effective survey questionnaire form.

FIGURE 5-2
Survey Questionnaire Form

Date: _____   Your assigned survey letter: (A)

Company Name: DEF Manufacturing Co.
Location: (City/State) Hartford, CT
Company Size: (# employees at this location): F/T____ P/T____

JOB TITLE(S)	PRIMARY DUTIES	SALARY RANGE		
		MIN	MID	MAX
_____	_____	$ ____	$ ____	$ ____
_____	_____	____	____	____
_____	_____	____	____	____
_____	_____	____	____	____
_____	_____	____	____	____

BENEFITS PROVIDED	COMPANY PAID	EMPLOYEE PAID
Medical	_____	_____
Dental	_____	_____
401(k)	_____	_____
Profit Sharing	_____	_____
Other Benefits (list) (such as apt. furnished, vacation pay):	_____	_____
	_____	_____

Pay increases based on Merit _____   Other _____

GENERAL COMMENTS:

At this point, you are now beginning to get a fairly good idea of the going rate needed to attract and keep good job candidates. Incidentally, no matter how thorough you are, your survey efforts will probably not cover each and every job title or position the company will have.

However, it will normally give you enough information to build wage ranges for your key jobs and to slot in the nonsurveyed jobs, based on their individual scoring analysis, which will be described later in this chapter.

WAGE AND SALARY GUIDELINES

At this point, a matrix or series of numerical grade levels can be constructed and a wage or salary range guideline can be assigned to each grade level. You can set up a table or chart of perhaps ten grade levels for nonexempt jobs and an equal number for the exempt job categories. There is no specific recommended number of grade levels but ten is a reasonable number to work with. A grade level table for executive jobs should also be created later, after the exempt/nonexempt wage tables have been constructed and placed in effect. Any number of grade levels may be selected for the wage and salary program, depending upon what you, as compensation manager, determine is right for the company and its wage and salary program. See Table 5-1 below for a sample illustration of what these wage and salary guideline tables might look like.

TABLE 5-1

Nonexempt Wage Schedule Guidelines
Hourly Rates (with Monthly Equivalents)

Grade Level	Rate Step 80	Rate Step 90	Rate Step J	Rate Step S	Rate Step T
1	7.25 (1,257.)	8.15 (1,413.)	9.05 (1,569.)	9.95 (1,725.)	10.90 (1,889.)
2	7.75 (1,343.)	8.70 (1,508.)	9.65 (1,673.)	10.60 (1,837.)	11.65 (2,019.)
3	8.25 (1,430.)	9.25 (1,603.)	10.25 (1,777.)	11.25 (1,950.)	12.40 (2,149.)
4	8.75 (1,517.)	9.80 (1,699.)	10.85 (1,881.)	11.90 (2,063.)	13.15 (2,279.)
5	9.25 (1,603.)	10.35 (1,794.)	11.45 (1,985.)	12.55 (2,175.)	13.90 (2,409.)

TABLE 5-1 (continued)

	Rate Step 80	Rate Step 90	Rate Step J	Rate Step S	Rate Step T
Grade Level					
6	9.75 (1,690.)	10.90 (1,889.)	12.05 (2,089.)	13.20 (2,288.)	14.65 (2,539.)
7	10.25 (1,777.)	11.45 (1,985.)	12.65 (2,192.)	13.85 (2,400.)	15.40 (2,669.)
8	10.75 (1,863.)	12.00 (2,080.)	13.30 (2,305.)	14.50 (2,513.)	16.15 (2,799.)
9	11.25 (1,950.)	12.55 (2,175.)	13.95 (2,418.)	15.15 (2,626.)	16.90 (2,929.)
10	11.75 (2,037.)	13.10 (2,270.)	14.55 (2,522.)	15.80 (2,738.)	17.65 (3,059.)

In Table 5-1, each grade level hourly range is constructed using flat 50 cent increases from grade levels 1 through 10 at the 80 step; and a 50 percent dollar spread from rate steps 80 through T, at each grade level. Each rate step is then rounded to the next higher 5 cent increment.

The various rate steps may be identified with any type of symbol, number, letter, etc. Here we have chosen to identify the steps as 80 (as in 80 percent of job standard); 90 (90 percent of job standard), J (normally referred to as job standard, the point at which the employee on a particular grade level is performing all phases of that job in a satisfactory manner); S (used to identify superior performance); and T (meaning top performance). T is the maximum point on the wage scale, and implies that the individual employee who achieves this rating is doing the job in an excellent or top-notch manner, or as well as it can possibly be done by anyone!

Current (July 24, 2009) Federal minimum wage—$7.25 per hour.

The wage schedule is constructed to increase the dollar potential for an employee who is promoted to a higher grade level. For example, employees on a grade level 3 job who have attained the J, S, or T step of that particular grade, and who are promoted to a grade level 5 job, increase their maximum potential from $12.40 per hour (grade 3

T), to $13.90 per hour (grade 5 T). This method of increasing money potential is also true in the Exempt Salary Schedule shown in Table 5-2 below.

TABLE 5-2
Exempt Salary Schedule Guidelines
Monthly Salaries (with Annual Equivalents)

Grade Level	Rate Step 80	Rate Step 90	Rate Step J	Rate Step S	Rate Step T
21	1975. (23,700.)	2220. (26,400.)	2465. (29,580.)	2715. (32,580.)	2965. (35,580.)
22	2175. (26,100.)	2445. (29,340.)	2715. (32,580.)	2990. (35,880.)	3265. (39,180.)
23	2395. (28,740.)	2695. (32,340.)	2995. (35,940.)	3295. (39,540.)	3595. (43,140.)
24	2635. (31,620.)	2965. (35,580.)	3295. (39,540.)	3625. (43,500.)	3955. (47,460.)
25	2900. (34,800.)	3260. (39,120.)	3620. (43,440.)	3985. (47,820.)	4350. (52,200.)
26	3190. (38,280.)	3585. (43,020.)	3985. (47,820.)	4385. (52,620.)	4785. (57,420.)
27	3510. (42,120.)	3945. (47,340.)	4385. (52,620.)	4825. (57,900.)	5265. (63,180.)
28	3860. (46,320.)	4340. (52,080.)	4820. (57,840.)	5305. (63,660.)	5790. (69,480.)
29	4245. (50,940.)	4775. (63,000.)	5305. (57,300.)	5835. (70,020.)	6370. (76,440.)
30	4670. (56,040.)	5250. (63,000.)	5835. (70,020.)	6420. (77,040.)	7005. (84,060.)

In Table 5-2, each grade level salary range is constructed using 10 percent increases from grade levels 21 through 30 at the 80 step; and a 50 percent dollar spread for each salary range, as from steps 80 through T at each grade level. Each rate step is then rounded to the next higher $5.00 increment.

The various rate steps may be identified with any type of symbol, number, letter, etc. Here as with the nonexempt wage schedule (Table 5-1) we have chosen to identify the steps as 80 (as in 80 percent of the job standard); 90 (90 percent of the job standard); J (normally referred to as the job standard, the point at which the employee on a particular grade level is performing all phases of that job in a satisfactory manner); S (used to identify Superior performance); and T (meaning Top performance), the maximum point on the salary scale. T implies that the individual employee who achieves this rating is doing the job in an excellent or top-notch manner, or as well as it can possibly be done by anyone!

The exempt salary schedule, similar to the hourly nonexempt schedule in Table 5-1, is also constructed to increase the dollar potential for an employee who is promoted to a higher grade level. For example, employees on a grade level 25 job who have attained the J, S, or T step on that particular grade, and who are promoted to a grade level 27 job, increase their maximum potential from $4,350 per month (Grade 25 T), to $5,265 per month (Grade 27 T).

Any type or combination of symbols, letters, and numbers may be utilized in constructing the wage and salary tables, but there must be some system of tables, charts, and wage cards in order for employees and managers to be aware of the guidelines for all jobs in the company. Once completed, the wage and salary guidelines should be distributed to all supervisors and managers for their use in compensating their employees. All company supervisors will appreciate the wage and salary tables printed on wallet-size cards and preferably laminated, for their convenience in usage.

Having constructed the tables based on the most accurate, current, and competitive information available, you should be sure to review them at least yearly and make adjustments based on inflation, cost of living, and wage increase data from the past 12-month period. The success of your entire wage and salary program is in many respects dependent on how up to date the charts and tables of the wage and salary guidelines are kept.

OTHER IMPORTANT TOOLS

The next and probably most complex part of the human resources compensation function involves the determination of just what jobs are needed in the program and how they are to be evaluated and described. In order to accomplish this, you will need some additional tools to help the compensation staff properly perform their analytical and evaluation duties. These tools include the following:

- Organization charts
- Questionnaire forms
- Personal interviews
- Job descriptions

Organization Charts

An organization chart is a graphic representation of all jobs in which the reporting relationships are delineated by boxes, circles, lines, captions, and so forth, to demonstrate how the unit is functionally organized. Normally prepared and approved by the manager of the department whose jobs are being evaluated, the organization chart provides the wage and salary analyst in the compensation group with an overview of the unit's organizational or reporting structure.

To assist the wage and salary analyst in gauging the weight or importance of lead, supervisory, or managerial jobs in the unit, the chart should also include the total number of employees classified in each job in order to determine the scope of any supervisory responsibility. See Table 5-3 for a sample organization chart.

In addition, the organization chart should have the signature approval of the respective department or line manager involved, which gives the compensation group the authority to begin the analysis and evaluation of the job or jobs in question. There is probably no greater source of frustration or waste of time and money than the discovery, after having completed or even partially completed a difficult job evaluation project, that top department supervision had *not* given final approval of the chart. The evaluation project might then be shelved either temporarily or permanently.

Table 5-3 is an example of an accounting department organization chart:

TABLE 5-3
Accounting Department Organizational Chart
(Example for organization with 500–1,000 employees)
Total Department Personnel: 15

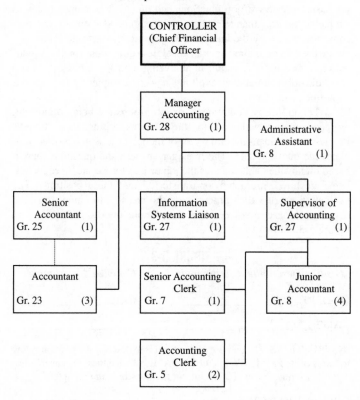

Questionnaire Forms

The questionnaire is a useful document that simply asks the incumbent of the job certain standard and basic questions regarding the job, such as

- the day-to-day duties and responsibilities of the job;
- the type and nature of the work;
- how often certain activities are performed;
- the frequency, nature, and level of contacts involved;
- the most difficult aspects of the work;

■■■ the type of decisions that must be made; and

■■■ the consequences of probable errors.

Designed by the compensation group, the questionnaire form requests current incumbent job holders of jobs being analyzed to fill out and return the form to compensation prior to the start of the job evaluation project.

The questionnaire gives the wage and salary analyst a preliminary yet basic overview of job functions and duties. It is intended only to supplement, rather than to replace, the recommended one-on-one personal interviews by the analyst with job incumbents and managers. While the questionnaire is not an absolute requirement for every evaluation, it is especially useful in analyzing highly technical jobs, and for multi-job evaluations involving new or completely reorganized departments or groups.

When company departments or job groups are being organized, reorganized, or reevaluated, and there are no incumbents in the jobs in question, the manager or director of the job or jobs in question completes the questionnaire. The manager answers the questions therein based on how he or she intends the job or jobs to operate, once incumbents are hired, promoted, or transferred into these positions. The evaluation process then proceeds on the basis of the input from the department head involved. See the sample questionnaire form in Figure 5-3 below.

FIGURE 5-3

Position Description Questionnaire (to be Completed by Manager)

CO/DEPT.:_____   DATE:_____

NAME:_____

INSTRUCTIONS: The purpose of this form is to describe the position below in terms of its PRIMARY AND FUNDAMENTAL duties, responsibilities, and other requirements. Please fill out the questionnaire completely.

CURRENT JOB TITLE:_____

THIS POSITION REPORTS TO:_____

PRIMARY/FUNDAMENTAL DUTIES (MOST ESSENTIAL
REQUIREMENTS) OF THIS POSITION: Indicate the percent of time
spent performing these duties daily. USE COMPLETE SENTENCES,
INDICATING THE DUTIES PERFORMED, WHY THEY ARE
PERFORMED OR HOW.

FIGURE 5-3 (continued)

OTHER DUTIES PERFORMED: (Marginal duties). Duties and responsibilities that are performed either very infrequently or that could be performed by others without altering the underlying reason the job exists. NOTE: A marginal function may be essential, however, due to the limited number of employees available to perform the particular duty(ies). Use back of this page to continue. *(Indicate the percent of time spent performing these duties daily.)*

SUPERVISION: LIST TITLES OF ANY SUBORDINATES REPORT-ING TO THIS POSITION, IF APPLICABLE.

1. WHAT IS THE MOST DIFFICULT OR COMPLEX PART OF THIS JOB?

2. WHO ASSIGNS DAILY OR REGULAR WORK? (IF NOT SUPER-VISOR, GIVE TITLE.)

3. HOW MUCH INSTRUCTION IS RECEIVED FROM THE SUPERVISOR IN DOING THIS WORK, AND WHAT PARTS ARE CHECKED BY THE SUPERVISOR?

4. WHAT KINDS OF DECISIONS OR JUDGMENTS DOES THE EMPLOYEE EXERCISE ON HIS OR HER OWN? (GIVE SPECIFIC OR CONCRETE EXAMPLES OF EACH.)

FIGURE 5-3 (continued)

5. WHAT CONTACTS DOES THE EMPLOYEE MAKE WITH PEOPLE IN THE PERFORMANCE OF THE JOB? (LIST DEPARTMENTS NOT NAMES.) TELL FREQUENCY, PURPOSE, AND TYPE OF CONTACT (WRITTEN, IN PERSON, BY PHONE).

6. WHAT PROGRAMS/PROJECTS IS THE EMPLOYEE DIRECTLY RESPONSIBLE FOR, IF ANY? (EXPLAIN THE PURPOSE OF EACH.)

7. PHYSICAL SKILLS: CHECK BELOW THE OFFICE MACHINES OR OTHER EQUIPMENT REQUIRED TO PERFORM THE PRIMARY/FUNDAMENTAL FUNCTIONS OF THIS JOB. INDICATE THE AVERAGE PERCENT OF TIME REQUIRED FOR EACH.

MACHINE	PERCENT OF TIME USED	DAILY	WKLY	MTHLY
a. Telephone systems				
b. Scanner				
c. PC/computer terminal				
d. Fax machine				
e. Forklift				

f. OTHER (list), for example, hand tools (hammers, screwdrivers); power tools, digital cameras/video recorders, etc.

8. INDICATE BELOW (X) THOSE PHYSICAL ACTIVITIES (ABSOLUTELY ESSENTIAL) TO THE PERFORMANCE OF THIS JOB. DESIGNATE THE PHYSICAL ACTIVITIES REQUIRING THE MOST EFFORT AND THAT ARE ABSOLUTELY NECESSARY TO PERFORM THE PRIMARY/FUNDAMENTAL DUTIES REQUIRED OF THIS POSITION.

FIGURE 5-3 (continued)

PHYSICAL ACTIVITIES

____Walking	____Jumping	____Running	____Balancing
____Climbing	____Crawling	____Standing	____Turning
____Stooping	____Crouching	____Kneeling	____Sitting
____Reaching	____Lifting	____Carrying	____Throwing
____Pushing	____Handling	____Fingering	____Feeling
____Talking	____Hearing	____Seeing	____Color Vision

____Depth Perception   ____Working Speed (as in assembler)

____Pulling   ____Grasping

If lifting or carrying is a requirement, what are the MINIMUM number of pounds required to be lifted or carried? _____

Is driving a motor vehicle a requirement of this job?_____

9. PHYSICAL REQUIREMENTS(DEMANDS): CHECK BELOW (X) WHICH ADEQUATELY DESCRIBES THE PHYSICAL EFFORT REQUIRED TO PERFORM THE JOB DUTIES):

a. Light tasks requiring a minimum of tiring physical effort. Performance of work provides intermittent sitting, standing, and walking._____

b. Light physical effort required in working with lightweight materials and office supplies. Occasional operation of office machines or equipment resulting in some fatigue._____

c. Almost constant or repetitive work of a mechanical or machine nature. Almost continuous sitting at computer terminal. Walking. Occasionally difficult working position. Small amount of lifting and carrying._____

d. SUSTAINED physical effort required in working with average or lightweight materials and/or office supplies with continuity of effort. CONTINUOUS SITTING OR WALKING. CONTINUOUS OPERATION OF OFFICE MACHINES OR EQUIPMENT RESULTING IN CONSIDERABLE FATIGUE._____

e. CONTINUOUS STANDING OR WORKING IN DIFFICULT POSITIONS. WORKING WITH AVERAGE OR HEAVYWEIGHT MATERIALS AND/OR OFFICE SUPPLIES._____

FIGURE 5-3 (continued)

10. WORKING CONDITIONS: CHECK BELOW (X) ANY WORKING
CONDITIONS THAT APPLY TO THE PRESENT WORK LOCATION
FOR THIS POSITION:

_____Work primarily inside _____Work primarily outside

____Hot ____Cold ____Sudden Temperature Changes ____Humid

____Dry ____Wet ____Dusty ____Odors ____Noisy

____Adequate lighting ____Adequate ventilation ____Vibration

____Mechanical hazards ____Moving objects ____Cramped spaces

____High places ____Exposure to burns ____Electrical hazards

____Explosives ____Radiant energy ____Toxic conditions

____Working with others ____Working around others ____Work alone

11. TRAINING: List any degree or on-the-job training essential to this
job (licenses, certificates, degrees). (Give minimum requirements.)

12. EXPERIENCE: What are the minimum years of job-related experience necessary to perform all of the normal duties required in this
position._____

13. CONFIDENTAL DATA: Does employee have access to confidential
data? YES____ NO____ If YES, what is the general nature of the
confidential data?

14. TRAVEL: Is the employee required to travel for business
purposes? YES____ NO____ If YES, approximately how many days
per year? _____

OTHER COMMENTS:

FIGURE 5-3 (continued)

MANAGER'S SIGNATURE

DATE COMPLETED:_____
CO./DEPT.: _____

NOTE: THIS QUESTIONNAIRE MUST BE RETURNED TO HUMAN
RESOURCES ALONG WITH A CURRENT ORGANIZATION
CHART APPROVED BY THE MANAGER'S VICE PRESIDENT,
GENERAL MANAGER, OR DIRECTOR.

Thank you,

HUMAN RESOURCES DEPARTMENT.

Personal Interviews

A critical responsibility of every good wage and salary analyst is to talk
with as many people as possible who occupy and perform the duties
of the jobs being evaluated. It cannot be performed at the analyst's
desk, but must be experienced out on the shop floor, in the engineering lab, at the office, or wherever else the job in question is being done.
Once again, if there are no job incumbents, then the respective manager
or department head must be interviewed by the analyst in order to determine how the job will interact and what its duties and responsibilities
are expected to be.

Although the personal interview may not be considered a tangible
tool of the job evaluation trade, the interviewing of those who are
already performing the job or jobs being evaluated becomes a formidable, *essential* aid in producing a good, well-written job description.

JOB DESCRIPTIONS

Job descriptions, which are the written products of the wage and
salary analyst's job evaluation process, should clearly and concisely
describe the duties and responsibilities of each of the jobs in question.

In the preparation of the job description, the experienced wage and
salary analyst uses the organization chart (see Table 5-3) to help determine the proper weight and credit for job-scoring purposes. Although
opponents of organization charts may deride them as being hanging
trees, bureaucratic red tape, artistic nonsense, and the like, they are
nonetheless valuable aids in writing realistic job descriptions.

Whether the job is an hourly wage, salaried, blue-collar, or white-
collar job does not change the process of analyzing the job. The only

practical and objective way a wage and salary analyst can prepare a clear, accurate, and comprehensive job description is to know the duties of the job *thoroughly*, and to skillfully and carefully describe those duties and responsibilities as they actually exist, not what one might suppose or assume them to be.

To fully understand and be familiar with the duties of the job under study, the analyst would be well advised to consider the following formula for success. As the human resources director, the wage and salary analyst, or whoever is evaluating the job, take the following steps.

1. Get up off your chair.
2. Take your portfolio or notebook in hand.
3. Leave your office.
4. Observe the incumbents (if any) on the job performing their work.
5. Make notes or an outline of your findings.
6. Ask for information or data from them as to *how*, *what*, *where*, *when*, and *why*, they do what they do.

Writing the Job Description

Assuming you now have an approved organization chart, have received your completed questionnaires from the department in question, and have conducted your personal interviews with job incumbents and/or the department manager, all that now remains is to begin your task of preparing a clear, accurate, and comprehensive job description.

You should also give credence and weight to anticipated future duties and responsibilities, even those that might not necessarily be a part of the job at the time it is first written.

A clear, concise, and well-written job description normally enables the reader to understand exactly what the job duties and responsibilities are. Ideally, it is written to describe what the duties of the job should be, as determined by the supervisor or manager of the job in question. A good rule is to write the job as generically as possible, as though there were no incumbent on it, and to build the description on the specific duties management expects future occupants of the job to perform.

This does not mean that you ignore the work that the incumbents are currently performing and what they tell us they do—far from it! However, you must always keep in mind the purpose and reason for having such a job at all, and where it fits into the overall department structure. This again is where preliminary job knowledge gathered from the chart and questionnaire can be of tremendous help in getting the feel for job duties and responsibilities before the actual analysis begins.

The format, or technical construction of the job description, also deserves your attention. You will find that the most effective techniques in writing a job description are

1. to summarize the duties and responsibilities of the job as clearly and completely as you can in the first paragraph, sometimes referred to as the topical or summary paragraph, and

2. to elaborate on these duties in the subsequent paragraphs.

The description should be concise, just long enough to adequately acquaint the reader with the essential duties and responsibilities of the job without unnecessary details. Contrary to some popular beliefs among wage and salary analysts, a sign of a good job description is not how long it is, such as, how many paragraphs or how many pages. Similar to Abraham Lincoln's famous comment that a person's legs should be just long enough to reach the ground, so should a well-written job description be just long enough to acquaint the reader with all of the principal job duties and responsibilities of the position. It rarely needs to exceed one page, with one-half to two-thirds of a page normally adequate to get your main points across.

The language should be simple, clear, and straightforward. It should not be sprinkled with oblique, flowery, or 64-dollar words. When you read a job description that does have such words, it's a fairly sure bet that the analyst who wrote it did not have a full grasp of the job and is probably just trying to meet an assigned quota of jobs written. Of course, it may also be an attempt by the analyst to get signoff approval of the description draft from his or her supervisor or checker by dazzling that person with big words and impressive language. The experienced analyst knows that tactic seldom works. Again, when too many big and important-sounding words are used in a job description, chances are pretty good that the analyst really didn't understand the duties of the job or what it was all about.

If you follow the above guidelines for researching and writing job descriptions, you will find it is the guaranteed, fail-safe way to success in the job description writing business.

Sample Job Descriptions

Figures 5-4 through 5-6 below are sample job descriptions illustrating the above-recommended methods of preparation.

FIGURE 5-4
Job Description

Job Title: OFFICE MANAGER   Grade Level: 7

Job Code: 1650   Exemption Status: NONEXEMPT

Company Name: ABC CORPORATION, INC.

Department Name: VARIOUS   Department No.: VARIOUS
(This job may be used in any department authorized to have a position of Office Manager on its staff.)

PRIMARY FUNCTION: Under the direction of the department manager, responsible for supervising office clerical personnel.

Supervise clerical personnel on the basis of economy and effectiveness. Maintain office and personnel records, and ensure that supplies and clerical support are available for staff. Gather data and prepare periodic reports. Assist with budget preparation and control. Select, train, and motivate personnel, initiate wage increases, promotions, and transfers, as well as disciplinary action including termination when warranted.

Conduct new-employee orientation and explain benefit programs. Must be familiar with ABC Corporation policies and procedures. Supervise the ordering of supplies and recommend the purchase of new office equipment or furniture.

Input special hours (sick time, vacation, and personal time off) into payroll system, and finalize payroll.

Perform other related duties as required or assigned.

PHYSICAL/MENTAL REQUIREMENTS: Flow of work and character of duties involve the coordination of manual dexterity and normal mental and visual attention. Activities: Fingering (55 percent of time spent on keyboard), seeing, sitting, talking, walking.

Wage and Salary Analyst:_____

Approvals: _____
                          (Name)   (Title)

                   _____
                          (Name)   (Title)

FIGURE 5-5
Job Description

Job Title: RECEPTIONIST/CLERK   Grade Level: 4

Job Code: 1675   Exemption Status: NONEXEMPT

Company Name: ABC CORPORATION, INC.

Department Name: WAREHOUSE   Department No.: 950

PRIMARY FUNCTION: Under the direction of the warehouse manager, or office manager, responsible for performing a variety of clerical duties, including one or more of the following:

Type reports, charts, graphs, correspondence, and memos. May take or transcribe dictation using dictating equipment. Enter data into computer terminal. Greet visitors or customers and direct them to appropriate individuals. Answer telephones. Take messages, answer questions, and direct callers to appropriate parties. Open and distribute incoming mail and prepare outgoing mail. Maintain office files, order office supplies, and operate a variety of office machines such as an adding machine, transcription machine, computer terminal, personal computer (PC), fax machine, and photocopier. Maintain good housekeeping in work area.

Perform other duties as required or assigned.

PHYSICAL/MENTAL REQUIREMENTS: Flow of work and character of duties involve the coordination of manual dexterity, and normal mental and visual attention, or part-time normal, and part-time concentration and coordination. Activities: Walking, stooping, reaching, talking, handling, hearing, standing, carrying, fingering (50 percent of time spent on keyboard), seeing, working speed, sitting.

Wage and Salary Analyst:_____

Approvals: _____
                    (Name)   (Title)

          _____
                    (Name)   (Title)

FIGURE 5-6
Job Description

Job Title: SHOP FOREMAN   Grade Level: 23

Job Code: 4427   Exemption Status: EXEMPT—EXECUTIVE

Company Name: ABC CORPORATION, INC.

Department Name: REPAIR SHOPS   Department No.: VARIOUS

PRIMARY FUNCTION: Under the direction of the shop manager, supervise the profitable operation of all repair activities at the shop. Select, train, supervise shop personnel and maintain training programs for new shop employees. Initiate wage increases, promotions, transfers, disciplinary action, and terminations. Ensure work area is maintained in a clean and orderly manner and that personnel comply with good safety practices and regulations.

Initiate methods of improving efficiency in the shop. Check progress of work performed, resolve problems, and provide technical information and assistance to shop personnel. Make final inspection of completed work. Review serviceability of completed work and ensure completion of all necessary paperwork. Keep shop manager apprised of delays or problems that may prevent meeting work deadlines.

Perform other related duties as required or assigned, and especially with regard to serving the customer.

PHYSICAL/MENTAL REQUIREMENTS: Walking, climbing, stooping, reaching, pushing, talking, depth perception, crawling, crouching, lifting (minimum 50 pounds), handling, hearing, standing, kneeling, carrying, digital dexterity, seeing, working speed, balancing, turning, sitting, throwing, feeling, color vision. Mental requirements include, but are not limited to, the ability to concentrate, take initiative, cope with stress, adapt to and stay alert in a business environment, and to use independent judgment to accomplish results.

Wage and Salary Analyst:_____

Approvals: _____
                  (Name)   (Title)

            _____
                  (Name)   (Title)

Testing the Job Description

The hallmark of a well-analyzed, well-planned, and well-written description is whether a person totally unfamiliar with the job itself could read the job description for the first time and understand in fairly general (if not specific) terms what is expected of the persons classified on this particular job.

Why Job Descriptions Will Remain Necessary

Although job descriptions have been an essential tool of wage administration for quite a few years, modern business practices as well as new governmental rules, laws, and regulations would seem to dictate that they are still vitally necessary and will continue to be a part of the business scene for many years into the future.

Americans with Disabilities Act (ADA/ADAAA)

The Americans with Disabilities Act (ADA) was revised January 1, 2009, as the ADA Amendments Act (ADAAA). The ADA, which originally became effective in 1992, has been greatly expanded to include many other disabilities heretofore excluded by law or legal interpretation. For example, the amended law now requires that disabled persons be covered under ADAAA even if their condition could be mitigated by medication, assistance technology and equipment, or learned behavioral adaptations. Such was not the case under the original ADA. In addition, the disability does *not* have to limit more than one major life activity, which in itself is broadened to include working, communicating, concentrating, thinking, reading, and other activities of central importance. And finally, ADAAA states that the limitation in question need not be significant or severe, but merely a "substantial limitation." However, transitory and minor impairments still do not qualify as disability.

These ADA/ADAAA provisions are a prime example of the continuing need for well-written, clear, and factual job descriptions. By clearly indicating in the description the duties of the job together with its mental and physical requirements related to lifting, walking, standing, job pressures, and so forth, and by reading or showing the job description to the employment applicant (nondisabled as well as disabled), the employer goes on record as affirming that these standards are an integral part of the requirements of the job being filled. If the applicant maintains that he or she can indeed perform the job as described, the employer is then obliged to include that person in the list or group of potential candidates being considered for the job. If a disabled applicant states that he or she can perform the job duties if some accommodation is made by the employer, and if, as the law states, such accommodation is considered a reasonable one, then the employer is also required under ADA/ADAAA to view that person as a viable job applicant.

In determining just what is a reasonable accommodation, its cost, as well as the inconvenience or disruption to the employer's operation if the disabled person is hired, are both relevant factors. In the meantime, the more that disabled persons are given the opportunity to demonstrate their worth, the sooner they and their new employers will benefit.

In any event, it should be clear that even in this one area of personnel management, companies that do not update their job descriptions to reflect the lifting, walking, standing, reaching, and other physical and mental requirements of each individual job—or that perhaps have no descriptions at all—can look forward to an uphill challenge in defending themselves against charges of discrimination involving disabled job applicants and current employees as well.

(Information on new ADAAA provisions courtesy of Council of Parent Attorneys and Advocates, Inc. [COPAA].)

Protection Against Other Discrimination Charges

Up-to-date, well-written job descriptions also provide protection against other types of discrimination charges involving sex, age, race, national origin, and religion. For example, it will be clear to government agencies, plaintiffs' lawyers, and the general public that this particular company, in its official documents stating the duties and responsibilities of each job in the company (such as job descriptions), makes no reference whatsoever to any factor relating to discrimination. Properly written job descriptions are sexually neutral, do not speak of age, race, religion, or creed, and speak only to the essential duties inherent in the job. The only stated requirements beside the normal skill and experience qualifications mentioned in job descriptions should be those physical or mental skills that are truly required of *any* person wishing to be considered for employment with the company.

Pay Equity. In today's world we are fortunate to have laws that require equal pay for equal work, regardless of the sex of the worker. In some countries, such as Canada, for example, existing laws and regulations require that workers performing jobs of equal value be paid equally. The Province of Ontario, Canada, has passed laws that require employers with male-dominated and female-dominated jobs to make adjustments to ensure that females and males, respectively, under these circumstances are paid equally, regardless of the type of work they perform.

One of the first pieces of legislation enacted by the Obama administration was the Lilly Ledbetter Fair Pay Act of 2009. This legislation addresses the pay equity concept, with particular emphasis on the timing and filing of a charge of discrimination in an equal-pay lawsuit. This law amending the Civil Rights Act of 1964 provides that the 180-day statute of limitations for filing an equal-pay lawsuit regarding pay discrimination resets with each new discriminatory paycheck delivered to the complainant. Prior to the passage of this legislation, the U.S. Supreme Court in the case of *Ledbetter v. Goodyear Tire & Rubber Co.*, 550 U.S.618, had upheld the statute of limitations for presenting an equal-pay lawsuit, that is, the date the pay was agreed upon, not the date of the most recent paycheck, as a lower court had ruled

Opponents of the Lilly Ledbetter Act argue that if an employee can wait for many years before submitting a claim of discrimination, the employer's reliance on non-permanent documents and memories will preclude any meaningful defense to the claim. But, in any event, Lilly Ledbetter is now law and HR professionals must adapt to its provisions.

Here again, although there can never be a 100 percent guarantee, well-planned and well-written job descriptions are just about the best defense any employer can have against charges of discrimination relating to equal pay, disability, or other forms of employment discrimination. Job descriptions support and back up various point-scoring or other evaluation systems that, in turn, justify different grade levels, with correspondingly different wage- or salary-range guidelines. The case can certainly be made that when the job description makes no reference to gender, men and women alike are eligible and considered for these jobs based on only one criteria, namely their ability to do the job, regardless of being either male or female!

Don't let anyone convince you that job descriptions are just another example of bureaucratic red tape, or again, merely artistic joy overriding commercial advantage, as we've heard before. To the contrary, you'll find them to be just about the most important weapon in your compensation and human resources arsenal.

The Importance of Updating Job Descriptions

Each job must then be kept up to date as substantive changes, whether additions or deletions of responsibilities or duties, occur. Even if no meaningful changes do happen, for example, within a year, it is still strongly recommended that all jobs be reviewed at least once a year by the compensation department in conjunction with the respective department supervisors or managers involved. By updating the descriptions, including any changes to the original set of duties, and obtaining departmental approval signatures, many problems are thus avoided.

Morale Building

When employees' jobs are systematically and periodically reviewed, their morale will in all likelihood improve when recognition is made of additional or expanded job duties and responsibilities, resulting in possible increases in wage- or salary-grade levels for the incumbents. It should also be recognized, however, that grade-level reductions, together with decreased salary potential, may also occur when significant duties are removed from the scope of any given job. Whether or not labor-grade changes result from the annual or periodic review, the very fact that the company recognized that, for example, duties *were* added to the job and subsequently to the job description, does tend to boost the morale of "our most important asset!"

Protection Against Misunderstandings

An accurate, understandable, and up-to-date job description also lets employees know what is expected of them in terms of their duties and responsibilities, and leaves little room for argument or contention that they were never really aware of what was expected of them. To further insure this knowledge, some companies feel that it's a good idea for all employees to be provided with a copy of their job description, and they require a signed receipt from employees stating they have received, read, and understood the description.

An Aid in Performance Evaluation

A current job description also becomes a valuable tool and aid for supervisors and managers at performance evaluation time. When employees are aware of exactly what is expected of them, supervisors have ready-made and built-in standards against which their people's performance may be measured. When descriptions are confused, hastily prepared, unclear, or not up to date—and certainly if no description exists at all—bosses have an uphill battle explaining and/or defending their evaluation of items in which employees may have fallen short in terms of their performance. So make your managers' collective lives much more pleasant—and your employees' lives as well—by having well-written, easily-understood, and current job and position descriptions for each and every job in your organization.

Please understand the distinction between having a job description for each job in your company, as opposed to having one for each employee. Most companies try to have as few job descriptions as possible. One very effective way of doing this is to use as many generic classifications as possible, such as accounting clerk, receptionist, data entry operator, or administrative assistant. They will have one description (in other words, one piece of paper) for each classification, regardless of how many employees may be classified on them, or the many depart-ments in which they may be used. If the work happens to be organized into different levels or degrees of complexity and grading, you may still have, for example, Accounting Clerk I, Accounting Clerk II, and even Accounting Clerk III jobs with progressively higher grade levels, if the increasing complexity of the work warrants such a distinction. These are still considered to be generic jobs that may be used in all departments.

A Foundation for the Wage and Salary Program

Having a well-written job description for every different job classifica-tion in your company should and must be the goal of every compen-sation manager. Once this feat is accomplished, you have laid the foundation for your wage and salary program.

CHAPTER PERSPECTIVE

This chapter concentrated on several, but not all, areas of responsibility of the compensation function of human resources. It defined the pro-fessional tools of the compensation specialists and explained how they are used. It provided an overview of how surveys are conducted and how wage and salary guidelines are constructed. It stressed the importance of having job descriptions to the company and explained how they are written. It also reviewed provisions of the Lilly Ledbetter Fair Pay Act of 2009, as it applies to pay equity.

Wage and Salary Administration: Job Analysis and Evaluation

INTRODUCTION AND MAIN POINTS

Chapter 6 continues to describe the job analysis and evaluation process that began in Chapter 5. It explains the purposes of a formal wage and salary program and focuses on the weighing and scoring part of the process. A detailed explanation of how to design and construct a formal wage and salary program is presented. Examples of standard factors and degrees help to illustrate the hands-on workings of this important task of compensation.

This chapter also discusses the valuable role of computers, both mainframe and PC networks, in storing and maintaining the data generated in the process of creating a wage and salary program.

After studying the material in this chapter:

▬ You will understand what the purposes and advantages of a formal wage and salary program are.

▬ You will know what the different steps in the job analysis and evaluation process are.

▬ You will be familiar with the basic terminology of the compensation function regarding the job analysis and evaluation process.

▬ You will be aware of the important role computers play in compensation's functions, especially in supporting the valuable database for vital statistical information that has been generated as a result of a formal wage and salary program and its maintenance.

THE PURPOSES OF A WAGE AND SALARY PROGRAM

Organizing, developing, and maintaining a sound wage and salary program is by no means an easy task. In case you or your boss, including the CEO of the company, should need convincing as to the useful purposes of all this effort, keep the following advantages in mind.

1) A wage and salary program will help insure your company's wage competitiveness in the geographic area in which your company operates.

2) As a logical, understandable system, a wage and salary program provides management with a means to control wages and salaries.

3) If properly designed, communicated, and maintained, such a program will establish internal equity of pay within your corporation.

4) Supervisors will find they have better knowledge and control of their groups by developing and utilizing written records of duty assignments and responsibilities.

5) Supervisors will find that the wage and salary program will assist them in their hiring, disciplinary action, and performance appraisal functions by allowing them to be much better organized and informed.

6) Management will be better able to detect overlapping job duties as well as unnecessary supervisory levels.

7) Managers and supervisors will come to find that a wage and salary program will result in a uniform, easy-to-maintain job titling system.

8) A wage and salary program becomes an invaluable database for vital statistical information.

THE JOB ANALYSIS AND EVALUATION PROCESS

The basic job evaluation process consists of the following steps.

1) Wage surveys of local companies are conducted in the areas in which your company's facilities are located.

2) Wage and salary range guidelines are built for key or so-called bellwether jobs, based on survey data.

3) A formal wage and salary plan is selected, preferably one with point scoring and factor evaluation systems.

4) Under the guidance of the human resources staff, company managers and supervisors develop organization charts for all departments and divisions within the company, showing the reporting relationships of all jobs involved.

5) Presidents, managers, and supervisors involved are requested to approve and sign each organization chart for which they are responsible.

6) Questionnaires are provided to all incumbents of the jobs being evaluated (and, if possible, also to their respective supervisors), to enable the wage and salary analyst to be aware of the essential aspects of the job or jobs under evaluation.

7) Be absolutely certain that, when at all possible, your wage and salary analysts conduct personal interviews with incumbents (not necessarily all of them; a meaningful sample will do), as well as with the respective supervisors and managers of the jobs under evaluation. No worthwhile job description was ever

written, and no "right-on-the-money" job analysis was ever made from a desk in the compensation department without the analyst having first seen the job being performed, or at least without having discussed it with management when the job or position is new, in the planning stage, or is untenanted.

8) Prepare complete, clear, concise, and straightforward job descriptions to account for each job being performed in your company, from basic operative jobs to the highest echelon of executive management positions.

9) Utilizing all of the aforementioned tools, the analyst is now in a position to appraise and grade the jobs properly, using established wage and salary procedures.

10) Once jobs are evaluated, written, scored, and approved, they must then be maintained (reviewed) on a periodic basis, or whenever there are substantial changes in job duties or responsibilities (either added or taken away). In the interim period after the job is first written, or between normal job description reviews, the job should also be promptly looked at if substantial duties or responsibilities are added to or deleted from it.

APPRAISING AND GRADING THE JOBS

The next and perhaps most subjective step in the process is the analysis, evaluation, weighing, and scoring of the information you've compiled. After you have carefully studied and reviewed your wage surveys, organization charts, questionnaires, and completed job descriptions, and have chosen the appropriate wage and salary plan, you can now begin the process of determining just what value or weight should be placed on each job description that has been written.

As a compensation analyst, you will assign the proper grade level to the job, which in turn determines its appropriate wage or salary range. This scoring and grading process is a very important and key operation in that it may actually determine how effectively your company will be able to attract and to retain competent personnel.

The Design and Construction of a Typical Wage and Salary Program

The design and construction of a typical, formal wage and salary program are explained in detail below. Although there is no perfect way to master this skill and no exact science involved, there is a process to understand. After reading these suggestions, you will have an overview of the process.

The wage and salary plan you've chosen to use may have a number of *factors* relating to the skills or requirements an applicant or employee must possess in order to do the job. Each of these factors will be further broken down into five or six categories known as *degrees*, which indicate whether the necessary job skills for that particular factor are relatively simple or complex. Each degree of every factor will have some sort of assigned point scoring or value placed on it by the plan—the higher the degree, the greater the scoring.

The wage and salary analyst selects and assigns the proper degree of each factor, based on the duties of the job. The combined total point scoring of all the degrees results in a specific grade level. Each grade level in turn has a wage and salary range guideline that you originally developed from your wage survey data (see "Surveying," Figures 5-1 and 5-2 in Chapter 5; and Schedule Guidelines, Tables 5-1 and 5-2 in Chapter 5). Incumbents of the job being studied are thus uniformly classified on the resulting grade level.

The following summary may assist the reader in better understanding the job evaluation process.

The wage and salary analyst
1) reviews and analyzes the job duties.
2) selects appropriate degree of each weighted plan factor.
3) adds total resulting point scoring.
4) determines, from the total number of points, the grade level of the job.
5) selects the appropriate wage and salary range guidelines from the previously established plan developed from wage survey data.
(See example of the job evaluation process in Figure 6-1, below.)

FIGURE 6-1
An Example of the Job Evaluation Process

Bob Jones, a wage and salary analyst in the compensation group of the human resources department of Honey Bee Equipment Manufacturing Company, has been requested by Bill Dailey, general manager of the Bee Bonnet division, to evaluate a group of jobs in a newly established department of that division. Mr. Jones has requested and received from Mr. Dailey an approved organization chart showing reporting relationships within the new department, as well as position description questionnaires for the jobs involved.

After reviewing the organization chart and studying the questionnaires, Mr. Jones visits the new department and conducts personal interviews with the job incumbents. Satisfied that he understands the job functions and their reporting relationships, he then proceeds to write accurate job descriptions and submits them to General Manager Dailey for his and other necessary approvals.

When the approved job descriptions are returned, Mr. Jones then begins his evaluation process to determine the exemption status of each job, and

FIGURE 6-1 (continued)

to arrive at a grade level by applying the proper point scoring for each factor (education, experience, job complexity, etc.). One of the particular jobs involved, for example, is titled net sewer. The analyst, based on his understanding and knowledge of the duties of this job, first determines that this is a nonexempt job—in other words, an hourly paid job, not exempt from the overtime and other provisions of the Wage and Hour Law.

He next reviews the different degrees that make up each factor (first degree—5 points, second degree—10 points, and so on), and based on his knowledge of the duties of the job, he then selects the correct degree for each. For example, one specific requirement of the net sewer job might be mechanical knowledge, specifically the ability to operate a professional Model X sewing machine. The applicable factor here would be the experience factor to reflect the amount of time required to professionally operate that machine or an equivalent. If the job required a minimum of two years of such experience, and since the company's wage and salary plan assigns different points to different levels of experience, the job analyst in this case would assign the third degree of the experience factor, which calls for one to three years' experience, and has a point value of 60.

After considering all the factors relating to the net sewer job, he then proceeds to assign the proper degree of each in order to arrive at the total scoring. Mr. Jones' point scoring summary might look like the following:

FACTOR	DEGREE	POINTS
Education	2nd	30
Experience	3rd	60
Job Complexity	2nd	30
Supervision Received	2nd	10
Errors	2nd	10
Contacts	2nd	10
Confidential Data	1st	5
Mental/Visual Demand	2nd	10
Working Conditions	3rd	15
	Total Points:	180

FIGURE 6-1 (continued)

Next he refers to the wage and salary point scoring manual, which has a predetermined range of points for each grade level. Table A below might represent a table from a typical scoring manual.

Table A

POINT SCORING RANGE	NONEXEMPT GRADES	EXEMPT GRADES
100 AND UNDER	1	–
105 – 130	2	–
135 – 160	3	–
165 – 190	4	–
195 – 220	5	–
225 – 250	6	21
255 – 280	7	22
285 – 310	8	23
315 – 340	9	24
345 – 370	10	25
375 – 400		26
405 – 430		27
435 – 460		28

Because the analyst has scored the net sewer's job at 180 points, he has determined that his scoring falls in the Labor Grade 4 range, so this job is officially designated as a Labor Grade 4. Because the wage range guidelines for a Grade 4, let us say, have a spread of $8.75 to $13.15 per hour, the net sewer's supervisor may then pay this employee an hourly rate of pay within that particular wage range (see Tables 5-1 and 5-2, Nonexempt Wage Schedule Guidelines and Exempt Salary Schedule Guidelines, in Chapter 5. These are only hypothetical wage and salary range tables, but they show suggested percentage of dollar spreads within each range as well as between ranges.)

FIGURE 6-1 (continued)

The wage and salary analyst then informs the division general manager of the final outcome of the job evaluation project. The analyst also provides copies of all completed job descriptions to authorized managers and supervisors.

PLAN FACTORS

Wage and salary plans normally have several standard factors. Any number of degrees may be included in each factor. In the examples below, five degrees for the education factor are delineated, while only four degrees are given for the errors factor.

Standard Factors

The Education Requirement Factor. One of the most common standard factors is the education requirement factor, which spells out the amount of education an applicant typically should have in order to successfully perform the job.

■■■ The *first degree* of the education requirement factor might, for example, call for a high school diploma or GED (high school equivalency program), and this degree of the factor would carry a value, perhaps, of 10 points.

■■■ The *second degree* might indicate that high school plus specialized training of some type is required in order to do the job. Let's assume your plan calls for a value of 15 points for this degree.

■■■ The *third degree* might specify a requirement for a college degree in a particular field. Let's have your plan assign a value of 25 points to this degree of the factor.

■■■ The *fourth degree* of the education requirement might contain a master's degree requirement and have a point value of 40.

■■■ The *fifth degree* would normally only apply in the case of a job requiring a Doctor of Philosophy (Ph.D.) degree in some specialized field, assuming that you had such a requirement. The point value here might be 60.

A Sample Evaluation. Focusing upon the education requirement factor, let's do a sample evaluation of a standard accountant-type position, not a bookkeeper or junior accountant, but a basic accountant job. After reviewing the duties and responsibilities of the job, the wage and salary analyst determines that in order for a person to be able to adequately perform the accountant job, the successful applicant would need a bachelor's degree in accounting, or its equivalent in years of experience. Normally, equivalency is determined by equating two years of experience to one year of college.

The education requirement factor may even specify a particular field of accounting (cost accounting, inventory accounting, tax accounting, or other) that the analyst believes is necessary. In any event, in the particular case under discussion the analyst would assign the third degree of the education requirement factor with its 25 points of scoring. In a like manner, the analyst would go through each of the other factors in the plan, assigning the proper degree and corresponding point scoring, exactly as we did with the education factor.

The Errors Factor. In all probability, an errors factor will be included in the wage and salary plan you have chosen. The errors factor addresses the type of error that the incumbent of the job could normally make (that is, has the possibility of making) during the performance of the particular job in question. The reader should clearly understand that this errors factor is not intended to measure that once-in-a-lifetime monumental error that is always possible in the performance of almost any given job, no matter how high or how low its position on the organization chart.

The degrees in the errors factor of your plan might look something like the following:

■ The *first degree* of the errors factor could provide for the commission of errors that may be of little consequence in the overall job. Such errors require little effort to redo or correct the work. This degree might be assigned 5 points.

■ Errors in the *second degree* might have an internal effect that would require some corrective measures by others. Let's assign this degree 15 points.

■ The *third degree* of the errors factor might be considered to be more serious. These are errors that require a great deal of effort by others to correct and/or redo the work. The point value here might be 30 points.

■ In the *fourth degree*, errors could be considered to be substantial, have an outside effect on the operation of the business, and require a great deal of additional effort to correct. Error in the fourth degree can also result in financial loss since the work normally needs to be redone and corrected. Let's have the plan assign a value of 45 points to this highest degree.

Based solely on the duties described in the job description, the wage and salary analyst now determines that the accountant job under study should carry the fourth degree of the errors factor. The reason is that this degree most nearly represents the typical consequences of any errors that accountants classified on this type of job and performing this set of duties might normally be subject to committing in the course of their work.

Combined Factors. You now have assigned 25 points of scoring based on the education requirement factor and 45 points from the errors factor, for a total of 70 points from these two factors. When you have considered all degrees of each of the remaining factors in your plan in like manner, you then total all the respective scoring points to determine the grade level of the job that, as explained above, gives us the appropriate wage or salary range guidelines to be used to compensate incumbents of the job. We repeat that there are any number of wage and salary evaluation plans that the human resources professional can use, but the scoring procedure just described should be somewhat typical or common to all of them.

STATISTICS, REPORTS, FACTS, AND FIGURES

The heart and lifeblood of any compensation function or department are the meaningful facts, figures, and statistics that group members will compile, collect, and categorize with regard to all phases of employee compensation. As we strive to become more of a paperless society, the more it will require us to mechanize and computerize these data.

In the past, data had been maintained almost exclusively on main-frame computers. While still used by larger companies and in certain circumstances, mainframes have largely given way to other micro-processor-based systems, including networked servers and mid-size systems utilizing a variety of operating systems, from Windows to various flavors of Unix.

This latter approach normally results in substantial cost savings after the initial investment, as well as practically total freedom and independence from mainframe software and systems. Advances in informational technology have proven to be a boon, both to human resources personnel as well as to compensation department users, whose programs do not always merit top priority in the project request waiting lines of management information systems and data processing departments.

PCs

The PC desktop and laptop computers and their related programs are the featured sales and marketing products of most hardware and software companies and vendors today. Complete, off-the-shelf PC software is available for just about any business application from fixed assets, accounts receivable, and inventory control, to human resources, compensation, benefits, and payroll functions.

These software programs allow their users nearly total control over their respective reports, surveys, statistics, and other data as they enter, store, and retrieve information that formerly lay exclusively in the domain of the overworked and usually understaffed data processing departments. The microplatform PC software will not solve all your information problems, but it will allow you the luxury of not having to depend exclusively on the availability and priorities of MIS programmers to supply the data you must have on a timely basis in order to do your job—and do it well! (Chapter 5 contains a listing of human resources software vendors with information on their products, services, and contact information.)

Taking the concept of separation of the user from technical considerations even further, one of the recent advances in software technology is known as "Software as a Service" (pronounced "saas"). A category of "Cloud Computing," SaaS involves a provider licensing an application to customers for use as a service on demand. SaaS software vendors may host the application on their own web servers, or download the application temporarily to the customer's device (e.g., PC). In addition to reducing complexity and IT infrastructure and support costs, on-demand licensing allows a firm to avoid purchasing a separate license for every device that will use the software. Application service providers (ASPs) may also use this concept to share licenses between firms.

CHAPTER PERSPECTIVE

The purposes and advantages of a formal wage and salary program were explained in this chapter. The weighing and scoring part of the job analysis and evaluation process were explained in detail. The basic concepts and terminology of this important compensation process were presented. The chapter also discussed the valuable role of computers in storing and maintaining the data generated in the process of creating a wage and salary program.

Employment Policies and Practices

INTRODUCTION AND MAIN POINTS

This chapter focuses on the employment function of human resources, which is responsible for hiring employees as well as for long-term staffing strategies and programs. The hiring process involves recruiting, interviewing, and screening applicants. The tools and resources of the employment specialists are the resume and application (including e-resumes and e-applications), the interview, preemployment aptitude and personality testing, and substance abuse testing. Practical guidelines on how to hire employees without having your company sued for discrimination are presented. Safeguards of a drug-free work operation are specified. The importance of recruiting personnel for the success of the company's overall performance is emphasized.

This chapter also discusses the unemployment insurance function, which is often advantageously combined with the employment function. The problem of timely responses to claims and suggestions on how to solve this costly problem through centralized processing are presented.

Finally, the need for employment personnel security is explained and several practical recommendations are made.

After reading the material in this chapter:

■ You will know what the employment function consists of, whether in a large corporate setting or a small business.

■ You will understand the importance of background checks and workplace security.

■ You will become aware of the importance of recruiting for excellence.

■ You will know what the tools of the employment specialist are and how to use them.

■ You will know how to avoid discrimination lawsuits against your company while recruiting, interviewing, and screening applicants.

■ You will become acquainted with some of the legal ins and outs of drug testing.

■ You will have a better understanding of the difference between independent contractors and employees.

■■ You will know what the unemployment insurance function is and its primary problems in responding to claims.

■■ You will become aware of the need for security in employment offices and you will learn how to increase security in such settings.

THE EMPLOYMENT FUNCTION

No matter how large or how small, every company has either a highly organized and formal staff of employment interviewers and/or recruiters or as few as one person (often the owner) whose duties include the employment function. Every company, from the Fortune 1000 to the corner independent drugstore or the Little Acorn Family Restaurant at some time or other needs to hire people to help run the business and serve customers. This is the *employment function*, and its importance in any enterprise should never be understated.

In larger companies, the employment function is usually an integral part of the human resources department, and it has the very critical responsibility of recruiting, interviewing, and screening job applicants, either directly or through divisional employment staffs in other geographic locations. In addition, the corporate employment manager normally has the mandate to design and implement the company's long-term strategic staffing plans and programs while, of course, remaining in compliance with state and federal employment laws and regulations.

If its employees are a company's most valuable asset, it follows that the success or failure of the enterprise can be greatly influenced by the quality of the employment group's recruiting and screening efforts. Competent, loyal, hardworking, and productive people, as well as those who lack these particular qualities, all apply at the employment office, submit e-resumes, or answer classified ads. The skill and conscientiousness of the employment staff basically determines which of these two groups will enter your work force, perhaps even to the extent of whether your company succeeds or fails.

Managerial Recruitment

A further refinement of the employment group's hiring responsibility lies in the area of managerial or supervisory recruitment. Many, if not most, companies adopt and adhere to the credo of promotion from within, and in many instances, due to the uniqueness of the company's product or service, promotions are necessarily based on the experience and demonstrated ability of a person within the organization. However, occasions occur in every company when it is practical and necessary to recruit from an outside source, as, for example:

▬ when expanding into a new line of business;

▬ when a particular department or even division is consistently failing to meet profit or other objectives; and

▬ when it is determined, in general, that only an infusion of new blood will correct the problem and put the entity back on the road to profitability.

In such cases, the employment group has the special task of finding and recruiting the particular type of management talent the situation calls for. Depending on the level of the executive or managerial position being sought, the employment department may do any or all of the following.

1) Advertise for the opening in either local or national newspapers, magazines, and trade publications.

2) Advertise current openings on company's Web site.

3) Participate in job fairs where such candidates may be present.

4) Coordinate their efforts with local employment agencies or executive search firms.

Regardless of the methods used to seek out and attract these managerial candidates, the employment staff must retain complete control of the recruiting effort at all times and must act as the catalyst in making the job search a successful one.

If the opening is for an upper-management position such as a divisional vice president, for example, the board chairman, chief executive officer, or the board of directors itself will normally communicate through the employment manager (or in some cases with the human resources manager or vice president), in order to determine the exact status and progress of the recruiting endeavor.

When a candidate has been selected, or in the event one or more applicants is invited to the company for interviewing and testing, it is often the responsibility of the employment manager to look to all the necessary details of travel, lodging, and interviewing schedules, as well as relocation and housing matters. It is that manager's responsibility to provide whatever assistance it takes to make things as convenient and helpful as possible for the applicants and for their families as well. All of this speaks well for the company regarding its thoughtfulness and concern for its people. Employment applicants—whether or not they are successful—cannot help but be impressed by your courtesy and, either as employees or future customers, they will not forget.

THE HIRING PROCESS

No matter what the size of the particular company involved or the number of job openings being filled, the hiring process is characterized by certain common denominators.

1) A given job opening is advertised on company home pages, on Web bulletin boards, in local newspapers, in trade magazines, by posting on company bulletin boards, or by word of mouth.

2) If a person applies for the job, the person is asked to fill out an application-for-employment form and return it to the employment department. This should apply to former employees as well as previously unknown applicants, so that they can account for their employment experience while away from the company.

3) The employment group then screens the applications to determine whose qualifications most closely fit the requirements of the job in question, calls the applicants in to be interviewed by the employment staff, and from these selects those to be referred to the supervisor or manager of the job being filled for interview and final consideration. Depending on the level of the job opening or the hiring practices of the individual company, the applicant may be interviewed several times before the actual hiring decision is made. This same process may also be used when current employees apply for transfer or promotion to an existing job opening.

4) Once the hiring decision is made, the applicant for our job should be checked for:

> Employment authorization to work in the United States
> Criminal history
> Credit history
> Previous employment history verification
> Education verification
> Driving record (including showing valid driver's license)
> Personal references

A signed release from the applicant giving the employer permission to check the above items is usually necessary; however, a statement giving such permission may be included on the back of the application form for the applicant's signature. Though sometimes cumbersome and time consuming, checking an applicant's past history to make sure they are who they claim to be is a long-term dividend by keeping problem personnel out of the organization, and protecting the company from employee actions for which it may be legally responsible.

5) Another recommended practice the employment group might follow is that of sending out a thank you letter or card to those who apply for employment, and especially to those who have been interviewed by HR and/or other department or line managers. When an applicant is rejected for a particular job, or the application is put on hold for consideration for other openings, a brief note or even form letter from the company thanking the

person for applying is always appreciated. Job applicants are also potential future customers, and they will not forget your courtesy. Unfortunately, many companies today do not follow this simple policy.

BACKGROUND CHECKS IN A POST-9/11 WORLD

The September 11, 2001, terrorist attacks on the United States' homeland that killed almost 3,000 people changed — at least temporarily — the employer-employee relationship. The average American worker especially related to the tragedy because those who died in these attacks were all people at work, performing their respective jobs. At the time of the attacks, many people in the media, as well as in corporate offices and boardrooms, said that our lives, including those of the average working man and woman, would be forever changed. And certainly so it then seemed. But with the passage of time since those tragic events, a closer look indicates that neither employees nor businesses have changed their habits, attitudes, or wants from what they were prior to September 11, 2001, and that a general business-as-usual attitude prevails — with one possible exception.

Employees in any occupation are now more keenly aware that terrorists can strike at any time, at any place, and at any employer, including their own. Throughout the country a major battle is shaping up between the need for our security and the rights of privacy for our citizens, the latter of which traditionally has been highly valued by all. But post-9/11, surveys are beginning to indicate that while employees still value their privacy rights, they are increasingly concerned that their employer is doing everything possible to keep inappropriate people out of the workplace. The majority of survey respondents believe that background checks of job applicants are not only acceptable but essential. Some would also like to see background checks done for current employees. There is special concern that ID procedures for entering workplaces and accessing computer systems should be strengthened and that more detailed background checks should be done on all job applicants. ID cards featuring photo, personnel data, and hand or fingerprint identification seem to be gaining popularity as a means of preserving and increasing workplace security.

In many companies, the security function falls within the responsibility of the human resources department. In others, especially larger organizations, a separate department and staff oversee that function. Now, however, with enhanced background checking and identification methods being of primary importance to most employees, HR professionals should be continuously involved in determining, monitoring, and taking a proactive role in the specific security needs of their particular company. For the foreseeable future, this need will continue, and conscientious HR involvement will help create not only a safer but a more effective and efficient work force by using background checking to uncover criminal convictions, fraudulent credentials, professional misconduct, and so on, of applicants and potential employees. One word of caution—HR professionals must be aware that under the Fair Credit Reporting Act (FCRA), if a third party conducts a criminal background investigation or credit check on applicants/employees of employers covered by the act, the employer is subject to all of the employee notice and consent provisions of the FCRA. For details see Federal Fair Credit Reporting Act, 15 USC &1681; and *www.ftc.gov/os/statutes/fcra.htm*.

TOOLS AND RESOURCES OF THE INTERVIEWER

Some of the key tools and resources that the interviewer needs and uses in the employment operation are

- the employment application.
- the interview.
- preemployment testing.
- substance abuse testing.

These tools and how the employment staff can use them to best advantage are discussed in the sections that follow.

The Employment Application

What May Not Be Asked. The employment application is normally the first step in the employment process. Most, if not all, employers are (or should be) aware of the fact that certain questions and inquiries may not be asked on the employment application, such as questions or items related to an applicant's

- Age,
- Sex,
- Number of children,
- Church attendance/membership,
- Marital status,
- Arrest record,
- Spouse's occupation,
- Applicant's or spouse's pregnancy, or
- Disability or any other health problems.

All such questions may not be asked of the applicant either verbally or on the employment application, or in any other document that the person is required to complete prior to actually being hired.

To say that certain questions may not be asked on the employment application, may be a technicality, in the sense that discrimination laws do not specifically forbid an employer from asking the things stated above, but if a company does decide, for example, to ask for the applicant's date of birth, it had better have an extremely valid reason for doing so. In the event that an age discrimination charge were to be filed against this particular company, its reasons for asking the above question should prove to be very interesting reading, to say the least.

Sources of Application Forms. Management services, such as the Bureau of National Affairs and Commerce Clearing House, as well as local stationery supply houses can provide valid, nondiscriminatory employment application forms for your use. Once you have adapted such a form to your own company requirements, you must continue to monitor and maintain it based on current as well as forthcoming employment legislation. (See also suggested Application For Employment form illustrated in Chapter 12.)

Accepting Employment Applications. In most corporations today, especially larger organizations, the paper employment application has been all but superceded by electronic applications originating from various field or store locations. And, prior to the issuance of the Uniform Guidelines on Employee Selection Procedures in 1978 (UGESP), HR professionals and company managers were advised to always accept an employment application from an individual who offers one, regardless of whether a job opening currently exists. This policy was designed to protect the company against charges of discrimination. However, since the issuance of the UGESP an employer may (probably should) define an applicant as someone who has the requisite skills and applies for a specific open position. The OFCCP (Office of Federal Contract Compliance Programs) in its rule concerning an Internet applicant allows employers to limit their definition to individuals who have the "advertised basic qualifications." The EEOC (Equal Employment Opportunity Comission) in the UGESP defines an applicant as someone "who is considered" for employment. So now the situation is basically reversed, that is, making all interested individuals applicants for employment, whether they are applying for specific open positions or not, may actually *increase* an employer's vulnerability to discrimination claims.

A Classification System for Applications. Once you have gathered a number of employment applications—and they will accumulate in large numbers after a time—you will be faced with the problem of classifying each application based on the skills and qualifications of each individual applicant. It is important to have ready access to the various job specialties and qualifications of applicants as future job openings and opportunities occur. The use of e-applications makes applications easier to retrieve and your classification system more efficient.

Fortunately, the employment specialist is now able to review applications and select potential candidates on an office personal computer with comfort, convenience, and a minimum expenditure of time, as it has become standard procedure for a number of human resources software packages to have built-in applicant-tracking functions.

If your own employment operation, however, is a relatively small one and you don't as a rule receive many applications, any clerical or manual filing system will probably suffice. The important thing, of course, is your ability to access and retrieve applications as new job opportunities occur.

Your classification system, whether computerized or manual, will also help you in complying with legal retention requirements of employment applications. They may be safely destroyed in a timely manner, if desired, based on application dates.

Employment Opportunities Posted on a Company's Web Site

Whether in good times or bad, companies are always looking for *good* employees. In fact, during periods of recession and lean economic times, recruiting some of the best candidates can help ensure a company's survival. And in boom times, frenzied competition for help requires optimum recruiting plans and programs.

In our current information technology era, any company that does not yet understand the fact that there are a lot of good, potential candidates in cyberspace faces an uncertain if not risky future. There are probably none but the smallest of companies today who do not have their own World Wide Web site, and there are few firms that do not include their employment opportunities on their Web site. In addition, company Web pages these days may include a summary of employee benefits as well as history, mission statement, principal officers, partners, or whatever else it might consider appropriate.

Human resources employment specialists understand that Internet recruiting also has such practical advantages as a meaningful reduction in often very expensive employment advertising; the immediacy in which job listings can be changed and kept updated; the worldwide scope of the Web, which increases the applicant pool (and the opportunity to reach the best talent) to an extent never dreamed of or possible before; and the reduction or total elimination of administrative costs when applications and other personnel data are put online. (*Note:* For a more detailed discussion, refer to "Recruiting Sources" in Chapter 16.)

Resume Scanning and Tracking Software and Programs

On the assumption that a human recruiter cannot look for standard skills and qualifications as fast or as efficiently as a computer can, many companies have turned to "virtual computers" (i.e., software programs that enable employers to convert resumes they receive into a data base that uses keyword search-and-retrieval software to fill job vacancies). Job candidates' resumes can be scanned into the database, which then sorts the data by job title, key words, educational qualifications, and various industry terms (e.g., "general ledger," "pay plan design," "applications designer").

This resume-scanning and tracking software is offered by any number of software vendors coast to coast. Databases constructed by such software may contain literally tens of thousands of resumes sorted by whatever criteria the individual company desires or requires, and may also be made available electronically to all managers in the company. Organizations using these tracking systems may wish to keep such resumes and applications on file for a specific period of time (60 days, for example) after which they would be deleted, and applicants would have to reapply if still interested in employment. Resumes and applications normally become "stale" after a while and the likelihood that a manager would retrieve an application that's "in the file" decreases with time.

A negative side of resume scanning and tracking, similar to other often-raised objections to the information technology revolution, is that computers can miss the human side of the candidate in question. Professional staffing personnel and recruiters can sense qualities of character, deportment, and demeanor that no computer can discern. The happy medium of using software databases controlled and monitored by one or more employment professionals can be the answer to such dilemmas. There is no question as to an employment data system's value in reducing advertising, agency, travel, and other related expenses while providing more time for HR and other managers for other duties, as well as keeping department administrative budgets under control.

As the use of resume electronic tracking and scanning continues to grow, hiring, recruiting, and filling job openings now appears to transition from an art to a science and from a luxury to a necessity in the always competitive business of attracting and retaining "good" employees.

The Interview

The employment interview is one of the most essential tools used in the hiring process. Supervisors, managers, and vice presidents, as well as presidents, all have occasion to interview job candidates, whether for new-hire or promotional purposes. And, of course, the employment staff itself interviews job applicants on a daily basis in the course of their work.

More often than not, the interview is probably the primary means of determining whether an offer of employment will be made to the job applicant. It is especially for this reason then that whoever does the interviewing must have a fundamental knowledge of the job requirements, especially the technical qualifications and the necessary personality characteristics.

What May Not Be Asked. Another especially important skill that all interviewers must have, of course, is the knowledge of what can and cannot legally be discussed in the interview. As with the application-for-employment, questions relating to age, disability, marital status, number of children, and dates of graduation from high school or college are just some of the subjects that must not, under any circumstances, be asked of or discussed with an applicant. Since basically all supervisors and managers interview job applicants from time to time, the HR professional should be certain that anyone in a supervisory capacity is informed, by whatever policy bulletins, memos, or counsel are necessary to keep them up to date about what may or may not be said to applicants, promotional candidates, or to any other employee for that matter. The uninformed interviewer risks the possibility of making innocent or offhand comments that might be interpreted as being discriminatory in content.

All supervisors must clearly understand that, regardless of their feelings or well-meaning intentions on the subject of civil rights and discrimination laws, if they ask any of these questions of an applicant, and the person is not hired—for whatever reason—your chances of defeating a discrimination charge or winning a related lawsuit realistically range from poor to none! Therefore, a training program for those who interview applicants and the establishment of good means of communication for keeping personnel up to date on related topics, should be priorities whether you are the employment manager or head of human resources.

The following guidelines illustrate what interviewers may not ask, as well as what they not only may but probably should ask when interviewing job applicants:

TEN QUESTIONS AN INTERVIEWER SHOULD *NEVER* ASK OF AN APPLICANT

1) How old are you?
2) What is your race or nationality?
3) Are you pregnant? (or, Do you have any plans to become so?)
4) Do you have a disability or any other health problem?
5) Are you married, divorced, separated, widowed, or single?
6) Do you have a family? (What are the ages of your children?)
7) Who lives in your household? (disabled or dependent parents, relatives)
8) What is your spouse's occupation?
9) What church, if any, do you attend? (What is your religion?)
10) Have you ever been arrested? (To clarify: Applicants must respond to the question of whether or not they have ever been *convicted* of a crime, but inquiries may not be made about an applicant's arrest record.)

These ten questions, and others asked in different ways on the same subjects, basically have no bearing whatever on whether or not a person is qualified to fill a particular job vacancy, and should not be asked by the interviewer. Prior to federal and state civil rights legislation, employers asked these types of questions (some still do) in an effort to determine how long applicants were likely to work for the company after the expense of training them, or making assumptions that women with families or young children would be likely to need more time off from work (as would also likely be the case if applicants were committed to caring for aging or ill parents and other relatives in their homes.)

Regarding disabled applicants, some companies held the prevailing viewpoint that they would be unproductive or disrupt the work of other employees. If people acknowledged a history of past or current medical or health problems, they reasoned this might, among other problems, adversely impact the company's medical benefit program costs.

They were also quite certain they could pay a female, for example, a lower wage and provide fewer benefits because her husband was employed. Racial, religious, and sex discrimination usually accounted for the remainder of their misguided inquiries.

TEN EXAMPLES OF QUESTIONS AN INTERVIEWER NOT ONLY *MAY* BUT *SHOULD* ASK A JOB APPLICANT

1) What was the nature of your previous jobs? What kind of work did you do?
2) What were your reasons for leaving your former (or present) job?
3) What did you like best (and least) about former jobs? (This is likely to give insight into one's occupational likes and dislikes.)

4) What are your work/career goals? Immediate? Long term?

5) What character or personality traits do you like in others? (These may also be the characteristics people like in themselves.)

6) Have you ever supervised or managed others? Did you like it? What was the largest number of people you supervised at any one time?

7) Have you ever had to fire someone? How did you go about it? How did you feel about it? (The answer may reveal something about the applicant's judgment, empathy for others, and the like.)

8) What do you already know about ABC Company? (The answers will probably show whether the applicant is interested in the company and has taken the time to research its products or services.)

9) Based on our discussion thus far, in what ways do you think you could make a contribution to our company?

10) If you did come to work for ABC Company, who do you think will pay your paycheck? (The desired answer, of course, "the customer.")

The interviewer (especially in a retail setting) may be able to tell from applicants' responses whether they really understand the importance to the company of serving and respecting the customer.

Experienced interviewers in human resources and other line or staff departments will find the questions in the guidelines above (often with their own particular modifications), a relaxed yet effective method of sounding out the applicant's personality traits, goals, and general thought processes. Coupled with the more tangible qualities of experience and education, they provide a more complete picture of the individual's ability to do the job while fitting into the corporate culture or mission.

Read the Application Carefully. Another word of advice might be in order for the less experienced employment interviewer, line manager, or supervisor: The employment application should be carefully read and studied by the interviewer. Gaps in dates of employment with previous employers, for example, might signal a problem in the applicant's history that might be worth questioning. It could mean a lengthy period of unexplained unemployment, a long-term serious illness or injury that might adversely affect the person's ability to perform the job in question (even with a reasonable accommodation), and, in a number of cases, further questioning of the applicant may reveal that some time had been spent in prison during this period.

Such inquiries of the applicant can and should be handled in a diplomatic and respectful manner, but, again, this is a potential employee, a company's most important asset, and when we make the hiring decision, we must have all the facts because the stakes are always high!

Preemployment Testing

Since the advent of modern civil rights legislation some 45 years ago, much has been written, debated, published, and legislated on the subject of aptitude and personality testing of applicants for employment in the private sector. Subsequent laws have been passed, Equal Employment Opportunity Commission rules and regulations abound, and U.S. Supreme Court precedent cases are handed down. Yet, in some respects, we seem to be no closer to clear and unambiguous guidelines than we were many years ago on this topic.

It is not the intent of this work to debate or even to give an opinion on the merits of this most complex matter of employment testing; the literature is truly saturated already. However, in the hope of focusing a small ray of light on the subject, it is noted that testing, particularly preemployment testing, does have its role in assisting a company supervisor or manager (as well as an employment manager or staff member, of course) to make the all-critical judgment as to whether or not this particular person should really be allowed the opportunity of joining the company as one of its most important assets — an employee. Some companies rightfully insist on calling their people associates, system members, or family members, further emphasizing the company's insistence that these *are* their important assets.

Not the Sole Determining Factor. Preemployment testing is and should be used as just one important item of evidence in considering and making the hiring decision. It cannot be emphasized too strongly that testing should not be the determining factor — nor should it even be a major consideration — for the interviewer. It should, on the other hand, be used to gain some further insight into the applicant's overall qualifications.

A wise move for the HR manager might be to caution all departmental and line managers that they must never be governed by so-called cut-off scores in applicant testing. Some veteran managers believe that they can predict successful job performance on the basis of a specific score on an intelligence or aptitude test. They believe that some specific score, for example, is a predictor of success in the company, whereas a score lower than that is not. In addition to not being a legal test validation, many a good potential employee is probably lost to the company as a result of such a practice.

As an additional tool for the interviewer, testing can often serve as a reliable predictor of successful job performance, and can even be used to validate the interviewer's instinctive feelings about an applicant. A preemployment test, on the other hand, can be safely used to disqualify an unqualified applicant from employment. For example, an applicant failing to pass a basic typing test for a job requiring typing skills can and should be disqualified. Likewise, a person applying for a job requiring mechanical aptitude who cannot pass the related test may be eliminated as a candidate for that job. But again, it is important to remember that HR professionals and other hiring managers must always be consistent in the use and application of preemployment testing.

Personality Profile Test. One of the more popular testing or assessment techniques in recent years has been the *personality profile test*, which purports to determine various trends or tendencies in an applicant's personality having to do with such issues as loyalty, truthfulness, social values, moral values (as they relate to theft), substance abuse, cheating, and falsifying company documents.

Proponents of these personality profile tests claim validity for them based on the fact that certain given test questions are repeatedly asked from a number of different angles and in various ways, making it almost impossible for applicants to slant their answers based on what they think the company is looking for in the test. Marketers of these tests (at least the more prominent ones) usually claim validation approval by the Equal Employment Opportunity Commission, and as previously mentioned, they are becoming popular with a growing number of employers. These tests should be considered just one more bit of evidence in the employer's overall, total assessment of the applicant's qualifications.

Using Aptitude and Personality Tests Skillfully. Those responsible for the hiring decision should be aware that, although tests can be excellent employment tools, they can also prove to be dangerous if misused, and that skillful administration and interpretation of employment testing can be a very important element in the hiring decision.

Substance Abuse Testing
In Chapter 10, substance abuse testing laws and regulations will be discussed in detail, with emphasis on the subject of preemployment drug testing policies in industry and business. However, it is appropriate that a preview of the advantages of mandatory preemployment drug testing to the company be presented here, as it relates to the employment function.

A Major Expense. Without a doubt, preemployment drug screening of all applicants is normally a major expense on a company's and human resources' operating budget.

One well-known company had arranged with a national testing laboratory to handle their preemployment drug testing needs for a volume-discounted fee representing a rock-bottom price so far as these tests were concerned. All applicants for employment, whether full time, part time, or temporary, in this company of over 10,000 employees, were required to pass a drug test between the time a job offer was made and before the person actually began work. Showing a negative drug test result (that is, no drugs are detected) prior to starting work was a hard and fast condition of employment, and there were no exceptions to this policy that also included applicants for top-level executive management vacancies.

The projected cost, or investment, for this drug testing program was budgeted at approximately $350,000 per year. This and all other expenses, including essential drug testing consulting services, were to be paid by the company. Due to unexpectedly heavy turnover experience in the first quarter of the year, requiring additional hiring and testing, costs outran budget projections, and total cost estimates were projected to top $500,000 for the year. Then, as might be predicted, the program was discontinued half-way through the fiscal year.

Nevertheless, the company remained convinced of the value of preemployment drug testing, and plans were made to resume preemployment testing beginning with the next fiscal year. The only basic difference when the program resumed was that the applicants for employment, rather than the company, were now responsible for paying for the drug testing themselves, consistent with state law. Although other companies are also starting to take this approach, it remains to be seen how and if the many foreseeable problems related to applicants paying for their own drug testing will be resolved.

The experience of the company described above can be considered to be typical of the vast majority of employers. Most companies want, if not insist on, having a drug-free environment throughout their organization, but the cost of attaining such an environment in many cases is more than they think they can afford. Fortunately, however, more and more companies, and especially larger companies, are now coming to the conclusion that they can't afford *not* to have a drug-free work environment. Drug testing then becomes a routine step in their hiring procedure.

A Consent and Release Form. If a company decides to include drug testing as part of its hiring procedure, it should also consider using another protection or safeguard: a consent and release form.

Applicants sign a consent and release form in which they voluntarily agree to the collection and testing of urine samples, and, at the same time, release and hold the company, its employees, representatives, and agents harmless from any liability whatever arising out of the drug-testing procedure. The form should also contain a statement that applicants authorize the confidential release of drug test results to the company. Legal counsel can prepare an appropriate consent-and-release form containing the above provisions, which is suited to the particular situation.

Other Safeguards of a Drug-Free Operation.

In addition to preemployment drug testing, many companies have also set up other safeguards in order to insure a completely drug-free work operation. For example:

1) Postaccident drug testing. A company may establish, of course, any type of drug testing program or procedure it chooses, consistent with applicable federal, state, and local laws. The following postaccident drug testing program can work very well and effectively.

Under this program, any company employee reporting a work-related injury, accident, or illness is required to submit to a substance abuse test within a stated number of hours after the occurrence of the incident. If such substance abuse test reveals a positive result (that is, drugs are detected), the employee is automatically classified as being on an unpaid, substance abuse (SA) leave of absence. The employee must then make arrangements to take another drug test at the original testing facility within 30 days from the date of the first positive drug test result.

If the employee refuses to take this second drug test (that is, within the 30 days), or if the employee tests positive (that is, if drugs are detected) on the retest drug screening, then the employee will be considered as having voluntarily resigned from the company. This latter point is most important in that a dismissal of the employee under these circumstances as opposed to a voluntary resignation could, in some states, be more difficult to defend in any subsequent legal action. While it would be foolhardy to even imply that there can be any such thing as a guarantee of winning a substance abuse or any other kind of lawsuit, your chances of winning your case will be greater if you have a policy similar to the one described above and if you have adhered to the letter of the policy.

If the 30-day retest drug screening in the above example is negative (that is, if drugs are not detected), the employee may be reinstated from the substance abuse leave of absence but would be subject to periodic follow-up drug testing for a period of time, perhaps for one year. A second positive drug test during this 12-month period would be considered a voluntary resignation on the part of the employee. Your policy might also include the provision that while on SA leave of absence, the employee involved would not be eligible for any sort of employee benefit coverage.

The above suggested policy on postaccident drug testing is only one example of policies of this type. Your own company's situation, together with the advice and counsel of your legal advisor, must determine the details of such a program. The policy is presented here so that the human resources manager may have a framework on which to build if it is to be proposed and submitted to company management.

2) Probable cause/safety-sensitive position drug testing. Drug abuse has been recognized for some time as a problem of national proportions, and one that affects almost all businesses. In the interests of protecting its employees, customers, and the general public, many companies have instituted drug testing safeguards applying to their current employee population. For example, if a company supervisor or manager has a reasonable suspicion that one or more employees are using, selling, in possession of, or impaired in any way by illegal drugs, alcohol, or abused prescription drugs, the company may request that the person suspected submit to a substance abuse test. As with most situations dealing with this sensitive area of drug testing, however, the supervisor or manager should first contact the company's human resources specialists to discuss the matter and decide on the most appropriate course of action.

In addition, more and more companies are requiring that those of their employees in selected high-risk occupations, such as various vehicle drivers and equipment operators, should be subject to mandatory, random drug testing for as long as they occupy such jobs. Following a series of highly publicized tragic accidents in public transportation in which marijuana and/or cocaine were involved, subsequent congressional action and supporting court decisions have given reassurance to the business community that such testing programs are not only legal but may even be necessary, as well.

3) Random drug testing. In their determination and zeal to maintain a drug-free environment in their workplace, some companies have instituted a system of unannounced, unscheduled random drug testing programs within their various organizations. Normally, the only known or announced element of this testing program is that each employee in the company will be periodically drug-tested on a random basis (perhaps two or three

times during the course of a year). An employee selected for such testing is usually given about one-half hour's notice to try to ensure that the employee will be able to provide an adequate urine sample for the test. Employees who refuse to participate in random testing are subject to termination; job applicants are not hired unless they agree to the conditions of such testing.

Random drug testing is the most controversial form of all substance abuse testing. Many employees—as well as nonemployees—staunchly maintain that urinalysis drug testing is an invasion of their privacy, and that any punitive measures their employer takes against them for refusal to be drug-tested constitutes wrongful discharge, intentional infliction of emotional distress, or even breach of contract. Random drug testing is the principal area of testing wherein the courts tend to support the employee rather than the company, especially where the job does not involve high-risk or security issues. Even in the low-risk area, however, several court decisions favor the employer's right to test randomly.

Similar to any other cost/value business decision, the risk versus reward of a random drug screening program should be carefully weighed as it is more open to challenge than other testing programs. Again, this is another facet of personnel relations wherein your legal counsel can play an important role.

APPLICANT RECRUITING

In many companies, particularly larger ones, the employment department includes a group of recruiting personnel. This group regularly visits colleges and universities and sets up and/or attends job fairs with the object of attracting the most qualified candidates for the organization. Large technology as well as aerospace firms, for example, have historically recruited large numbers of technical as well as engineering personnel during expansionary periods, but even in lean economic times, they must still recruit a certain amount of new talent in order to keep up with the latest technology and to remain competitive.

Even if yours is a relatively small company and you have no formal employment recruiting staff, you must still be constantly on the alert for the high-tech or highly skilled superstars who could really be an asset to your company, consistent with budgetary and financial considerations. Classified help wanted ads, job fairs, and membership in various personnel management associations can all be helpful in continually striving to recruit the best talent your company can afford.

It is often the case in business that companies always seem to have the financial means to purchase the latest computer hardware and software (certainly not inexpensive items), as well as the most recent models of production or processing equipment, but, for some strange reason, when the unplanned expenditure involves buying, so to speak, highly skilled personnel talent, there never seems to be enough money in the budget to do so. There are not necessarily a large number of people who need to be recruited; sometimes, even one person can make the difference between black or red ink on the company's profit and loss statement. We normally get what we pay for, regardless of the commodity or resource we're buying.

The simplified model of industrial or corporate organization is a useful concept in understanding the relative importance of business components. A company's organization structure, or table of organization, is normally supported by four separate and distinct columns or legs, the first leg being marketing, the second, manufacturing, the third, money or finance, and the fourth being the personnel leg, or people. Many company CEOs and boards of directors tend to concentrate on and support the first three legs, while deemphasizing or at least giving low priority to the fourth or people leg of the table; in some cases, they even allow the fourth leg to practically atrophy. We all know what happens when one leg of a table is weaker or shorter than the others or, in some cases, missing altogether. The table is seriously unbalanced and may collapse completely, as any number of companies have already experienced to their sorrow and regret.

TEMPORARY STAFFING—INDEPENDENT CONTRACTOR VERSUS EMPLOYEE

In recent years many companies have found it easier and financially expedient to hire needed help on a temporary basis (i.e., just for the duration of the project, program, or assignment involved) rather than as a full-time or part-time "permanent" employee. When the employer develops such a need, it contacts a temporary staffing agency which, under contract, provides the requested number of persons, at a specific price, to be available at a specific time and location. When the work in question is completed, the "temps" leave the job and return to the staffing agency to become available for their next temporary assignment with another employer.

Other advantages to this type of employment include the opportunity for the employer to observe the work habits and performance of temps and to hire qualified ones as full-time or part-time employees if contractually in agreement with the staffing agency. In addition, employers can immediately remove or replace nonperforming or problem employees by informing the staffing agency that their services are no longer needed, thus reducing or eliminating the risk of charges of wrongful termination. But probably the most attractive aspect of hiring temps from a financial standpoint is that the employer is not subject to paying its share of social security, Medicare, unemployment taxes, health insurance, and other benefits for these people, and with no need to withhold and deposit federal income taxes on the temporary workers.

As with most facets of life and the business world, there can be a downside to hiring temporary employees as some companies have discovered. (See the Microsoft case below.) Temporary hires as a class could include consultants, clerical, computer, service, janitorial help . . . or any other type of assistance. Companies may try to refer to these temporary workers as "independent contractors," but the Internal Revenue Service (IRS) has established fairly specific criteria for a person to be a bona fide independent contractor, and the burden of proof rests with the employer to prove it has complied with the IRS regulations. (Note: In addition to the IRS test for independent contractor status, other laws, for example, FUTA (Federal Unemployment Tax Act), state unemployment insurance, and state workers' compensation, have separate and often different definitions.)

The degree of the company's control as well as the individual's degree of independence are critical factors and must be thoroughly examined before any determination is made as to independent contractor status. Behavioral control, financial control, and the type of relationship between the parties are the major categories to be considered. The IRS lists various so-called "common law" rules to be used by employers in determining whether or not a person qualifies as an independent contractor. These rules generally relate to the extent to which the business directs and controls the worker in doing the job; the type of instructions as to how, when, and where to do the work; the degree and type of training involved; the extent of the worker's investment in the tools or facilities used in performing services; whether or not the worker makes his/her services available to other businesses; method of payment used (i.e., whether a flat fee or periodic payment); the type of relationship involved including written contracts, any employee-type benefits provided and the permanency of the relationship; and, finally, the extent to which services performed by the worker are a key part of the company's business.

THE MICROSOFT CASE

As mentioned above, the determination of independent contractor status by a business is anything but an exact science as some companies—and in particular Microsoft Corporation—have discovered. After an 8-year legal battle, in December 2000, Microsoft announced it would pay $96.9 million to settle two lawsuits brought by thousands of Microsoft workers who contended that the software giant classified them as temporary employees in order to deny them the employee benefits regular Microsoft employees received. The case eventually was heard by the Ninth Circuit Court of Appeals, and in two separate decisions in 1996 and 1997, the court ruled that based on the merits of the case, these temporary workers could not be excluded from Microsoft's benefit plan because they were considered by the court to be common law employees and not independent contractors.

Now, briefly, let's examine just how a giant company like Microsoft ultimately found itself faced with such a costly settlement. Being a large corporation, Microsoft over the years hired thousands of people whom they classified as temporary workers. At the time of entry, the company had these temps (sometimes referred to as "perma-temps") sign agreements indicating they were independent contractors and thus not entitled to the company's benefit plan. Since they were not considered to be employees, no Social Security or other payroll taxes were withheld, all of which is appropriate for bona fide independent contractors, except that Microsoft did not comply with the common law rules listed above and a clear contracting relationship was not established. Microsoft instead chose to maintain an employer-like control over these workers, insisting on the same responsibilities, reporting requirements, and identification as if they were "real employees."

When a subsequent IRS audit in 1989 and 1990 determined that these temps were in fact employees, Microsoft agreed to pay back FICA (Federal Insurance Contributions Act), FUTA (Federal Unemployment Tax Act), and other withholding taxes and overtime. Upon learning of the IRS's payroll tax determination, a number of the formerly misclassified workers demanded full employee benefits for the time they had worked as independent contractors. The Washington Department of Labor filed suit on behalf of these individuals and approximately eight years later Microsoft paid $96.9 million in reparation for their mistakes. (See *Vizcaino v. Microsoft Corp.*, 120 F.3d 1006 (9th Cir. 1997).)

When an industrial giant such as Microsoft goes down on the issue of independent contractors, it is not difficult to imagine the shock and fear experienced by other companies, large and small, who utilize temporary workers or independent contractors. Extreme caution as well as knowledge of and compliance with the common law rules of employment is most essential; however, for those businesses interested in more peace of mind or a "safe harbor" for their temporary/independent (non-employee) program, it is strongly recommended that such organizations submit their plan to the Internal Revenue Service for approval of the status of the workers in question. (See IRS Form SS-8, Determination of Employee Work Status for Purposes of Federal Employment Taxes and Income Withholding.) Concurrence by the IRS assures the company involved that it may proceed with its temporary staffing program with impunity and with the assurance that no future problems will be encountered so long as it adheres to the original program.

THE UNEMPLOYMENT INSURANCE FUNCTION

In some companies, the unemployment insurance function may be a separate department, or it may be a section under the employment department and therefore report to the employment manager. A combined employment and unemployment operation is advantageous since there is often a commonality of information and communication in both groups relating to, for example:

- Reasons for termination
- Exit interview programs
- Files and computer data bases
- Contacts with corporate and field managers and supervisors

The joint operation also gives the employment manager a much better grasp and control of the overall employment picture, including having access to reasons for termination of former employees and knowing where more resources and effort must be directed as staffing or turnover problems become apparent in the various company locations.

In Chapter 10, unemployment compensation laws will be defined, and their role as a form of income insurance protection and how they apply to both employers and employees will be discussed. The value of a conscientious unemployment compensation staff cannot be stressed too strongly. Such a staff continually strives to represent the company's best interests by doing the following:

- Answering unemployment claims promptly and completely
- Strongly contesting frivolous or inaccurate claims
- Protesting and appealing decisions unfavorable to the company by the various state unemployment compensation boards
- Attending and representing the company at state unemployment hearings
- Carefully auditing periodic statements of charges from state agencies

The unemployment compensation group's sole purpose is to decrease the company's unemployment experience rating, as this is the basis upon which states assess charges to the company. Through its efforts, this group can save its employer considerable sums of money, which it would otherwise be legally required to pay.

Responding to Claims

One practical problem that many unemployment compensation groups face is that of responding in a timely manner to employees' unemployment claims received from the state. This is especially true of multistate employers. In most cases, the employer faces a double-edged problem when answers to unemployment claims are not returned to the state on time. Although only one state charges its employers a late filing fee ($15 per claim in Maryland), more importantly, a late response is normally considered no response at all, and the exemployee claimant is automatically granted unemployment benefits unless the company can show good cause as to why the response to the claim was late. Examples of good cause might be if the claim was originally sent to the wrong address by the state, or if there was no mail delivery on a certain date that resulted in the claim being received late. If there are other substantive reasons for late claims responses, the unemployment staff should aggressively pursue the matter with the state.

Centralized Processing of Claims

Occasionally, for one reason or another, when the state sends the unemployment claim notice to the local company office or facility, it ends up in a desk drawer or under the counter, and no company response gets sent back to the state. This particular circumstance has prompted employers that operate in various geographic areas to arrange with states to send unemployment claims directly to the corporate human resources (unemployment claims) office. To achieve this, human resources notifies the state unemployment agencies of its intention, and informs the state of the correct corporate address to which all unemployment claims are to be sent in the future.

It is also just as important for all company supervisors and managers to understand that *all* unemployment claims will now be handled by corporate human resources or at other designated locations. With this arrangement, delay is reduced to a minimum since the claims come directly to a central location. The corporate staff then calls the local company or office to determine the circumstances of the employee's leaving the company, and the response is forwarded by corporate unemployment in a timely manner to the appropriate state.

Using this method doesn't mean you'll never have a late unemployment claim response again; however, giving this method a try, you will find that:

- your chances of a timely answer will increase considerably;
- your late charges will drop; and
- the percentage of claims you win should show a considerable improvement.

Sometimes, even with this arrangement for central processing and handling, the state may occasionally still send the claim to your local facility, or their new computer may have the wrong corporate address, but, all things considered, centralized processing of unemployment claims works for the company. It will free up local store, shop, or office supervision to concentrate on managing their own marketing, repair, or clerical functions.

EMPLOYMENT PERSONNEL SECURITY

We live in a challenging and, in many respects, a dangerous world. Within any given business organization, the employment personnel staff—the manager, the interviewers, receptionist, or clerical personnel—can be and often are exposed to the same degree of risk as the employees at the company's retail stores, inasmuch as they both deal with and face the general public. In retail situations, it is not uncommon, of course, for an occasional customer to become irate about some facet of a sales or rental transaction, and to vocally express displeasure in no uncertain terms to anyone willing to listen. If the matter is not satisfactorily and quickly resolved, what started as a low-key disagreement could escalate into a full-scale shouting match with the potential for violent and sometimes tragic consequences.

This same type of scenario can also occur in a personnel employment office when, for example, an unsuccessful job applicant (on occasion with a knife strapped on the leg or sporting a gun in a holster!) in no uncertain terms loudly yells to the receptionist something like, "What do you mean I'm not qualified for the job?" and then, "And I want to talk to the idiot who made that decision!"

For those who have been in the trenches of personnel or human resources management for a while, the above example will not appear to be too much of an exaggeration. In those states where carrying an unconcealed weapon is permitted, the possibility becomes anything but remote. It is, therefore, advisable to make sure that your employment group, even if that's only one person, has some means of protecting itself as much as possible from the rare (but real) unbalanced applicant who can cause annoyance, disturbance, and occasionally tragedy in a personnel or human resources employment office.

The human resources employment office or some other area designated to receive applications should be located on the first floor of your building complex for two basic reasons.

1) You don't have to worry about applicants for employment wandering around on other floors of the building.
2) Most important, disgruntled applicants can be quickly ushered out of the building if they become rude or unruly.

Always have a prearranged procedure set up with your security personnel to handle such situations as they arise. Closed-circuit TV cameras or some type of concealed buzzer or alarm system connected to the company's security or building management department, for example, gives a certain amount of protection as well as feeling of security to the employment staff. If such arrangements are not available or practicable, it would certainly be good policy to have other HR staff members alerted to provide assistance when anything out of the ordinary occurs with an applicant. Should an emergency occur (an applicant or other person in your office becoming seriously ill, for example, or suffering some type of seizure) it is important to have at least one HR staff member trained to react quickly to such emergency situations. Once the situation is judged to be serious by a staff member, there should be no hesitation in calling for police or security personnel assistance immediately.

The human resources department constantly deals with the most complex organism ever invented or discovered—a human being. In our modern society where people seem to be more concerned about rights and privileges than duties and responsibilities, sometimes a termination or the awarding of a job or promotion to someone else—even the slightest perceived offense—can be enough to cause the individual to lose control and the unthinkable happens. News media stories of department managers, supervisors, and personnel staff members being physically attacked or even murdered in a company office, store, or shop are, unfortunately, not uncommon.

While there can be no guarantee of complete protection, it is to the benefit of the management of all companies, large and small, to install the necessary systems and procedures to protect their employees as much as possible. It is an investment, not an expense, in the security of their people as well as that of the company itself.

WEAPONS IN THE WORKPLACE

In addition to a growing host of problems concerning security in the workplace, a new and more serious challenge for human resource managers is the phenomenon of employees, contractors, or visitors of any kind bringing guns, illegal knives, explosives, or any other type of weapon prohibited by law into the workplace. Since no fewer than thirty-five states now have laws permitting licensed individuals to carry a concealed handgun—and in Vermont and Alaska anyone can carry a concealed weapon without any license or permit—the enormity of the problem of keeping guns out of the office, shop, factory, or other workplace becomes most obvious to security and human resource professionals alike. Similar to the approach to its already full plate of other responsibilities, HR must design (in accordance with applicable state laws) a sensible, logical, and understandable response to this added function of workplace safety and security.

Two specific measures are generally recommended by legal authorities to counter this security challenge:

1) There should be implementation of a workplace safety program, with specific emphasis on the problem of guns in the workplace. Highlighting the program would be the publication and guaranteed enforcement of a no-weapons policy prohibiting weapons anywhere on company premises.

2) Notices prohibiting weapons on company property should be posted at usual building entrances, in parking lots, or wherever the employer desires the policy to be enforced.

BUT—and please note this caution—a small but growing number of states have passed laws that *prohibit* an employer from prohibiting weapons in the workplace: HR professionals must keep up-to-date and aware of any changes in no-weapons laws in the particular state or states in which they operate, and design creative no-weapons policies as necessary.

A suggested sample no-weapons policy is presented in Figure 7-1 below. The policy should be signed by the company president/CEO, and posted on company bulletin boards and in conspicuous places throughout the property. Some employers may wish to provide a copy of the policy to each employee and request that it be signed, acknowledging receipt.

FIGURE 7-1

ABC Company Policy Regarding Weapons in the Workplace

Discussion: The ABC Company desires to make its employees specifically aware of its position regarding the matter of weapons in the workplace. If, after having read this policy statement, you have any questions, you are urged to refer it to the human resources department.

Policy: All persons entering company premises at any time for any reason, regardless of whether or not the person is licensed to carry a weapon, are prohibited from carrying a handgun, firearm, or prohibited weapon of any kind onto the property. Police officers, security guards, or other persons with written permission by the company to carry a weapon on the property, will be the only exceptions to this policy.

Definitions:

1) Prohibited weapons include any type of weapon or explosive restricted under local, state, or federal regulation, including all firearms, illegal knives, or other weapons covered by law.

2) Company property as stated in this policy includes all company-owned or leased buildings, parking lots, and company vehicles.

Searches: In an effort to maintain a safe and productive work environment for ABC and its employees, ABC reserves the right to conduct searches at the company's discretion. Therefore, every employee will be required, upon the company's request, to submit to a search of any pocket, package, purse, briefcase, toolbox, lunch box, or other container brought onto company property; to submit to a search of a desk, file, locker, or other container provided by the company; and to submit to a search of any vehicle brought onto company premises. The company reserves the right to conduct searches without the employee being present. By coming onto ABC property, an employee consents to a search; an employee's refusal to consent to such a search can lead to disciplinary measures, up to and including discharge.

Albert B. Collins
President and CEO
ABC Company

As noted above, posting of notices at all entrances would also notify visitors that weapons of any kind may not be brought onto company property.

Some examples of posted notices might include those shown in Figure 7-2 below.

FIGURE 7-2

ABC Company Sample Posted Notices

NO WEAPONS ALLOWED

THIS NOTICE APPLIES TO ALL PROPERTY BEYOND THIS SIGN AND TO LICENSED HANDGUNS

VIOLATORS SUBJECT TO PROSECUTION FOR TRESPASS

NO PRIVATE RESPONSIBILITY FOR ENFORCEMENT

Up until recently, more often than not, the courts supported the position of the employer who prohibits employees and others from bringing weapons onto company property. But as previously stated on page 104, "Weapons in the Workplace," a small but growing number of states have passed laws *prohibiting* employers from prohibiting weapons in the workplace. Because of these new state laws and other considerations, it would therefore be expedient to consult legal counsel before publishing or attempting to enforce a no-weapons workplace policy.

CHAPTER PERSPECTIVE

In this chapter, the employment function and the unemployment insurance function were explained. These functions draw upon much of the same information and are often advantageously combined in one unit. The importance of recruiting to the overall success of a company was emphasized. The procedures of employment's hiring process are detailed, and the tools of the employment specialist are discussed from a legal perspective. How to go about attaining and maintaining a drug-free work operation was described.

The chapter also discussed the primary problem of the unemployment insurance function — responding to claims on time — and offered a proven solution. In addition, this chapter explained the need for security in employment offices and suggested several procedures for increasing it. The chapter also discussed weapons-in-the-workplace policies as well as new trends in state law affecting such policies or programs.

Discrimination, Affirmative Action, and Equal Employment Opportunity

INTRODUCTION AND MAIN POINTS

This chapter is concerned with the problems of discrimination in the workplace as well as the development of company strategies for avoiding costly lawsuits. The human resources department has the primary responsibility for protecting and defending the company against charges of violation of discrimination law. Specific strategies include the development of a written policy statement and its communication to management and staff. A sample Equal Employment Opportunity policy statement is presented.

The effects of civil rights legislation on business organizations with fifteen or more employees are discussed. Affirmative action plans are defined, and human resources' need to employ an EEO staff member is demonstrated. Reverse discrimination is defined and three landmark U.S. Supreme Court cases are presented as examples of the complexity of this subject.

Finally, sexual harassment in the business environment is defined and discussed. Included are a sample Sexual Harassment Policy Statement and a sample Notice to All Employees.

After reading the material in this chapter:

■ You will understand what discrimination in the workplace is and why civil rights legislation is necessary.

■ You will be aware of the importance of developing an Equal Employment Opportunity policy statement and educating management and staff concerning its contents.

■ You will understand that the primary responsibility for protecting and defending the company against discrimination lawsuits lies with the human resources department.

■ You will know the U.S. Supreme Court's stand on reverse discrimination and affirmative action.

■ You will know what sexual harassment is and how it can be discouraged.

DISCRIMINATION

Discrimination and its unfair practices have been a part of our existence from the time we first appeared on earth. People who were old, young, disabled, female, or belonged to different races, tribes, nationalities, or religions all undoubtedly experienced some form of discrimination, prejudice, or harassment. In more modern times, working people who wanted to organize into groups to bargain collectively with employers about wages, hours, work rules, and other conditions experienced the same discrimination and resentment.

Although much has been said, many things written, and some progress made in alleviating the causes as well as the effects of discrimination, especially in the latter half of the twentieth century, the substantially discrimination-free society is not yet a reality. Indeed, unless much greater effort at understanding and tolerance is made by all manner of companies, governments, groups, and especially by individual people, it may never become a reality.

Many of the difficulties that arise between nations and individuals today as in the past, can be linked to a misunderstanding of—and often the lack of desire to understand—the motivation and reasons why we human beings act as we do. In other words, *why* did my neighbor do what he or she did, or say what he or she said? Would I have said or done the same thing under similar circumstances? And even more to the point perhaps is, have *I* actually said and/or done the very same thing to my neighbor that I now resent in his or her conduct toward me?

Even as a nation, we might ask the same question when another country acts in any given situation, such as, would my country have done the same thing under the same conditions? And all of this, of course, might lead us to agree that we should certainly "put ourselves in the shoes" of minorities, the disabled, the aged, women, the oppressed, and the homeless, and make an effort to try to understand their point of view as well as their conduct in any given situation or circumstance. Yes, we have heard it all before, but we must continue to remind ourselves that the age of true and absolute nondiscrimination must be preceded by a new and universal age of understanding and reason.

Laws as Interim Need

We in human resources must be pragmatic and practical enough to know and believe that great efforts involving universal understanding and tolerance are still needed before all forms of discrimination cease. In the meantime, assuming this reality may not occur in the near future, governments pass laws in an attempt to make it happen by establishing penalties for those companies and individuals who still choose to discriminate against people in covered classes or groups.

Primary Responsibility

Normally, the corporate guardian, protector, and defender of the company's best interests as they relate to discrimination laws and practices is the human resources department. As discussed in Chapter 2, the successful human resources department creates an environment in which employees consider human resources neutral territory where their concerns are addressed and fairly acted upon, and that by so doing, the human resources department represents even more effectively the best interests of the corporation.

Some people, such as associates in the legal profession, might challenge the previous statement that the human resources department is the focal point in defending the company against charges of violation of discrimination law. Some may feel that the company's in-house legal staff or retained outside counsel should really be the key area and have the primary responsibility of assuring corporate compliance with the myriad of federal, state, and local discrimination laws and regulations.

Where the basic responsibility should lie is governed by the environment or situation. For example, if your company is relatively small and you, with a small staff, handle the human resources function, then you must rely heavily either on qualified company lawyers (if they exist) or on discrimination specialists from local law firms to assist you in representing and defending your company in the event discrimination charges are filed by your employees. Your strategic defense under such circumstances is, as it would be for any other legal charge or suit, essentially in the hands of the lawyers. This by no means implies that you have abdicated your responsibility for handling and defending such charges to your legal counsel; in fact, you may just choose to handle these matters personally, or hire an Equal Employment Opportunity (EEO) coordinator to assist you. If not, then legal counsel must necessarily play a vital and key role in interpreting the law, analyzing the circumstances of the case in question, and advising you as to the wisdom of either fighting or settling the current charge at issue.

Some smaller companies feel it is prudent to rely upon legal advice and assistance when discrimination or other types of charges are filed against the firm. It is, of course, essential to be represented by counsel if a lawsuit involving discrimination or any other charge or complaint is filed by an employee or customer. However, depending on the size of the human resources staff, and its overall experience in handling such matters, discrimination charges may sometimes be investigated, handled, and resolved exclusively by human resources with little, if indeed any, professional legal advice involved. In any event, and under any conditions, where a functional human resources department exists in the company, corporate policy should require that it assume the primary (not to be interpreted to mean exclusive) responsibility of protecting and defending the best interests of the company when charges of discrimination of any kind are filed against it.

STRATEGY FOR FIGHTING DISCRIMINATION

An Official Written Company Policy

The keystone of every company's defense in protecting itself against any type of employee relations law violations, charges, claims, and lawsuits, is a clear, unambiguous, and forthright written company policy signed by the president of the company and stating the company's support of and intention to strictly adhere to the provisions of the particular law in question.

All employees should be provided with a copy of this official policy, which should also inform employees of the procedure to follow and the proper company official or department to contact in the event they have any complaints, problems, questions, or feedback. In addition, employee handbooks, new-hire data packets, supervisors' and managers' personnel policies manuals, and related materials should all contain similar references to the company's position regarding personnel laws, and encouraging employees to advise management if they have questions or encounter problems.

Any number of human resources magazine articles and books, as well as management services of the Bureau of National Affairs (BNA) and the Commerce Clearing House (CCH), contain sample personnel policies. These resources can help the human resources professional in providing at least the framework for developing the company's written position on the policy. In addition, more and more data and assistance regarding HR matters is available through the Internet or so-called Information Highway (see Chapter 16 for more detailed discussion of human resources and the Internet).

The likelihood of a court suit or at least a discrimination charge is very real in most companies today, regardless of size. The courts, the Equal Employment Opportunity Commission, or any other government agency, for that matter, will normally want to see your official company policy on discrimination and equal employment opportunity early on in the proceedings. You will be fortunate, indeed, if you are able to present to the agency in question an up-to-date, well-written company policy that makes it clear that your company not only supports the law in question but also urges its managers and employees to do the same.

Another important point is that company statistics on the numbers of minorities, women, and disabled persons in its work force and in management positions speak much louder than all the protestations the human resources vice president or other company officials may make as to how this particular corporation supports and encourages equal employment opportunity. While it is true that your actions do speak much louder than your words, a strongly worded policy statement directed to each employee indicates your company's official commitment to equal opportunity and becomes a vital element in defending against discrimination claims and charges.

Figure 8-1 below contains an example of an equal employment opportunity policy statement that has been used and found effective in communicating in simple but direct language the position of the company on this particular subject.

FIGURE 8-1

Sample EEO Policy Statement

ABC Company
Policy Statement
Equal Employment Opportunity Policy

As an equal employment opportunity employer, ABC Company believes in and practices fair and equal employment opportunities for everyone.

Certainly, one of the most complex challenges still confronting our nation in general and industry in particular is to provide full and equal opportunity for all people without regard to sex, age, race, color, national origin, religion, or disability.

While civil rights laws have been enacted for some time to assure such equality, many individuals and institutions continue to be negligent in meeting the requirements of the laws, and to that extent equal opportunity for all is still not a reality.

It is most important, therefore, that we all strive aggressively to assure the entry and growth of minorities, women, and disabled persons in our work force until it is unmistakably clear that equality of opportunity at ABC is a fact as well as an ideal. It is obviously not enough to simply claim that we support equal opportunity; as the law and the courts have stated and continue to state again and again, results count far more than intent. To achieve these results, our efforts toward equal employment opportunity for all our people should go beyond the letter of the law and result in total commitment to this goal on the part of every ABC employee.

Your cooperation and support in this matter are most essential in assuring that true employment opportunities will exist in all ABC entities.

Albert B. Collins
President and CEO
ABC Company

You'll notice that the chairman of the corporation signed this policy statement. It is absolutely essential that no less important an official than the chair of the company sign all policy statements in order to ensure that employees, customers, vendors, suppliers, and others understand that this policy has the backing and total support of the top official of the organization.

CIVIL RIGHTS LEGISLATION

These laws were conceived and created by Congress and/or the presidents of the United States in response to the existing blatant patterns and practices of discrimination against minorities and women in our country, especially in the areas of hiring, promotion, termination, and transfer—in other words, in practically every facet of employment.

The Civil Rights Act of 1964 was the legislative response to the demeaning effects of discrimination, particularly in the workplace. As with the National Labor Relations Act, passed almost 30 years earlier, a specific body or commission was created by the law to enforce and oversee the provisions of the new act. This body, known as the Equal Employment Opportunity Commission, was delegated the power to do the following.

- Receive complaints from employees.
- Mediate and settle disputes related thereto.
- Bring suit against companies for egregious discriminatory conduct or willful disregard of the employment rights of their employees covered by the law.

Generally speaking, any company with fifteen or more employees that is engaged in an industry affecting commerce is subject to the Civil Rights Act. Federal, state, local public employers, and educational institutions were added in 1972 to increase the scope of coverage of the law.

AFFIRMATIVE ACTION PLANS AND PROGRAMS

Many companies that are not government contractors voluntarily institute affirmative action plans in order to demonstrate their support of and compliance with civil rights legislation. Such plans generally indicate the company's current minority population and stipulate its future plans and programs for increasing minority as well as female participation in hiring and promotion. The government encourages sincere and realistic voluntary affirmative action plans, and employers will find such plans helpful in preventing as well as defending against future charges of discrimination.

Your company is considered to be a government contractor if it:
- Has fifty or more employees;
- Has a contract with the United States of $50,000 or more; or

■ Has a subcontract of $50,000 or more which is necessary to a primary contractor's performance of a covered federal contract;

■ Has government bills of lading that in any 12-month period total, or can reasonably be expected to total, $50,000 or more;

■ Serves as a depository of government funds in any amount; or

■ Is a financial institution that is an issuing and paying agent for U.S. savings bonds and savings notes in any amount.

If your company meets any of these criteria, you are required to have a formal affirmative action program documented by a written affirmative action plan. Lack of such a plan, or failure to properly maintain or carry out the provisions of it, could result in loss of the current government contract with possible disbarment from future government contracts.

HUMAN RESOURCES EEO STAFFING

Depending on the size of the company involved, even the most inexperienced human resources managers or professionals will recognize that the complexity and importance of properly handling discrimination charges and dealing with the federal Equal Employment Opportunity Commission, as well as state, county, and municipal civil rights agencies, require at least one full-time staff person. The person in this full-time position would be responsible for the preparation of affirmative action plans and of statements of position, which are written statements to the EEOC or to state or local agencies explaining and defending the company's actions in answer to discrimination charges filed by employees.

If the budget allows, the company might consider hiring an equal employment opportunity coordinator, a position that would report directly to the personnel director or vice president of human resources. Depending on the size of your organization, the coordinator may eventually need an auxiliary staff of one or two part-time or perhaps even full-time people to:

1) Compile related payroll and/or human resources data for affirmation action purposes.
2) Write computer programs.
3) Take statements from witnesses.
4) Handle phone calls, letters, and personal meetings with employees regarding discrimination matters.
5) Draft position statements.
6) Perform the many, many other support services related to defending the corporation when charges are brought, or legal action taken in discrimination matters.

Although the human resources function first and foremost represents the best interests of company management and ownership, HR personnel also assist employees to the best of their ability. Nevertheless, human resources is ethically and morally bound to defend the employer against discrimination charges and court actions—especially the frivolous and vexatious ones—to the best of its collective ability.

REVERSE DISCRIMINATION

If your company hasn't yet experienced reverse discrimination charges, that is, nonminorities or males charging discrimination, you will probably be confronted by such charges sooner or later. The law is very specific in that it prohibits discrimination in any form, against any race, color, creed, sex, national origin, and so forth. It does not state, nor was it ever intended to forbid, discrimination only against a particular race, creed, sex, religion, or anyone who happens to fall in some covered or specified class of persons.

Quotas

The law as written, interpreted, and amended, however, does prohibit the establishment of such things as *quotas*, which dictate that a given company, for example, must strive to employ and promote a specific percentage quota of minority and female employees in order to make amends for the past evils of discrimination. Legislative as well as judicial pronouncements on the subject all stress that such quota systems may not be used, since "the two wrongs can never make it right," nor even adequately begin to atone for the racial sins of the past.

Landmark Cases

The reading of several landmark United States Supreme Court cases that involved reverse discrimination might assist the human resources practitioner in better understanding this concept as well as the Court's reasoning in arriving at its decisions. In particular, each of five following Supreme Court cases decided between 1978 and 2003 presented new and different aspects of the reverse discrimination problem to the Court, and each also added to the body of legal knowledge concerning affirmative action.

- *The Bakke Case*—Bakke, a white student, was rejected for admission to the University of California medical school at Davis. He brought suit, alleging that except for a special minorities admissions program which reserved 16 slots for minority applicants to increase minority representation in the student body, he would have been admitted. He claimed this racial preference violated his constitutional rights under the Equal Protection Clause of the Fourteenth Amendment, as well as Title VI of the Civil Rights Act of 1964, and the California Constitution.

The Court concluded that Bakke was improperly denied admission to the medical school on racial grounds; but also held that race may be given some consideration in an admissions process in order to create a diverse student body to further the education process. (*Regents of the University of California v. Bakke,* 438 U.S. 265, 17 FEP 1000 [1978])

* ***The Weber Case*** — A collective bargaining agreement between Kaiser Aluminum and Chemical Corporation and the United Steelworkers of America provided for an on-the-job training program to train selected employees in craft skills. One black employee and one white employee were to be alternately selected as training vacancies occurred. The selection process was to be maintained until the percentage of black craft workers at Kaiser approximated the percentage of black employees in the local labor force in each Kaiser plant area. Weber, a white worker, filed suit challenging the program when he was passed over for this training in favor of a less senior black employee.

The Court decided that the training program was valid under Title VII, holding that the law was not intended to prohibit voluntary affirmative action. (*United Steelworkers of America v. Weber,* 443 U.S. 193, 20 FEP 1 [1979])

* ***The Fullilove Case*** — A provision was included in the 1977 Public Works Employment Act that required that, absent an administrative waiver, at least 10 percent of federal funds set aside for local public works projects must be used by state or local grantees to procure services or supplies from minority business enterprises [MBE].

Several contractors sought legal relief from the Court, alleging that the MBE preference was unconstitutional.

The Court approved the 10 percent MBE set-aside because it was considered to be equitable and reasonably necessary to redress discrimination that had been identified. (*Fullilove v. Klutznick,* 448 U.S. 448 [1980]).

Three recent and relevant U.S. Supreme Court cases:

* ***The Grutter Case*** — Under the University of Michigan Law School's admissions policy, certain racial minorities were given special consideration for admission. In 1996, Barbara Grutter, a

115

white Michigan resident with a 3.8 GPA and a 161 Law School Admissions Test (LSAT) score, was rejected for admission into the University of Michigan's Law School. The Center for Individual Rights filed suit on her behalf in December 1997, alleging that the university had discriminated against her on the basis of race in violation of the equal protection clause of the Fourteenth Amendment to the U.S. Constitution and Title VII of the Civil Rights Act of 1964. Grutter said she was rejected because the law school used race as the main factor giving African-Americans, Hispanics, and Native Americans a significantly greater chance of admission than white and Asian-American applicants with similar credentials, and that the university had no compelling interest to justify that use of race.

In March 2001, the U.S. District Court ruled that the admissions policies were unconstitutional because they "clearly consider" race and are "practically indistinguishable from a quota system." In May 2002, the Sixth Circuit Court of Appeals reversed the decision, citing the *Bakke* decision, and allowing the use of race to further the "compelling interest" of diversity. Plaintiffs subsequently requested U.S. Supreme Court review. The Supreme Court agreed to hear the case, the first time the court had heard a case of affirmative action in education since the landmark Bakke decision 25 years prior.

On June 23, 2003, the U.S. Supreme Court held that the Law School's narrowly tailored use of race in admission decisions to further a compelling interest in obtaining the educational benefits that flow from a diverse student body is not prohibited by the Equal Protection Clause, Title VII, or s1981, pp. 9-32 (438 U.S. at 318–319) (*Grutter v. Bollinger et al.*, No. 02–241 [2003]).

- *The Gratz et al. Case*—Petitioners Gratz and Hamacher, both of whom were Michigan residents and Caucasian, applied for admission to the University of Michigan's (University) College of Literature, Science, and the Arts (LSA) in 1995 and 1997, respectively. The LSA considered Gratz well qualified and Hamacher to be within the qualified range, but both were denied admission. Petitioners then filed this class action alleging that the University's use of racial preferences in undergraduate admissions violated the Equal Protection Clause of the Fourteenth Amendment, Title VII of the Civil Rights Act of 1964, and 42 U. S. C. §1981.

The University's Office of Undergraduate Admissions (OUA) considers a number of factors in making admission decisions, one of which is race. It automatically awarded African-

American, Hispanic, and Native American applicants 20 of the 100 points needed for admission.

Writing for the 6-3 majority opinion, Chief Justice William Rehnquist stated: "We conclude, therefore, that because the University's use of race in its current freshman admissions policy is not narrowly tailored to achieve respondents' asserted compelling interest in diversity, the admissions policy violates the Equal Protection Clause of the 14th Amendment" (Jennifer Gratz and Patrick Hamacher, *Petitioners v. Lee Bollinger, et al.*, No. 02-516 [2003]).

- *Rici v. DeStafano*—In this most recent (2009) U.S. Supreme Court decision on affirmative action since the *Bakke* case—despite some elements of opinion to the contrary—the Supreme Court has said clearly and decisively that employment law only rarely permits racial preferences to remedy racial imbalance. The background of the case follows:

In 2003, in the city of New Haven, Connecticut, fire department, fifty-eight whites, twenty-three blacks, and nineteen Hispanics took tests to determine who would qualify as captains and lieutenants. Seventeen white firefighters, two Hispanics, and no blacks had test scores high enough to qualify for promotion. The city's Civil Service Board refused to certify the test results, invalidating them because none of the black firefighters who passed the exam had scored high enough to be considered for the promotions. The City stated it feared a lawsuit over the test's disparate impact on a protected minority, but the complainants (seventeen white candidates and one Hispanic) contended they were denied promotions because of their race, that is, a form of racial discrimination.

The U.S. Supreme Court heard the case on April 22, 2009, and issued its decision on June 29, 2009. In a 5-4 decision, the Court held that New Haven's decision to ignore the test results violated Title VII of the Civil Rights Act of 1964. In rendering its decision, the Court held that before an employer can engage in intentional discrimination for the asserted purpose of avoiding remedying an unintentional disparate impact, the employer must have a strong basis in evidence to believe it will be subject to disparate-impact liability if it fails to take the race-conscious, discriminatory action. Because New Haven failed to demonstrate such strong basis in evidence, the City's action in discarding the tests violated Title VII. The Second Circuit Court of Appeals reversed and remanded.

Associate Justice Kennedy, writing for the majority, concluded that "The record in this litigation documents a process that, at the outset, had the potential to produce a testing procedure that was true to the promise of Title VII: No individual should face workplace discrimination based on race. Respondents thought about promotion qualifications and relevant experience in neutral ways. They were careful to insure broad racial participation in the design of the test itself and its administration. As we have discussed at length, the process was open and fair. The problem, of course, was that after the tests were completed, the raw racial results became the predominant rationale for the City's refusal to certify the results. The injury in part arises from the high, and justified, expectations of the candidates who had participated in the testing procedure on the terms the City had established for the promotional process. Many of the candidates had studied for months, at considerable personal and financial expense, and thus the injury caused by the City's reliance on raw racial statistics at the end of the process was all the more severe. Confronted with arguments both for and against certifying the test results—and threats of a lawsuit either way—the City was required to make a difficult inquiry. But its hearings produced no strong evidence of a disparate-impact violation, and the City was not entitled to disregard the tests based solely on the racial disparity in the results.

"Our holding today clarifies how Title VII applies to resolve competing expectations under the disparate-treatment and disparate-impact provisions. If, after it certifies the test results, the City faces a disparate-impact suit, then in light of our holding today it should be clear that the City would avoid disparate-impact liability based on the strong basis in evidence that, had it not certified the results, it would have been subject to disparate-treatment liability" (U.S. No. 07-1428, *Ricci et al v. DeStefano et al.*) (U.S. No. 08-328, *Ricci et al. v. DeStefano et al.*, also on certiorari to the same court).

The preceding references and discussions of six of the major reverse discrimination/affirmative action cases decided by the U.S. Supreme Court are intended only to acquaint the human resources professional with the basic issues in each. There were quite a number of concurring as well as dissenting opinions rendered in these cases, and the curious reader may wish to review the Court's intricate but interesting rationale (both pro and con) regarding this complex and often divisive subject of national interest.

SEXUAL HARASSMENT

As stated at the beginning of this chapter, sexual harassment is one of those forms of discrimination that began far back in the calendar of our existence. Indeed, it is possible that sexual harassment might perhaps claim the dubious title of the oldest discriminatory practice, first in social, then in business relationships.

The perpetuation of sexual harassment's long history, especially in the business world, is owing to the fact that those being harassed have been coerced into tolerating such behavior under threat of loss of employment or promotion. Many victims of sexual harassment endure a hostile working environment, acquiring an unjust reputation of being a prude, a square, or just a plain weirdo, when they reject the unwelcome sexual advances or refuse to go along with the fun. (For purposes of discussion here, we will assume that the victim of sexual harassment is a female and that the harasser a male, even though the law does not make that distinction, and only addresses the harassment of one sex by a person of the opposite or same sex.)

Sexual harassment is probably one of the most insidious and cruelest forms of discrimination. Although the majority of HR professionals may have no specific admiration or affection for the host of personnel-related laws in our country today, the one exception to this must be that law that prohibits sexual harassment in the workplace in any form. Many strongly feel that it should have been on the books many years before its actual enactment. Harassment on the basis of sex was first mentioned as a violation of Section 703 of Title VII of the 1964 Civil Rights Act. The Equal Employment Opportunity Commission issued the first guidelines on sexual harassment in 1980, and in 1988 and 1999 the guidelines were supplemented by an EEOC policy statement.

HR support of this particular legislation is probably influenced by the many charges of this nature that HR staff investigates, as well as to some extent by related phone calls. Typically, such calls are from a female employee tearfully relating the usual story of unwelcome sexual advances by her male supervisor or coworker, stressing how badly she needs her job, and in some cases describing the sexual talk, jokes, or pictures at the company facility where she works. Despite repeated entreaties and guarantees of confidentiality, she will often not disclose her name or company location due to her extreme fear of losing her job or incurring the supervisor's wrath if he discovers she has complained to human resources.

The harasser involved is not always but quite often the employee's supervisor or manager who apparently never paid attention to company policy bulletins or manuals regarding discrimination, never read newspapers, books, or magazines, never watched television, or heard of the Internet. Otherwise, he would certainly have known of the literally millions of dollars' liability to which his actions were subjecting his company, for whom he acted and represented. This liability does not even address the issues of moral and ethical behavior that most corporations would encourage in those who supervise their organization's most important asset.

In many companies today, a discussion or even mention of the subject of sexual harassment often brings smiles, sometimes laughter, and frequently humorous remarks. When these elements, together with off-color jokes and remarks, do exist in the workplace, other employees sometimes join in the laughter and go along with this kind of conduct for fear of losing their jobs or being thought of as squares, wet blankets, or of just not possessing a sense of humor. However, the reality of the situation is that when the victim is terminated or demoted, even for legitimate business reasons, or if she perhaps did not receive an anticipated wage increase in a timely manner, the laughter suddenly ceases, a charge of sexual harassment is filed, and the victim's work performance or lack thereof is completely overshadowed by the allegation that an atmosphere of sexual harassment existed at that particular company, and that this was the real reason for her termination, demotion, or failure to receive a wage increase. At this point, the company finds itself with a serious problem involving a possible financial settlement, or facing an expensive court trial and the definite possibility of substantial compensatory and punitive awards to the plaintiff.

Sexual Harassment Defined

It is probably safe to say that the general public, and perhaps even many company managers and supervisors, are in most cases still not clear as to what is actually meant by the term *sexual harassment*. We read quite a bit about it in magazines and newspapers, and probably one of the most landmark and high-profile sexual harassment cases in recent memory occurred in 1991 when Anita Hill accused Judge Clarence Thomas of sexual harassment. The case was televised before a Congressional committee in Washington, DC, and obviously drew nationwide attention. Anita Hill, a former legal associate of Judge Thomas, accused him of sexually harassing her during the time they both worked for the Equal Employment Opportunity Commission in Washington, DC. To a great extent, the approval or rejection of Judge Thomas' nomination to the U.S. Supreme Court hinged on the committee's decision as to whether or not he was in fact guilty of sexual harassment as alleged by Ms. Hill. These hearings and subsequent multi-million dollar settlements of sexual harassment class actions by large corporations put the rest of the country on the alert that sexual harassment is a reality, and that it is indeed a punishable offense under the law.

Despite the abundance of information on the subject of sexual harassment, most people, including some human resources practitioners, are still confused as to the precise meaning of the term. Therefore, let's look at the EEOC's stated and official definition of just what *sexual harassment* really means. The U.S. Equal Employment Opportunity Commission's definition of sexual harassment follows.

Sexual harassment.

(a) Harassment on the basis of sex is a violation of Sec. 703 of Title VII.[1] Unwelcome sexual advances, requests for sexual favors, and other verbal or physical conduct of a sexual nature

constitute sexual harassment when (1) submission to such conduct is made either explicitly or implicitly a term or condition of an individual's employment, (2) submission to or rejection of such conduct by an individual is used as the basis for employment decisions affecting such individual, or (3) such conduct has the purpose or effect of unreasonably interfering with an individual's work performance or creating an intimidating, hostile, or offensive working environment.

(b) In determining whether alleged conduct constitutes sexual harassment, the Commission will look at the record as a whole and at the totality of the circumstances, such as the nature of the sexual advances and the context in which the alleged incidents occurred. The determination of the legality of a particular action will be made from the facts, on a case by case basis.

(c) Applying general Title VII principles, an employer, employment agency, joint apprenticeship committee or labor organization (hereinafter collectively referred to as "employer") is responsible for its acts and those of its agents and supervisory employees with respect to sexual harassment regardless of whether the specific acts complained of were authorized or even forbidden by the employer and regardless of whether the employer knew or should have known of their occurrence. The Commission will examine the circumstances of the particular employment relationship and the job functions performed by the individual in determining whether an individual acts in either a supervisory or agency capacity.

1. The principles involved here continue to apply to race, color, religion or national origin.

(d) With respect to conduct between fellow employees, an employer is responsible for all acts of sexual harassment in the workplace where the employer (or its agents or supervisory employees) knows or should have known of the conduct, unless it can show that it took immediate and appropriate corrective action.

(e) An employer may also be responsible for the acts of non-employees, with respect to sexual harassment of employees in the workplace, where the employer (or its agents or supervisory employees) knows or should have known of the conduct and fails to take immediate and appropriate corrective action. In reviewing these cases the Commission will consider the extent of the employer's control and any other legal responsibility which the employer may have with respect to the conduct of such non-employees.

(f) Prevention is the best tool for the elimination of sexual harassment. An employer should take all steps necessary to prevent sexual harassment from occurring, such as affirmatively raising the subject, expressing strong disapproval, developing appropriate sanctions, informing employees of their right to raise and how to raise the issue of harassment under Title VII, and developing methods to sensitize all concerned.

(g) Other related practices: Where employment opportunities or benefits are granted because of an individual's submission to the employer's sexual advances or requests for sexual favors, the employer may be held liable for unlawful sex discrimination against other persons who were qualified for but denied that employment opportunity or benefit.
(45 Fed.Reg. 74677, 11/10/80.)

What Steps to Take

Heeding the advice of paragraph (f) in the above definition of sexual harassment: "An employer should take all steps necessary to prevent sexual harassment from occurring, such as affirmatively raising the subject, expressing strong disapproval, developing appropriate sanctions, informing employees of their right to raise and how to raise the issue of harassment under Title VII, and developing methods to sensitize all concerned," a company needs to promulgate its official feelings via the company policy route and to issue an official statement that might read, for example, something like the policy statement in Figure 8-2 below:

FIGURE 8-2

ABC Company Sexual Harassment Policy Statement

It is ABC Company's policy that sexual harassment of its employees or its customers by company personnel will not be tolerated. All employees, whether supervisors or nonsupervisors, are responsible for ensuring that the workplace is free of sexual harassment. All personnel must avoid any action or conduct that could be in any way viewed as sexual harassment. In addition, any person who has been sexually harassed at work by anyone—including supervisors, coworkers, customers—must promptly bring the problem to the attention of his or her immediate supervisor or an official of the company. In the event that the complaint involves the person's immediate supervisor or someone in the employee's direct line of command, that employee should go to a higher supervisor or manager, or should contact the vice president of human resources.

In order that all company personnel may understand exactly what is meant by the term *sexual harassment*, I have listed below four points that should be helpful in recognizing and defining the subject.

1) Unwelcome advances, requests for sexual favors, and other verbal or physical conduct of a sexual nature that affects employment decisions, interferes with work performance, or creates a hostile work environment.

2) Deliberate or repeated unsolicited verbal comments, gestures, or physical contacts of a sexual nature that are unwelcome or offensive to a reasonably sensitive person. Included in this category are innuendoes, jokes, sexually oriented comments, or any other tasteless action of a sexual nature.

3) Any repeated or unwanted sexual comments, looks, suggestions, or physical contacts that are objectionable or cause an employee discomfort on the job, or the condoning of a working environment in which such actions occur.

4) Any of the above activities between a direct supervisor and subordinates whether you think the activities are welcome or not, or are wanted or not.

It must be also understood that when a company leader, supervisor, manager, vice president—any company official—receives a complaint of sexual harassment, it must be investigated promptly and documentation placed in applicable personnel files. When a manager or supervisor becomes aware of a sexual harassment problem, the following steps are to be taken immediately to resolve it.

1) Interview the person complaining of harassment. Ask the details of the specific instances of harassment, the dates and locations of each incident, and the names of any witnesses.

2) Encourage the complaining person to put the complaint in writing.

3) Make a thorough investigation. Talk to witnesses and other employees. Contact the human resources department for any assistance you may need.

4) Once the details of the complaint have been determined (and within no more than 24 hours, if possible), the person against whom the complaint is being made must be confronted by the supervisor and questioned about the alleged incidents of harassment. It is recommended that the complaining party not be present at this interview, unless that person specifically requests to be present.

5) When the entire investigation is complete, take immediate necessary corrective action and apply whatever disciplinary measures may be necessary and appropriate.

Special safeguards should be applied in handling sexual harassment complaints in order to protect the privacy of the complainant as well as the accused party. Discussing the matter with other employees or persons who do not have the need to know (especially coworkers of the complainant), could lead to legal problems relating to embarrassment or even slander of an individual's reputation, and the identity of the party or parties involved should be therefore kept strictly confidential. The charging party should also be reassured by management that there will be no retaliation of any kind by any supervisor or manager for having brought the complaint to the attention of management or the human resources department.

Enclosed with the policy statement is a notice to all ABC employees regarding the company's policy and attitude on sexual harassment. This notice is to be posted on all company bulletin boards throughout the organization so that employees may read it at their place of work.

Albert B. Collins
President and CEO
ABC Company

Mr. Collins, in order to be sure that each and every one of his employees is aware of the company's feelings on sexual harassment, wisely directs that the policy notice in Figure 8-3 below be displayed in conspicuous places throughout the organization:

FIGURE 8-3

ABC Company Notice to All Employees

ABC Company is an equal opportunity employer. The employment policies and practices of this company are to recruit and hire without discrimination based on race, creed, color, national origin, disability, religion, age, or sex. This policy applies to all terms, conditions, and privileges of employment.

It is ABC policy that sexual harassment of its personnel or customers by company personnel will not be tolerated. All employees—supervisors and nonsupervisors alike—are responsible for insuring that the workplace is free of sexual harassment. All personnel must avoid any action or conduct that could be viewed as sexual harassment. Any person who has been sexually harassed at work by anyone, including supervisors, coworkers, or customers must promptly bring the problem to the attention of his or her immediate supervisor. Sexual harassment can be committed by a coworker as well as by a supervisor or manager. If supervisors or managers are aware of sexual harassment in the workplace and make no effort to stop it, they are subject to immediate termination by their superiors. (If the complaint involves someone in an employee's direct line of command, the employee should go to a higher supervisor or contact a personnel staff member or the vice president of human resources at the corporate office.)

Sexual harassment demeans and offends individuals who are subject to such conduct. It creates unacceptable stress for the entire organization and imposes significant costs including a decline in company morale and work effectiveness. *This company will not tolerate sexual harassment of its employees or customers.*

If you believe you have been sexually harassed, please report any and all incidents to your supervisor immediately. Our company takes these complaints very seriously, and its policy is to take prompt action to resolve the matter. I can assure you it is also company policy that anyone complaining to the company of sexual harassment need have no fear of retaliation either in the form of job security or having to endure a hostile work environment. If it is your supervisor who is harassing you, or if your complaint to your superior does not bring results, please speak with me, the president of the company. If you wish, you may also contact the vice president of human resources at the corporate office.

Remember, sexual harassment disrupts the work environment and is grounds for immediate termination. *There will be no exceptions.* I ask that you please do your part in helping us maintain a positive, healthy, and pleasant work environment.

Albert B. Collins
President and CEO
ABC Company

Despite the fact that sexual harassment does exist in many areas of our society—and probably especially in the business world—there is definitely a growing awareness on the part of the public, and with legislatures in particular, that this is another of the modern-day societal problems and evils that must be controlled and eradicated as much as, and as soon as, possible. Some states also require posting of information specifically indicating that sexual harassment is illegal, and stating the remedies available to its victims. The states of California, Connecticut, and Maine (and the Virgin Islands) already require private employers to provide harassment training to all employees. And Colorado, Massachusetts, Rhode Island, and Vermont have laws that "encourage" employers to conduct sexual harassment training, but they impose no penalties for failure to do so. Human resource managers in these four states, however, need not have majored in "rocket science" to understand the intent of these state legislatures regarding sexual harassment training. But whether *all* states eventually require such training or not, prudent employers will consider including sexual harassment training in *all* employee training programs as a defensive step against potential future claims.

From a managerial standpoint, sexual harassment often seems to be an occupational hazard, especially for newly appointed supervisors and managers. In one particular company, no matter what type of company training programs these management trainees attended—including specific, required courses in preventing sexual harassment—within six months to a year after their managerial appointment, a number of male managers of demonstrated ability and great potential were accused of sexual harassment by one or more female staff members at their new locations. Unfortunately, after thorough investigations, the accusations in most cases were determined to be true, and the illustrious but short-lived management careers of these particular managers at this company were ended. They had lost their jobs, the company lost competent, experienced personnel, and employee morale had to be rebuilt. Nobody won. Nobody ever does when sexual harassment infiltrates a company or organization.

It would be somewhat naive to believe that this tendency toward sexual harassment began with these particular managers at the time they assumed their new supervisory duties. Undoubtedly, they had a realization of the status of their new positions and were under the impression they could use their new power with impunity, especially in the area of employee supervision and management. In most cases, it was found that the sexual harassment tendency was present in these people long before they were selected as candidates for any management training program. Intelligence, competency, hard work, and dedication are and should be essential qualifications for promotion. However, company management and those involved in the selection process must be absolutely certain by whatever means available that a sexual harassment tendency is not an element in the candidate's makeup or personality.

The consequences of this cruel form of discrimination in terms of company liability can be financially staggering and could conceivably result in the demise of the company and the loss of employment for many employees, not only those whose actions created the problem in the first place.

The battle against sexual harassment will not be a quick or easy one since, as previously stated, the root causes go far back in our history. But it will eventually be largely eliminated—at least in the workplace—and in all likelihood those most responsible for the victory will be the chief executives of America's business corporations who have the power to require their managers, supervisors, and employees to comply with this as well as all other policies deemed to be primarily in the best interests of the business entity. In truth, however, their customers, employees, and the general public will be the real winners in overcoming this most vicious of discrimination evils.

CHAPTER PERSPECTIVE

This chapter dealt with several types of discrimination in the workplace, and it stressed the need for business organizations to develop written policies regarding discrimination. Sample policy statements on equal employment opportunity and sexual harassment set forth in detail the ground that needs to be covered in such documents. While the existence of the policy statements is a legal protection to the company, the dissemination of their contents to all employees is part of the company's training.

Civil rights legislation was also discussed in this chapter. Reverse discrimination and affirmative action were defined and explored in six U.S. Supreme Court examples. The chapter also presented a thorough discussion of what sexual harassment in the workplace consists of and how it can be discouraged.

Employee Benefits Function

INTRODUCTION AND MAIN POINTS

This chapter discusses the importance of employee benefit programs. It examines the many different types of benefits that a company might offer to its employees in regard both to their effectiveness and their popularity with employees. At the top of the list are medical insurance coverage and other group insurance coverage, family friendly benefits, employee savings plans, and paid time off, but numerous other benefit programs are evaluated. How legislation affects certain benefit programs is explained. Practical advice on the implementation of several programs is offered.

After you have read the material in this chapter:

■ You will have a thorough overview of the most important employee benefit programs.

■ You will understand the relative value of benefit programs during various economic conditions.

■ You will be aware of which programs are mandated by law and which are voluntary.

■ You will know which benefit programs work best and why.

■ You will understand how highly employees value benefit programs and the importance of implementing only those that can be continued.

THE CHANGING PRIORITY OF EMPLOYEE CONCERNS

The three most important aspects of modern-day employees' working relationship with their employers are most likely as follows.

1) Rate of pay
2) Job security
3) Employee benefits

The order of importance of these items to any given employee tends to vary, usually depending on the business and/or economic environment that prevails at the time.

In Boom Times

While rate of pay or salary is never unimportant to an employee, in periods of booming economic expansion values may shift. Inflation during these periods causes merit, promotional, as well as cost-of-living increases to become a major if not primary concern to employees. Acquiring more liberal and comprehensive employee benefits is normally also considered to be a high-ranking priority so long as boom times continue.

In Times of Recession

When the economy loses its steam and recessionary times follow, personnel layoffs and reductions in force are common and the issue of job security tends to take on a more important meaning for most employees. Once again, their priorities as to pay, security, and benefits are revised and reshuffled.

As of this writing, the economic and financial outlook for the United States and indeed the entire world can only be described at best as only slightly improved over the economic and financial devastation of the last two years, when major financial institutions disappeared either through breakup, bankruptcy, or acquisition; or perhaps barely survived, thanks to the federal government's financial stimulus policy known as the Troubled Asset Relief Program (TARP). Dwarfing the 2003 "technology bubble," the 2008 "housing bubble," with its highly inflated housing prices, and sub-prime mortgage loans (and their unique packaging schemes), blew apart with such force as to rival Emerson's famous poem of the "shot heard round the world!" And, indeed, the effect was felt by the whole world and was awesome. In the United States and most countries around the world, massive layoffs and the elimination of great numbers of jobs mark this recession as one of the worst in recent memory. The unemployment rate in the United States, for example, currently tops 10 percent.

So, returning to our favorite subject, the HR profession, the challenges resulting from our current financial predicament have undoubtedly impacted all HR professionals as it once again underscores the key role of human resources in helping their companies cope and survive.

In All Economic Conditions

Whether economic times are good or bad, the subject of employee benefits is always a priority item for a majority of the American work force. At the top of the list of the many different kinds of benefits employees enjoy, you will usually find medical benefits, both for the employee and for his or her spouse and dependents. The ever-increasing costs of health care coverage and the potential for financial ruin as a result of catastrophic illness, accident, or disease are well known to most people who work for a living, and the company that offers the best program of medical coverage and protection at reasonable costs often has the best chance of attracting the most competent and qualified individuals in the job market.

As the country moves from a strictly work-for-a-living culture to a more realistic social and family values working environment, employee benefits are becoming the centerpiece of employment relationships. In addition, the current Obama administration has been and will without question become a factor for change in many phases of the human resource function, from employee benefits to union matters to health care, with anticipated changes affecting employees, their families, and employers alike. Yet, contrary to the opinion of a growing number of consultants in the human resources field, the old adage of "a good day's work for a fair day's pay" is far from obsolete. The employee should certainly have the right, if not the duty, to participate in decisions involving work methods, scheduling, policies, and procedures, and this area has seen more and more good results, especially in the concept of teaming. Nonetheless, this trend is still not inconsistent with employers retaining responsible power and control over their employees' actions, so long as companies are cognizant of current and revised personnel and employment labor laws and regulations. But employers must also consider modern-day stresses on employees, especially those related to family and dependent-care responsibilities with which many employees must cope. And, regardless of company size, the knowledgeable and caring employer emphasizes and gears the company's benefit program to this need. (See discussion of family-friendly benefits below).

THE COST OF EMPLOYEE BENEFITS

A 2009 employee benefits survey by the Society for Human Resource Management indicates that organizations spent an average of 20 percent of an employee's annual salary on mandatory benefits (including payroll taxes, workers' compensation and unemployment), 19 percent on voluntary benefits, and 11 percent on pay-for-time-not-worked benefits. Company size was not especially significant as to the cost of employee benefits except in the area of voluntary benefits, which ranged from a low of 15 percent in companies with one to ninety-nine employees, to a high of 21 percent for larger companies with employment of 500 or more. Most employee benefits offerings have experienced a slight downward trend over the past year. As I point out later in this chapter, employees consistently rate benefits as one of the key factors in employee job satisfaction and it is therefore so important for an employee benefits package to be attractive to both current and prospective employees as well as be cost effective, especially in this current downturn. A recent U.S. Chamber of Commerce survey states that as the economy slowed in 2007, employers of all sizes began scaling back on employee benefits. The average dollar amount that employees received in benefits decreased from $21,527 in 2006 to $18,496 in 2007. Randel Johnson, the U.S. Chamber's vice president of Labor, Immigration, and Employee Benefits says, "This study shows the ever-increasing cost pressures businesses of all sizes are facing in their efforts to provide health insurance to employees."

The above figures indicate that benefit costs are *real* and are always an additional cost of doing business. Employee benefits, unlike wages and salaries, are often taken for granted by covered employees and their value and worth may not be fully realized until such time as they find themselves out of work and can't believe the premium they must now pay, for example, to retain medical coverage under a COBRA (Consolidated Omnibus Budget Reconciliation Act [1985]) program. The human resources staff has an important obligation to make certain that their company is getting the most mileage for its benefit dollar, and regular benefits communications to employees via the company house organ, videos, brochures, the intranet, and so forth go a long way toward achieving this objective. (See discussion of New COBRA provisions on page 174 of Chapter 10).

SOME POPULAR EMPLOYEE BENEFITS

Spurred by employee desires as well as union pressures, the importance of benefits to employees continues to be evident as the number and scope of such benefits increases from year to year. The following are some of the more popular, well-known employee benefits:

Medical Insurance Coverage

Most HR professionals would undoubtedly agree that the single, most-valued company benefit to the average American worker is medical coverage for his or her family and dependents; and without regard to an employee's status — whether laborer or executive — is of primary concern for all who earn their living. And to be free of the worry of catastrophic medical costs is obviously a real benefit for employees and their families.

Medical care coverage is equally (if not more) important to those not-so-affluent employees who typically support young families, and who have 35 to 40 more years of work before even thinking of retirement. In the past, medical coverage was especially valued by those with chronically ill or disabled dependents who would probably not be covered for extended periods of time if the employee changed jobs. Consequently, these workers were often forced to remain in uninteresting, underpaid, and non-challenging jobs simply because their medical coverage stopped on their last day of work. Fortunately, laws were subsequently enacted that remedied this problem: In 1996 the Health Insurance Portability and Accountability Act (HIPAA) was passed that extended new protections for workers, the self-employed, small businesses, and the uninsured. In effect, employees with medical coverage could now move to another job and literally take their health coverage with them.

The expansion of the health-care umbrella by this law included the following provisions:

1) It guarantees that a person who currently has health insurance coverage through work can change jobs without fear of losing coverage, even if that person or a family member has a chronic illness. (Employees with preexisting medical conditions must start a new job within one year in order to obtain insurance coverage.)

2) It prohibits group insurance plans from dropping coverage for a sick employee, or for a business with a sick employee.

3) It sets up some tax-deductible medical savings accounts (MSAs) for small businesses, the self-employed, and the uninsured.

4) It increases tax deductibility for health insurance premiums for the self-employed from 30 percent to 80 percent by the year 2006.

Even prior to HIPAA, the Consolidated Omnibus Budget Reconciliation Act (COBRA), which became law in 1985, permitted employees who were laid off, or terminated without gross misconduct, to purchase health insurance from their former employer for a period of 18 months. And although eligible out-of-work employees had this option under COBRA, quite often the cost was unaffordable to them and they and their families had no medical insurance coverage until and unless they obtained new employment. But then in 2009, the American Recovery and Reinvestment Act (ARRA) considerably liberalized COBRA, primarily by providing government subsidies of 65 percent of the cost of medical coverage for eligible employees for a period of 9 months. And among other provisions of the law, it provided employers with a credit against payroll taxes for the cost of the subsidy. (See more details of the ARRA revision of COBRA under "The Cost of Employee Benefits" section on page 131.)

Notwithstanding the above-referred-to laws improving the access to and affordability of medical insurance, most HR professionals (and the public in general) would probably agree that some type of major health-care reform is needed in our country. Even for those with health-care coverage by employers or who can afford private health insurance, the cost of coverage continues to escalate; and though U.S. health-care is considered to be of the highest quality, there are still millions of our citizens who have no health care coverage whatsoever. And at this writing, the 111th U.S. Congress has passed comprehensive health care reform. Problems, of course, still exist. Considering the scope and purpose of the legislation, that is, that *no* citizen be without access to medical coverage, the cost of such a program and how to obtain necessary funding becomes one of, if not *the* major challenge of the legislation. Other considerations such as taxpayer funding of abortion, the roles of medical providers, employers, *and* the federal government make for many, many diverse opinions, as one might imagine. In the past—as well as in current public opinion polls—the American people have made it abundantly clear that though our health-care system stands in need of improvement, socialized medicine in any form is not the answer and not their wish.

Preventive Health Care. Some logical, sound proposals and potential answers are now also coming from prominent physicians and other medical experts who continually crusade for the cause of preventive health care by the individual person rather than the super-expensive corrective and curative measures needed once the person becomes ill. Overcoming bad habits, such as lack of exercise, smoking, eating too much, and improper nutrition is the focus of preventive medicine. These experts are confident that if people kept themselves in better health and adopted sensible lifestyles, the need for hospitals and doctors to acquire expensive and sophisticated medical equipment and technology needed to cure them would decrease, and health care costs would probably plummet accordingly. As an additional benefit, we might even be a healthier and happier society, as well.

In the meantime, until this attitudinal change concerning individual health care does occur, the medical insurance coverage benefit will remain extremely important to all workers and their families.

Although of major importance, health care is only one example on the list of employee benefits. Now let's look at some other benefits and assess their relative importance to employees.

Other Group Insurance Benefit Coverages

These might include the following benefits.

Dental coverage is always important to employees with young families. This benefit normally has a waiting period of one to two years after the start of employment to guard against people getting all of their dental work done (as well as that of their families) when they're first hired and then leaving the company.

Life insurance, of course, gives financial protection to an employee's family in the event of the employee's death. Limited life insurance coverage may also apply to employee's spouse and dependent children. Employee's life coverage is generally based on one, one and one-half, or two times the base salary, up to a maximum of $50,000.

Disability insurance provides salary income protection for employees who are totally disabled from performing their jobs as a result of injury or illness. Disability payments may be provided on a short- and/or long-term basis, and can cover a tax-free percentage of the employee's salary up to a specified maximum monthly limit. For example, disability coverage based on 60 percent of one's salary (tax free), up to a maximum monthly limit of $10,000, often makes the employee whole, and the tax-free disability payment largely offsets the loss of wage or salary income.

Travel/accident insurance provides coverage to employees who travel on company business of a multiple (usually two or three times) of their annual base salary, up to a maximum limit.

Accidental death and dismemberment insurance is designed to provide one-half of an employee's annual base salary up to a specified maximum, for loss of life, limb, or eye, as a result of accidental injury caused directly and exclusively by external, violent, and purely accidental means.

Workers' compensation insurance laws require that every employer carry industrial-accident insurance for all company employees. (Four states and the U.S. Virgin Islands and Puerto Rico have their own state-funded workers compensation programs to which employers must contribute. These four states (known as monopolistic states) are North Dakota, Ohio, Washington State, and Wyoming.) Any injury or illness requiring medical attention that is incurred by an employee, out of and in the course of his or her employment, is covered under workers' compensation insurance, making the employer generally immune from damage suits arising out of occupational injuries.

Employers should make certain that their supervisors and managers understand they may not retaliate in any way against any of their employees for having filed a workers' compensation claim; that is, they may not terminate, harass, or unjustly discipline their employees as a result of having filed a workers' compensation claim.

Employee Savings Plans Benefits

This type of benefit might include any of the following plans.

Employee profit-sharing plans enable employees to share in the company's profits that they help create. Employee sharing may consist of a percentage of the profits based on salary, or on a fixed dollar amount for each eligible participant.

401(k) plans are based upon Section 401(k) of the Internal Revenue Code, which allows eligible employees to contribute a percentage of their salary on a tax-deferred basis into a company-administered investment program. The company may also match employee contributions using a defined formula method in order to increase employee participation in the plan. These types of savings plans are designed to encourage individuals to provide for their own financial needs at retirement through the deferral of taxes on wages and on earned income from company-sponsored investment plans.

Employee stock ownership plans (ESOP) allow an employer to declare a percentage of profits to the ESOP fund and literally give employees an ownership share in the company through company stock. Employees who participate in the ESOP benefit as profits grow and company stock increases in value. They thus become owners of the company, and in some companies the employees literally do own the entire company. Contributions to the ESOP are tax deferred to the individual employee. The tax code also allows favorable tax treatment to companies that borrow money in order to set up such ESOP plans.

Many companies consider an employee stock ownership plan to be the flagship of their entire retirement benefit program. Once an employee passes the required number of years for 100 percent vesting (for example, five to ten years of employment), all monies allocated by the company to that participant become the property of that person. Participating ESOP members who resign or are discharged or laid off prior to being fully vested receive a pro rata share of their ESOP account.

Regardless of what happens to the employee in the future (such as discharge, layoff, or resignation), under the federal Employee Retirement Income Security Act (ERISA), the monies credited to that individual's ESOP are 100 percent his or hers, and are not subject to attachment or garnishment.

As with every aspect of personnel management, it is most important that employees understand and comprehend what an ESOP is and especially how much of a benefit it is now (tax deferral), and can be in the future (secure retirement), for every participant. The human resources benefit group, therefore, has the number one responsibility to communicate with the ESOP participants using every means it can devise in order to get the message across, such as paycheck stuffers, posters, letters to participants' homes (preferably signed by the company president), and any other type of communication human resources can devise to clearly explain the ESOP concept, with special emphasis on two basic precepts:

1) When you are an ESOP participant, you actually do own a portion of the company.

2) By the collective and individual hard work and effort of each ESOP participant, profits can increase and the amount of money contributed by the company to the ESOP therefore can be greater.

In times of recession, companies' stock values can be and often are adversely affected, and those workers planning retirement in the near future might face severe financial problems. But in the long term, the ESOP can generally be a good motivational benefit for the company and certainly a strong financial incentive to the employee.

Paid Time Off

This is one of the more important benefits that modern-day employees enjoy and that, according to most survey results, are so meaningful to them. This trend is likely to continue and expand in the future and employers might be well advised to consider allocating more for this particular benefit, even where the employee-benefit budget dollar is a tight one. Some examples of paid time off include:

Vacations were probably one of the first so-called fringe benefits that employees enjoyed. Vacations are usually based on length of service, with the majority of vacation policies granting two weeks' vacation after one year of service, and three weeks after five years with the company. Vacation allowances of more than three weeks tend to vary with individual employers.

Holidays are welcome work respites eagerly anticipated by employees. The number of paid holidays varies with individual companies, but common practice is to grant between seven and ten paid holidays annually. In addition, floating holidays, which are used at the discretion of the individual employee or the company, seem to be a popular practice and serve as morale builders and motivators for many employees.

Other examples of paid time off include jury duty, voting time, funeral or bereavement leave, and sick leave (often for nonexempt employees only), as well as serving as a court witness, in military summer camp, and as an election official. (Compensation or fees received by the employee for jury duty, court witnessing, election officiating, and military summer camp are normally coordinated with employees' salaries so they do not lose or gain money as a result of participating in these events.)

Family-Friendly Benefits

Child Care, Corporate Day Care. More and more successful companies are adapting to the premise that since they are located in a given community or communities, they are literally a corporate member of that community and should act as any other "good citizen" would. This responsibility goes even beyond observing laws prohibiting pollution of the community's lakes, streams, and air; supporting various civic, cultural, and charitable projects; paying its fair share of taxes; and operating its business with honesty and integrity, as it becomes more aware of and the need for so-called family friendly benefits, which are of paramount importance to those employees with child care and/or elder care responsibilities.

Especially in the larger companies, the number of company-sponsored on-site day-care centers had been increasing but due to current recession-related cutbacks is certainly not now increasing by "leaps and bounds." And again, since larger companies often have multiple locations, in most cases access to the on-site day-care facility is limited, perhaps being available only at the more populated headquarters operation. The U.S. Department of Labor states that some employers offer child care benefits to their employees, recognizing that the unavailability of child care is a barrier to the employment of many parents, especially qualified women, and that the cost of benefits is offset by increased employee morale and productivity and reduced absenteeism. Some employers sponsor child-care centers in or near the workplace, while others provide direct financial assistance, vouchers, or discounts for child care or after-school or sick-child care services. Still others offer a dependent-care option in a flexible benefits plan.

On the beneficial side, on-site day care can be especially valuable for employee recruitment and retention, cut absenteeism, and be a large boost to worker morale and job performance—as well as boosting a company's image in the community. Such a program results in a better concentration on job duties by employees since they know their child (or children) is being cared for nearby by professionals. A "Bright Horizons" survey indicates that 97 percent of top-performing employees who use the child care center stay with their organizations, and that turnover among child care users was reduced by nearly 50 percent, resulting in a $3.4 million cost savings.

It is no secret, of course, that on-site day care as a benefit can be a rather expensive investment for the employer. Over and above space, staffing, and equipment requirements, the organization must ensure that, in order to attract and satisfy parents, the operation is one of high quality. It serves no purpose to offer day care if employees are not happy with the program. Day care staff (or professional providers) must be screened and selected carefully, as well as paid adequately, with salaries sometimes reaching $35,000 per year and beyond for top personnel. But again, day care proponents will continue to point out the significant advantages to the worker and the company.

Another problem may develop when employees cannot afford the expense of having a child in the on-site workplace. In some cases, offering day care to the outside community is a method of reducing costs, especially at smaller companies. Some lower level and lower paid workers (i.e., receptionists, administrative assistants, and clerical personnel) cannot afford daycare, even with a sliding scale or subsidies, which a number of companies use. Subsidies may in themselves create a backlash from childless employees and cause potential resentment if a firm offers financial assistance to lower-paid workers. Higher-paid people and those similarly paid who do not participate in day care may also complain about the perceived inequities of the program. In reality, however, few companies report visible signs of such resentment and employees in general—even childless employees— believe on-site day care to be a worthwhile benefit and would even be willing to contribute a percentage of their salary toward the upkeep of such a facility. Overall, although the adoption of work-site daycare programs by companies has not been rapid, its future as a viable employee benefit seems assured.

Elder Care. Elder care benefits present a somewhat different scenario and challenge to the employer. Elder care is normally defined as giving care to family members over fifty years of age. It can take many different forms and can range from helping Mom or Dad with meals or groceries once a week to providing 24-hour-a-day care for a parent in the final stage of Alzheimer's disease. Such caregivers who are otherwise employed full time may well find themselves faced with the 24/7 requirements of caregiving as well as job pressures, tight schedules and in many cases child responsibilities.

Recent surveys by MetLife and AARP reveal that people-oriented companies (e.g., AstraZeneca, IBM, Fannie Mae, the Principal Financial Group, S.C. Johnson, Michelin North America, Mercy Health System) recgonize the situation and the needs of such workers and offer employee benefit plans that include relief for these "sandwich generation" workers.

In addition to causing career problems for working caregivers, their immediate job responsibilities can also be adversely affected as a result of normal worry and concern for elderly parents or relatives. Recognizing this fact, these companies know that without elder care benefits, productivity losses can be staggering (estimated to be as high as $33 billion at the national level), and they are beginning to view it as mutually beneficial. For example, though extremely difficult to measure, the goodwill and company loyalty of caregiving workers who qualify for such benefits cannot be overlooked. Once again, as such plans become more and more popular, human resource professionals are challenged to investigate thoroughly all aspects of elder care, work/life programs if their company is considering such a benefit.

Long-Term Care Insurance. Long-term care (LTC) insurance refers to the services and assistance a person may need on a long-term basis as a result of illness, an accident, or age. As the name implies, long-term care means care for a lengthy period of time either in the home or in a facility that provides LTC services. The January 2009 issue of *HR Magazine* indicates that according to the 2008 National Compensation Survey conducted by the U.S. Department of Labor's Bureau of Labor Statistics, the percentage of workers in private industry with access to long-term care insurance through their employers has doubled since 1999, from 6 to 12 percent, though the coverage is much more prevalent among companies with 100 or more employees. Currently, 20 percent of workers have access to long-term care insurance. Today's Americans are living longer and healthier lives, but since there is no immunity to the toll longevity and aging take on the human body, many of today's workers will eventually face reduced mental and/or physical ability and will require some level of LTC. Some insurance coverage for LTC may also be applied to family members. Based on the demographic trends of the last few decades, many experts predict that LTC insurance will continue to grow in importance as an employee benefit. Individuals subject to paying part or all of LTC premiums should also be aware that they are normally quite expensive and that much consideration should be given as to the absolute need for such coverage. Another caveat for the prospective buyer might be in order: select an LTC insurance carrier that will live longer than you do!

529 College Savings Plans. The 529 college savings plans refer to qualified tuition programs as described in Section 529 of the Internal Revenue Code. They offer numerous benefits to families and individuals facing college tuition costs and can be opened by a parent, grandparent, any other relative, or friend—or even by one's self. From a tax standpoint, the investment grows tax free so long as the money stays in the plan. Withdrawal of funds for qualified college expenses are free from federal income tax. All fifty states have a 529 plan, and in some states one may even qualify for state income tax exemption for qualified withdrawals. Many states allow deduction from state income taxes in the amount of the contribution. The account owner maintains complete control of the distribution and disposition of the invested funds, and generally has the ability to invest in one or more professionally managed portfolios. Contribution limits for 529 college savings plans are considerably much higher than other types of higher education funding vehicles, and for some people this is a decided advantage. At the moment, 529 plans are not exactly a "hot" item insofar as employer benefit plans are concerned, but they will receive more attention from companies and human resource planners as the current recession eases and competition for talent again increases.

Coverdell Education Savings Accounts. Coverdell Education Savings Accounts (ESAs; formerly known as Education IRAs) are another tax-advantaged way to pay for college expenses. Unlike 529 plans, investment options are virtually limitless, and except for life insurance contracts, you may buy and sell whatever you want whenever you want. They can be set up at any brokerage firm, mutual fund company, or other financial institution. Earnings in ESAs are tax deferred, and withdrawals that are used for education expenses are tax free. Another ESA advantage is the ability to make tax-free withdrawals to pay for private elementary or high school expenses, as well as postsecondary expenses. In other words, one option might be to use an ESA for private schooling while using a 529 plan for college.

Other features of Coverdell ESA's include contributions up to $2,000 per child per year; contributions are nondeductible; eligibility varies, depending upon the income level of the contributor; beneficiary may have more than one account in his or her name; and account may be withdrawn until the beneficiary reaches age thirty.

Flextime. Flextime is an alternative work arrangement option that permits an employee to work daily hours using nonstandard flexible starting and ending times. Normally, flextime is scheduled around core hours but even variations to core-hour scheduling are sometimes permitted. Flextime benefits may be granted on a short- or long-term basis, and an employee's benefits are usually not affected by a flextime schedule. Together with dependent care and flexible spending accounts, flextime is one of the three most popular family-friendly benefits.

Flexible Spending Accounts. A Flexible Spending Account (FSA) plan is an IRS Section 125 cafeteria plan that allows employees the option of pre-tax payroll deduction for various insurance premiums, unreimbursed medical expenses, and child/dependent care expenses. Employees in an FSA plan determine at the beginning of the plan year the amount of their out-of-pocket medical or child or dependent care expenses they will need for that particular year and arrange with the employer to deduct that amount from their paychecks. During the year, the employees pay for such expenses out of pocket, submit their claim for reimbursement to their employer who will then issue them a tax-free check. Both the employer and employee benefit since no Social Security, federal income tax, or state and local taxes are deducted from the reimbursed amount. A majority of employers now offer the FSA benefit as a means of attracting and retaining qualified employees.

This almost "no-lose" benefit, however, does have one caveat: employees' estimates of how much to have deducted from their pay for their flexible spending account must be carefully considered since one of the most important IRS guidelines for FSAs is the use-it-or-lose-it rule, meaning that because of the FSA tax benefit, any monies left in the account at the end of the year cannot be refunded or rolled over to the next plan year. Obviously, careful planning on the individual's part is most essential.

Corporate Sabbaticals. While sabbatical leaves have been the exclusive domain and indeed part of the fabric of higher education for over 100 years, they are now becoming almost commonplace in corporate America. The beginning of such workplace sabbaticals in the business world probably dates back to the 1970s, especially when firms in the Silicon Valley of California (e.g., Apple Computer, Tandem Computers) initiated this type of leave program in order to counter technical obsolescence and engineering burn out. The Society for Human Resource Management (SHRM) has estimated that 11 percent of large American companies have formal paid sabbatical leave programs, which in essence do not vary greatly from the traditional academic leave. Salary and benefits continue, those on such leaves return to their same jobs, and they usually have an obligation to remain with the organization for a designated period of time. SHRM also estimates that 29 percent of large companies have formal unpaid sabbatical programs.

Participants in these leave programs often acquire new skills, enhance their own expertise in their profession, perhaps redirect their careers in staff reductions, or just experience temporary relief from the corporate high-tech grind. In many cases, after returning to work, the person on sabbatical may share acquired knowledge with colleagues via training programs, seminars, and so on. Some larger companies may possess their own educational centers for sabbaticals, but others contract with various colleges and universities to provide off-site learning.

Examples of well-known companies offering sabbatical leaves include Apple Computer, Intel, S.C. Johnson, Hewlett-Packard, Frank Russell Company, Nike, Silicon Graphics, AT&T, IBM Corporations, and PricewaterhouseCoopers.

Employee Assistance Programs. Within varying degrees of formal or informal policy, most larger companies offer confidential 24/7 counseling and information services to their employees. Such counseling is often necessary in the event of such tragic events as natural disasters, violence and killings in schools, terrorism (e.g., the September 11 tragedy), and other catastrophes, whether in workplaces, schools, or the community at large.

Many companies offer an employee assistance program (EAP) to assist employees in coping with stress or other personal or work-related problems that might otherwise seriously affect their personal lives as well as impair job performance. Companies may use in-house psychologists or trained specialists or contract with outside EAP counseling firms, depending on the nature and gravity of the problems being handled. Counseling may also be extended to family members and others directly involved or affected by the events in question. In some organizations, EAP counseling may consist simply of HR referring employees with drug- or alcohol-related problems to local or national substance abuse agencies for assistance.

Human resource specialists must keep in mind that properly designed and implemented EAPs should be supportive rather than punitive. If illegal substances, for example, are detected in random or periodic drug screenings—or if employees voluntarily ask for company assistance with their alcohol or drug problems—we should be careful to strike a balance between helping the individuals in question and taking whatever action is necessary to guarantee a safe and drug-free environment for the protection of the rest of the organization.

Service Awards

This type of benefit is made to company employees, whether full time or part time, upon the completion of specified milestones of company service, normally in increments of 5, 10, 15, 20, 25, 30, and more years. They are normally highly regarded by employees as recognition by the company of their performance and contributions during their years of service. The form of the service award is not of the greatest importance to the employee, but the recognition is.

A number of companies go to great lengths to demonstrate to their employees that management also highly values these awards. In many cases they will provide elaborate, full-color catalogs and/or brochures featuring a large variety of quality gift items from which employees select the service award gift of their own choosing. Other organizations, although still highly valuing the concept of recognition, simply offer a more traditional pin, necklace, bracelet, ring, or watch whose intrinsic value increases in proportion to the number of years of company service or employment.

Severance Pay Program

This benefit is one that most employees hope they never have to use. A severance pay program is set up in most companies to assist employees who, through basically no fault of their own, have lost their jobs and need some financial help to bridge the gap while they are seeking other employment. The company should consider a severance pay company policy normally based on a formula geared to the number of years of service. In the event of a layoff caused by a reduction in work force, organization restructuring, or similar event, the severance policy should be utilized. Also, if an employee's termination results from his or her inability to do the job even though the employee has demonstrated conscientious effort and a generally good attitude, company managers should be authorized to grant severance pay as provided by company policy.

Although severance is normally not paid when a person resigns voluntarily, the severance policy should not be so rigid and unbending that supervisors and managers do not have the leeway to exercise their own judgment in this regard. They are the people on the spot, and they should know better than anyone else whether or not the person has been a conscientious employee, whether there was any dishonesty or willful misconduct involved, and what the circumstances were in case an individual legal challenge is made.

Regarding severance pay plans, it is important to know that under ERISA, a severance pay plan is considered to be a welfare program and, as such, must be reported to the U.S. Department of Labor in the same manner as the retirement plan document, and other employee benefit plans that are defined as welfare programs. Form 5500, "Annual Return/Report of Employee Benefit Plan," must also be prepared and submitted by the company, normally the responsibility of the human resources benefits staff. The company has complete freedom to set up its severance program as a discretionary one, based on whatever provisions it thinks appropriate for its operation. However, the notification and 5500 form must be submitted to the Department of Labor on an annual basis.

Don't let the ERISA reporting requirement stop you from advocating a severance policy. The paperwork, as always, is cumbersome but not excessive. The severance policy will be appreciated by your employees and their families, and though it is a voluntary or nonstatutory benefit (similar to vacations, for example), it can often become meaningful in the competitive market for competent employees.

A severance pay formula as described in Table 9-1 below might look something like this:

TABLE 9-1
Severance Pay Formula

Years of Service	Severance Pay
After one year of service	1 week
2 but less than 6 years	2 weeks
6 but less than 10 years	3 weeks
10 but less than 15 years	4 weeks
15 but less than 25 years	5 weeks
25 years or more	6 weeks

It should also be noted in your severance policy that, in addition to severance pay, employees discharged or laid off will also be paid for any unused vacation and sick pay for which they are eligible (unless there is evidence of willful misconduct). This makes it clear to employees and supervisors alike that other payments such as vacation and sick pay should not be used as substitutes for, or in lieu of, severance pay.

Educational Assistance Programs
Most companies, recognizing the value of continuing education to the personal development of their work force, will often establish an educational assistance benefit program. Such a program may be designed to assist their employees in becoming better performers on their current job, as well as to prepare them to qualify later for other higher-level jobs within the organization. In addition, educational assistance programs also give the individual employee a better sense of self-esteem and pride in accomplishment—and it certainly is no secret that a company cannot help but benefit from a better-educated work force.

No specific guidelines or standards exist regarding what a company should cover in an educational assistance program. Some companies will pay the entire cost of tuition, books, and other associated fees. Others allow 100 percent reimbursement for college courses that benefit the employee's current position, and 50 percent, perhaps, for those taken for the purpose of preparing for new job responsibilities or advancement within the company. On the other hand, a company may choose to pay for only the employee's tuition, and then not always at the 100 percent rate. Often, a company will require that employees must be approved for the tuition program by their manager; that the employees must attain passing grades; and, to lessen the chances of schoolwork interfering with their job performance, that no more than two courses be taken at any one time. Other provisions or conditions, of course, may be added at the discretion of the individual management.

When we speak about educational assistance benefit programs, we are usually implying a system of reimbursement to the participant: After the tuition is paid at the beginning of the course and the course is completed in accordance with tuition policy provisions, then the employee is repaid by the company.

Some companies that require employees to take certain courses related to their job allow for advance tuition payments whereby the company prepays the cost of the course or courses for those who might not otherwise be able to pay. In addition to the other provisions of the policy, employees given advance tuition must then sign a statement agreeing to reimburse the company from their last paycheck in the event of termination for any reason before courses are completed. Advance tuition reimbursement should be used sparingly as it will otherwise tend to become the rule rather than the exception, and the human resources department runs the risk of becoming a collection agency (along with the related administrative problems and complaints), which it was never designed to be.

Education for the Competition. One final comment on this particular benefit: A viable, well-administered educational assistance program is an excellent benefit for any company, large or small, to have and to support. The human resources manager, however, must be watchful of the program to be sure that, as sometimes happens, the company is not simply training and educating the work force to qualify for higher-level and better-paying jobs with the XYZ Company located across the street. The XYZ Company may extend open arms to your employees who have completed a portion or even all of their college education through the good offices of your generous educational assistance program sponsored and underwritten by your company.

Of course, a company cannot legally bind its employees to continue employment with it once they have their education behind them, because verbal or even signed agreements are not normally practical or enforceable in situations of this kind. So, how do we cope with such a problem? The old fight-fire-with-fire doctrine might have some application here, in that if the XYZ Company sees value and promise in these people, why can't the ABC Company (your company) do likewise? And since they are your employees, you certainly have the inside track.

Rewarding Employee Achievement. The problems in the ABC Companies of the world on the subject of employee education are more ones of complacency and inattention to the progress of these usually ambitious members of the company. They are determined to get their education and probably just as determined to get ahead in the world of business. In other words, they're good employees! The human resources department can be very effective in making another contribution to the company by, firstly, giving personal recognition to those completing associate's (A.A. or A.S.) and bachelor's (B.A. or B.S.) degrees through the company's educational assistance program. Since human resources administers this program, it knows who the participants are, what courses they're taking, and when they expect to complete their studies. Well-designed and highly embellished Certificates of Achievement, for example, would certainly be in order. Pictures of the graduates in the company newspaper or magazine, and on company bulletin boards, in other words, a little attention, recognition, and publicity is never in bad taste. It might even encourage their fellow workers to also try their hand at this education business.

Second, and probably most important, keep in touch with your employees in the education program, and encourage their supervisors and managers as well to work with them, to notice them, and especially to keep them in mind as new job openings and promotional opportunities arise. After all, you're paying for their education—why not take advantage of your investment? As the complexity of business and technology continues to increase, in coming years the companies with better work force education levels will be the winners as the competition surges. Your educational assistance program may not be the deciding factor, but look at it as one of the more important employee relations investments you will make in your most important asset.

Credit Unions

Although not always considered by employees to be a true benefit, which in fact it is, a credit union is an excellent way for company employees and their families to join together to save at high dividend rates, and to borrow at low interest rates. Credit unions are chartered and regulated by the federal government, and members' savings are insured up to $250,000 until the end of 2013 by the National Credit Union Administration (NCUA), an agency of the U.S. Government.

Credit unions also offer the convenience of payroll deductions for both savings and repayment of loans. Special savings plans such as Christmas clubs and vacation clubs can also be included for the convenience of its members. Savings in a credit union are usually known as shares, in that they represent ownership, but unlike stock, because of federal insurance of members' funds, there is no risk. Also, credit union dividends usually exceed interest rates paid by banks on similar demand deposit savings.

For the above reasons, employees in any company, even a relatively small one, will appreciate having a credit union available to them and their families. Company presidents (and human resource managers, in particular), should make certain their business takes advantage of this low-cost, worthwhile employee benefit.

U.S. Savings Bonds

U.S. Savings Bonds are another excellent employee benefit that may currently be offered through the ease and convenience of payroll deduction. Payroll withholding provides an easy and systematic means for the individual to purchase savings bonds for future needs and goals. If not available through an employer, savings bonds can be purchased at most financial institutions, or online at *www.savingsbonds.gov*.

Savings bonds have distinct advantages of risk-free growth, tax exemptions and security over many other investments. They are guaranteed by the full faith and credit of the U.S. government and pay competitive interest rates which are reviewed every six months to reflect national interest rate trends. The interest rate is applied monthly and compounded semiannually. All interest earned is exempt from state and local income taxes, and federal tax reporting may be deferred until the bond is redeemed. In addition, federal taxes may be reduced or eliminated when proceeds are applied to parents' or children's higher education. Savings bonds have an interest-earning life of 30 years and may be redeemed at any time after one year from issue date if the bond was issued on or after February 1, 2003. (All bonds issued prior to this date can be redeemed after six months.) Two types of savings bonds—Series EE and Series I—are currently available for purchase, ranging from $50.00 to $10,000.

In most companies, a savings bond program is considered to be an employee benefit and is administered by the human resources department. Savings bonds do not normally compete with an employer's 401(k) program since there is no employer match and withholding is not with pre-tax dollars. In addition, savings bonds normally serve pre-retirement needs such as home and automobile purchases, college education expenses, and medical or other emergency needs. And while benefiting the employee, savings bond purchases also help the country in that they help to underwrite federal monetary needs. They help fight inflation by supplying dollars that would otherwise have to be borrowed, typically at higher costs. It is officially estimated that $1 billion in savings bonds saves the U.S. Treasury (and taxpayers) about $17 million. Recent annual sales have been in the $10 billion range.

Note: The U.S. Treasury Department has implemented an all-electronic system known as Treasury Direct for the purchase and redemption of Series EE and Series I savings bonds through electronic fund transfers, and the familiar paper savings bonds will eventually be discontinued. The full range of all other U.S. Treasury securities will also be available through Treasury Direct, and account holders will be able to buy and manage their securities 24/7 from any computer with Internet access. Companies with current payroll deduction for savings bond programs will be notified as to their status when Treasury Direct is fully implemented. For further information and details, HR staff should contact *www.treasurydirect.gov*.

Direct Deposit

The direct deposit of payroll checks is a benefit that most companies can make available to all of their employees. And for those who do take advantage of it, they will undoubtedly find it a very important as well as convenient one. This program allows employees to authorize automatic deposits from their paychecks directly into their checking and savings accounts, and the only requirement is that the person have or open a checking or savings account with any financial institution.

Each payday, employees on direct deposit receive a nonnegotiable check as their pay stub, and their deposit is posted to their checking/savings account normally before payday. Direct deposit is convenient and virtually risk free. When employees are on vacation, ill, or just too busy to get to the bank on payday or lunch hour, they have no worries if they have signed up for their company's direct deposit benefit. The company also benefits from this program since employees on direct deposit no longer need to stand in line at their local bank while on short lunch hours, or to frantically run to the bank, perhaps on company time, upon receipt of their paycheck in order to cover some prematurely written personal checks.

There will always be the diehards who will resist the direct deposit program because they "like the feel of the paycheck in their hand," or some other such rationalization. This is one employee benefit that some companies even insist be administered on a mandatory basis for their entire employee population.

Payroll Cards

In their continuing efforts to cut payroll costs—and hopefully to benefit employees as well—payroll managers are continually devising new methods of compensating workers (e.g., the direct deposit system mentioned above). Now comes another innovative idea to compensate employees known as the payroll card. Under this plan, the worker's money (credit) is downloaded onto a piece of plastic resembling a credit card, and one can then make ATM withdrawals and debit-like purchases. The payroll card thus makes standing in line to cash a check and carrying around a lot of cash a thing of the past.

Payroll cards have been around since the late 1990s, and in terms of sheer numbers of cards in use, the Pelorus Group, a management research and consulting firm, expects some 17.5 million pay cards to be in use in 2010, compared to just 2.2 million cards back in 2004. Many low-income people who now rely on check-cashing facilities (sometimes with substantial fees) would also be potential users of the payroll card. Another use of the card for people without credit or debit cards is the ability to use it to shop on-line. And, as might be expected, there are some transactional fees associated with the payroll card, but these tend to be somewhat modest. Employers subsidize many of the expenses involved, but card users may have to bear some of the costs.

Primarily owing to a lack of awareness by those who would most benefit, the payroll card has not yet revolutionized payroll processing or operations, but the trend continues as more people take advantage of it and more banks recognize the marketing opportunity of working with corporate clients while increasing their own customer base.

Employee Parking

This is probably one of the very few employee benefits more effectively administered outside of the human resources department. If your company provides parking for your employees' vehicles, and especially if it is free of charge to your people, then you, as the human resources manager or director, would be well advised to be sure your building services, security department, or some other authority handles your company's parking program.

Exceptions may exist to this recommendation, particularly if yours is a small company and if parking is not a problem. However, if you have large numbers of employees and parking spaces together with car and van pools, visitor spaces, customer spaces, reserved, covered and uncovered parking, and other variations, you and your human resources staff will spend a good deal of your time immersed in parking problems, a traditional no-win situation. If you have a building management or services group or person, try to include parking as a function in their job description. They are usually much more qualified and equipped to handle it, and you will be doing yourself a favor.

Due to the problems that arise from the parking benefit, it is always wise for the company to charge at least a token amount for employee parking. In this way, people regard the parking space as their personal property as well as responsibility. Pride of ownership usually resolves any number of situations before they become problems or complaints.

Leaves of Absence

When a need arises for employees to be absent from work for a prolonged period of time, most companies will grant them the benefit of a leave of absence, and such leave is normally considered to be a form of employee benefit to the person involved. Employees may request various types of leave such as medical (including maternity), family, personal, and military leave. With the exception of military leaves and those qualifying under the Family and Medical Leave Act (1993), an employer is not required to guarantee reemployment at the time the person is ready and able to return to work. Let's discuss the various kinds of leaves of absence:

Medical leave is normally granted to employees in order to allow them sufficient time to recuperate from a disabling injury or illness incurred on or off the job. The length of the leave is usually based on a physician's recommendation as well as the type of injury or illness involved. It is always advisable to have a company policy that requires that the employee involved must provide the company with a written doctor's release before that employee may return to work from a medical leave of absence. Having such a policy protects the company from the liability associated with the employee returning to work prematurely. Strong Recommendation: Never under any circumstances allow any exceptions to this policy!

Maternity leave is usually considered in the same category as a medical leave of absence. It is designed to allow sufficient time to prepare for and recuperate from childbirth. Most companies permit the employee to continue working up to the date recommended by her doctor, so long as her job performance is satisfactory, but the employee should not be allowed to continue working past the date indicated in her doctor's statement. Again, similar to any other medical leave, no employee should be allowed to return to work from maternity leave without a written doctor's release. The word *written* is an especially important one, both in consideration of the employee's health, and for the protection of the company against lawsuits and legal challenges in the event of serious health problems of the mother before or after childbirth or pregnancy.

Family leave is supported by the Family and Medical Leave Act (FMLA), which provides for a family leave for employees who wish to take a leave for the following reasons.

- Birth of a child
- Adoption of a child
- Care of a child, spouse, or parent with a serious illness

The length of the leave may not exceed 12 weeks per year, and the employee must have been employed for at least one year, and have worked for a covered employer for at least 1,250 hours over the previous 12 months. The Act also applies if the company has at least fifty employees within a 75-mile radius.

While on family leave, the employee's seniority is protected and that employee must be reinstated in the same (or a similar) job held prior to the leave being granted. In addition, persons on family leave are entitled to the same medical coverage they had prior to the leave.

Executives and others in key positions may be refused family leave under certain specified provisions of the act. As with any personnel legislation, your human resources professionals must be very familiar and conversant with this law in order to answer anticipated questions from supervisors, managers, and employees. (*Note*: In 2009, FMLA was amended to include military family leave entitlements—see Chapter 10 for details.)

Personal leave is probably the most controversial and misunderstood of all the leaves of absence. Employees as well as supervisors are not always clear on when or even if a personal leave should be granted. In some cases, personal leaves are used as a disciplinary technique and even a device to terminate employees by putting them on a personal leave and then not bringing them back to work on the basis that company policy does not require their reinstatement. This type of usage is highly questionable since it reflects on the judgment, integrity, as well as courage of a manager, supervisor, or even the company itself that resorts to this method of eliminating employees from the work group.

One of the first principles of personnel management is that all managers and supervisors in the company base their disciplinary and termination policies on the truthful reasons for the action involved and not on the easy-way-out method. Examples of the latter might include laying off employees who clearly should have been discharged for nonperformance, misconduct, or insubordination. The long-term consequences of such decisions may come back one day to haunt them, particularly in a court of law.

So long as company policy permits the granting of personal leaves, the granting or denial of such a request should be primarily the decision of the immediate supervisor or even the next level of supervision. The supervisor or manager involved must look at each such request on an individual basis, considering the employee's length of service, performance, attendance, and, of course, the nature and reasons for the request.

Companies may consider granting their people personal leaves of absence for the following reasons.

Death in the immediate family
Settling family estates
Compelling personal matters
Religious needs
Educational purposes
Service in public offices or governmental agencies

Ordinarily, employers should make every effort to grant personal leaves, primarily as a benefit or morale factor, but they should be highly selective on the basis, as stated above, of the individual's performance (including attitude and cooperation), attendance, length of service, and reasons for the request. It will then be recognized by others as a genuine and valued employee benefit.

It is essential that every company establish policies stating the conditions under which a leave of absence will be granted, and what effect a leave will have on the benefits of the employee on leave. It will then be necessary for the human resources department to advise these employees as to what effect their leave will have on their medical and dental coverage, life insurance, retirement savings and pension plans, vacations, sick leave, and any other facet of the employment relationship. As federal laws regulate the conditions under which military as well as family leaves of absence are granted, human resources staffs must be thoroughly familiar with these regulations and how they relate to company policy.

Miscellaneous Employee Benefits

Although the major employee benefits listed previously are the ones that employees as well as employers should be primarily concerned with, some lesser benefits that employees seem to regard highly should also be mentioned. Let's discuss some of these benefits and how they might apply to an individual company and its employees:

Holiday bonuses are a benefit that many companies provide their employees with, in the form of cash bonuses, gifts, or other recognition at holidays and other special times. It is a gesture to their people that they appreciate their hard work and loyalty during the course of the year.

Some corporations concentrate on their employees' children, and they put on elaborate holiday parties for them complete with candy, balloons, and decorations, and a substantial toy (reflecting age and gender) presented to each child.

The cost of such an affair, depending upon the size of the company, can be considerable; but the expense is more than justified in terms of employee morale including the involvement of the employee's entire family. Such events often make a lasting good impression on all concerned when they are properly orchestrated and every effort is made for the enjoyment of the children, in particular.

If you as manager, director or vice president of human resources propose such an event to mark the holiday season for your organization's employees and their families, you may get at least one or two objections from upper- or mid-level management that since employee loyalty is currently eroding and will eventually be a thing of the past, why waste money on such an affair? The correct answer to that is a resounding, "Don't you believe it!" Employees are still people, and your company's most important asset.

Despite what you may read or hear, the quality of loyalty remains alive and well in the modern American business community, as those companies with genuine concern for their employees as well as their families have long since discovered and encouraged. Of course, many companies, large or small, downsized or rightsized their work forces during recent recessionary years, and some are continuing to do so. Such layoffs are often interpreted by employees as a tangible lack of loyalty on the part of management to its people. While this is probably the case in a number of instances, many other companies who were also forced to cut staff did so while being as supportive to their employees as possible by job sharing, outplacement, assistance with resumes, as well as job and career counseling. Equally as important, they objectively and effectively communicated to their people the economic or budgetary reasons that made the cutbacks necessary. Most HR managers would perhaps agree that if a company really wants the loyalty of its employees, it will always find a way to earn and deserve it.

Thanksgiving turkeys are simply another means of showing appreciation to employees and their families. Some companies give gift certificates for turkeys, ham, bacon, or other foodstuffs at Thanksgiving, while other companies believe that the actual purchase and distribution of frozen turkeys, to their employees, brings home the message of the company's caring in a more tangible way.

Some human resources personnel may downplay the idea of distributing turkeys to employees at Thanksgiving or during the holiday season, but even in the modern, so-called sophisticated employee environment, people will be just as impressed with the thoughtful employer who takes the time to mark the season with this simple, inexpensive, yet meaningful gesture of appreciation. If this is currently your practice, don't even think of stopping it as a belt-tightening or some other such cost-cutting measure. This type of action often boomerangs on the company that does so, with an offsetting effect of employee ill will and bad morale on the bottom line of the P&L statement. Once again, remember the lesson of never taking away a benefit once given, no matter how small that benefit might be!

Employee discounts usually means giving percentage discounts on company products and services. This benefit has a number of advantages, including feedback from employees as to how they were treated and received as a customer, how the product performed, and other useful data. And, of course, the dollar savings will not be overlooked by your employees as a genuine company benefit.

You will find that extending this privilege to your retired employees also will be much appreciated by them both from a practical as well as goodwill gesture on the part of the company. It also serves to make them feel they are still a part of the organization.

Casual Day. This is one of the less formal yet much appreciated employee benefits on the modern scene. Also called *dress-down Friday*, it is a benefit that a number of companies now use as either an outright benefit or an incentive reward program.

An HR manager of a large corporation was once approached by his staff to discuss the possibility of the office force dressing down and wearing jeans to work every other Friday. Since the manager had for some time been on a low-key crusade to discourage smoking in the office, he not only agreed to jeans every other Friday but, as an incentive, offered dress-down day *every* Friday to everyone, so long as they were nonsmokers. The program worked for a time and a number of staff members did give up smoking, but eventually, the remaining smokers felt the policy was unfair to them and the nonsmoking requirement was dropped. The Friday jeans day remained in effect and was overall regarded as a positive benefit by the HR staff.

Corporate Gym–Wellness Policies. Many corporations now stress the importance of healthy lifestyles of their employees by offering subsidized or discounted memberships in various health and exercise clubs, and providing periodicals, magazines, and posters on healthy foods, diet, exercise, and other information on how to stay healthy. Some large companies are also convinced that building and underwriting their own exercise facilities, gyms, and equipment for employees and their families is a good investment to contain medical care costs while providing employees and families the opportunity of remaining in good health. (See Chapter 13 for a further discussion of corporate wellness policies.)

The Company Picnic. Prior to the ever-increasing recognition of the human resources/personnel function as an integral part of corporate management and direction, the traditional company picnic was just another of those unimportant, usually overhead items relegated to the personnel department. Over the years, though normally still handled by the human resources department, the company picnic seems to have come into its own as a result of added management emphasis on employee relations, corporate image, and worker morale.

Most employers hold HR responsible to see that employees, their families and guests enjoy the outing, and that the location, food, and other fun activities are up to expectation. Many companies also see the picnic as a good opportunity for employees to meet and socialize in an informal setting with other employees with whom they normally do not have contact in day-to-day business operations.

The company picnic is another of those benefits that, while relatively inexpensive, has real meaning for employees and their families.

THE NEED TO CAREFULLY SELECT BENEFITS
All of us can probably think of many other types of benefits or privileges that employees might appreciate. No matter how incidental a proposal for a new benefit may seem, serious consideration should be given to its implementation provided it fits within the overall company employee benefit strategy and budget. Employees, in many cases, value their benefits as much as they do their paycheck, and in the case of their medical benefits, perhaps even more so.

As benefits are highly regarded by the average employee, companies must make every effort to insure that their benefit program is meaningful, effective, and, not least of all, competitive. This, of course, is all well and good. However, great care must be taken to insure that your benefit program is not too rich or too generous. If a recession or hard times strike the organization and you can no longer afford particular benefits, you will be forced to cut them out or reduce them, thereby creating serious morale problems.

There is a long-standing tenet in the human resources field that you never take away an employee benefit once it has been granted. All human resources managers should consider the consequences of possibly having to rescind a new benefit currently being considered, at some point in the future. As with any other important human resources tool, each employee benefit must be handled in such a manner that both the company and the employee do benefit from its use.

EMPLOYEE ELIGIBILITY

In most companies, employee benefits eligibility is a function of the length of time a person has worked for the company, that is, seniority. The longer service, of course, equates to greater benefits. Though required time periods to qualify for benefits vary with individual corporate policy, Table 9-2 below lists typical qualification periods, depending upon the size of the company and whether employment is governmental or private.

TABLE 9-2
Example of Employee Benefits Eligibility Policy

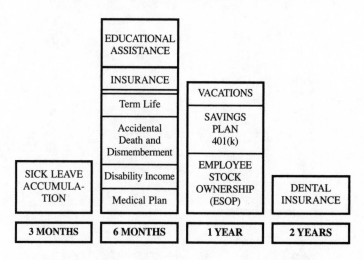

FINAL THOUGHTS ON BENEFITS

HR staff must be careful about recommending employee benefit cuts in order to pare expenses in difficult economic times such as the present (2010), and monthly savings may translate into dissatisfaction and morale problems in the long run. But, again, sometimes the company has no other choice but to reduce benefits, should it be the day-care or fitness facilities, the Educational Assistance program, or (and don't laugh) the Thanksgiving turkey (which sometimes can cause disproportionate morale problems...?). Balance is everything and HR professionals must be able to closely estimate the effect of such cuts on the employees of their particular company. Such situations again emphasize the importance of honest, frequent communication with employees that may dull or lessen the impact of the damage when the news is bad.

CHAPTER PERSPECTIVE

In this chapter, the importance of employee benefit programs, both to employees and to the companies that wish to attract and retain excellent employees, was discussed. Fourteen of the most popular types of benefit programs were defined and evaluated. Several practical tips on their implementation were offered. The discussion included specific legislation affecting several employee benefit programs. The importance of instituting benefits thoughtfully and carefully was stressed.

Legal Compliance Role of Human Resources

INTRODUCTION AND MAIN POINTS

This chapter summarizes the most important laws relating to personnel/human resources functions. Federal laws range from the National Labor Relations Act of 1935 to the American Recovery and Reinvestment Act of 2009. Topics cover many aspects of the employer-employee relationship from what constitutes overtime to the validity of polygraph testing. State and local laws covering Workers' Compensation, Unemployment Insurance, Health Insurance, and those regulating substance-abuse testing and smoking are included in the discussion. Relevant concepts such as exempt status, protected concerted activity, and employment-at-will are explained under the appropriate law.

The necessity for human resources practitioners to become knowledgeable about those laws in order to perform their work well is emphasized. A company's correct compliance with the law not only precludes penalties but also often avoids the possibility of lawsuits or strengthens the company's position in the event of a lawsuit. Helpful suggestions concerning timely responses to complaints and disclaimers—how to word them and where to place them for maximum effectiveness—are offered.

After reading the material in this chapter:

▬ You will have an overview of the most important laws that impact on the personnel/human resources function, including the Sarbanes-Oxley Act of 2002.

▬ You will understand the concepts upon which many of these federal, state, and local laws are based.

▬ You will see the necessity for becoming knowledgeable about these laws in order to correctly comply with them.

▬ You will be aware of the importance of formulating written policies and disclaimers in protecting your company from lawsuits.

LEGAL COMPLIANCE

Job evaluation and wage and salary administration form the basis of yet another critical aspect of compensation, namely, compliance with a myriad of federal and state laws dealing with employee compensation and employee relations. A discussion of those laws most frequently encountered by human resources practitioners is important in order to have a general understanding of how they directly or indirectly affect compensation as well as the overall human resources function.

FAIR LABOR STANDARDS ACT (WAGE AND HOUR LAW) OF 1938

The Fair Labor Standards Act (FLSA) is the principal federal law that establishes minimum wage, overtime pay, record-keeping, and child labor standards affecting full-time and part-time workers in the private sector and in federal, state, and local governments. Nonexempt workers covered by the Act are entitled to a minimum wage of not less than $7.25 an hour. Overtime pay at a rate of not less than one and one-half times their regular rates of pay is required after 40 hours of work in a work week.

The FLSA, as amended, and more commonly known as the Wage and Hour Law, is essentially the keystone of employee compensation. Its provisions are relatively clear and generally well known by employers as well as by most employees. The FLSA covers the following employees:

- All engaged in interstate or foreign commerce
- Those producing goods for interstate commerce
- All engaged in commerce or in the production of goods at an enterprise of not less than $500,000 in gross sales

In effect, practically all U.S. workers are covered under the Fair Labor Standards Act.

See "Proposed FLSA Revisions and Changes" in Chapter 11.

OVERTIME PAY REQUIREMENTS

In addition to its minimum wage standards and requirements, the overtime feature of the law is the one most generally associated with it and the one most familiar to and understood by employees and employers alike. It provides that all nonexempt employees, such as those who are not exempt from the provisions of the law, must be paid at one and one-half times their base hourly rate of pay (their regular rate of pay), for all hours worked in excess of 40 per week. Paid vacation, sick time, or other compensated hours are not counted in the calculation of overtime. Only hours actually worked in excess of 40 per week are counted in overtime determination.

The law's overtime payment provisions are rigid, and employers must be fully prepared to comply with them, even to the extent of paying time and one-half premium pay if a nonexempt employee takes work home without the knowledge or permission of the supervisor. (When it is discovered that an employee has taken work home without authorization, the supervisor should make it clear to the person involved—preferably in writing—that this must never be repeated without the specific approval of the employee's supervisor. If the situation does occur again, discipline should be assessed up to and including possible termination.)

MINIMUM WAGE

At the time of this writing (2009), fourteen states and the District of Columbia had minimum wage requirements that exceeded federal minimum wage standards. (See Table 10-1 below.) In any of these situations, the higher minimum wage rate will always apply. In most cases of conflict or overlap between state and federal wage laws, the one most benefiting the employee normally prevails.

TABLE 10-1

States with Minimum Wage Laws Exceeding Federal Minimum Wage
(Based on Federal Minimum Wage of $7.25 per Hour,
Effective June 2009)

State	Minimum Hourly Wage $
California	8.00
Colorado	7.28
Connecticut	8.25
District of Columbia	8.25
Illinois	7.50
Maine	7.50
Massachusetts	8.00
Michigan	7.40
Nevada	7.55
New Mexico	7.50
Ohio	7.30
Oregon	8.40
Rhode Island	7.40
Vermont	8.06
Washington	8.55

Figure 10-1 below illustrates the progress of federal minimum wage legislation since its inception in 1938:

FIGURE 10-1
The Federal Hourly Minimum Wage Since Its Inception

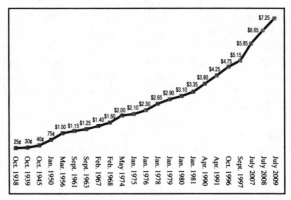

In several states overtime wage laws differ from the federal law, and again the more liberal provisions apply. For example:

■ California law requires the payment of time and one-half for all hours worked after 8 hours per day, and double time after 12 hours per day. California also requires payment of time and one-half for the first 8 hours worked on the seventh day of work in any one week, and double time in excess of 8 hours worked on the seventh day. (To qualify for seventh-day overtime, however, the employee must have worked all 7 days of the work week.)

■ In Colorado, time and one-half must be paid for all hours worked over 12 per day, or over 12 consecutive hours without regard to the start or end of the work day.

■ Kentucky requires time and one-half payment for all hours worked on the seventh day of the work week, so long as the employee works more than 40 hours in that 7-day period.

■ Nevada law requires payment of time and one-half for all hours worked over 8 hours per day.

EXEMPT STATUS

We have briefly referred to exempt and nonexempt classifications of employees under the federal wage and hour law. The exemption feature of the law basically provides that employees who meet certain compensation or duties standards or tests may be considered exempt from the payment of overtime and from the other provisions of the FLSA. The most common classifications of exemptions (so-called White Collar exemptions), under the wage and hour law are for

Executives
Administrative employees
Professionals
Computer-related occupations
Outside sales employees
Highly compensated employees

The FLSA also provides certain criteria or tests for each of the above categories in order to determine their exemption validity. The United States Department of Labor (USDOL) has eliminated the "long test" for determining whether an employee is exempt from overtime, and has, instead, made a single test for each of the categories. This means employers no longer have to determine whether an exempt employee is devoting more than 20 percent of his or her time performing nonexempt duties. In addition, the salary limit for these categories has been rasied to $455 per week. Criteria for the five categories are highlighted below. It should be understood that the exemption criteria provided here are not to be relied upon as complete or legally defensible in any exemption question dealing with individual circumstances.

TYPES OF EXEMPTIONS

Executive Employees

To qualify for the executive employee exemption, all of the following tests must be met:

■ The employees must be compensated on a salary basis (as defined in the regulations) at a rate of not less than $455 per week;

■ The employee's primary duty must be managing the enterprise, or managing a customarily recognized department or subdivision of the enterprise;

■ The employee must customarily and regularly direct the work of at least two or more other full-time employees or their equivalent; and

■ The employee must have the authority to hire and fire other employees, or the employee's suggestions and recommendations as to the hiring, firing, advancement, promotion, or any other change of status of other employees must be given particular weight.

Administrative Employees

To qualify for the administrative employee exemption, all of the following tests must be met:

■ The employee must be compensated on a salary or fee basis (as defined in the regulations) at a rate not less than $455 per week;

■ The employee's primary duty must be the performance of office or nonmanual work directly related to the management or general business operations of the employer or the employer's customers; and

▬ The employee's primary duty includes the exercise of discretion and independent judgment with respect to matters of significance.

Professional Employees
Learned Professional
To qualify for the learned professional employee exemption, all of the following tests must be met:

▬ The employee must be compensated on a salary or fee basis (as defined in the regulations) at a rate not less than $455 per week;

▬ The employee's primary duty must be the performance of work requiring advanced knowledge, defined as work that is predominantly intellectual in character and which includes work requiring the consistent exercise of discretion and judgment;

▬ The advanced knowledge must be in a field of science or learning; and

▬ The advanced knowledge must be customarily acquired by a prolonged course of specialized intellectual instruction.

Creative Professional
To qualify for the creative professional employee exemption, all of the following tests must be met:

▬ The employee must be compensated on a salary or fee basis (as defined in the regulations) at a rate of not less than $455 per week; and

▬ The employee's primary duty must be the performance of work requiring invention, imagination, originality, or talent in a recognized field of artistic or creative endeavor.

Computer-Related Occupations
To qualify for the computer employee exemption, the following tests must be met:

▬ The employee must be compensated either on a salary or fee basis at a rate not less that $455 per week or, if compensated on an hourly basis, at a rate not less than $27.63 an hour; and

▬ The employee must be employed as a computer systems analyst, computer programmer, software engineer, or other similarly skilled worker in the computer field performing the duties described below:

▬ The employee's primary duty must consist of:

1) The application of systems analysis techniques and procedures, including consulting with users, to determine hardware, software, or system functional specifications;

2) The design, documentation, development, analysis, creation, testing, or modification of computer systems or programs,

including prototypes, based on and related to user or system design specifications;

3) The design, documentation, testing, creation, or modification of computer programs related to machine operating systems; or

4) A combination of the aforementioned duties, the performance of which requires the same level of skills.

Outside Sales

To qualify for the outside sales employee exemption, all of the following tests must be met:

■ The employee's primary duty must be making sales (as defined in the FLSA), or obtaining orders or contracts for services or for the use of facilities for which a consideration will be paid by the client or customer; and

■ The employee must be customarily and regularly engaged away from the employer's place or places of business.

Highly Compensated Employees

The regulations contain a special rule for "highly compensated" workers who are paid total annual compensation of $100,000 or more. A highly compensated employee is deemed exempt under Section 13(a)(17) if:

■ The employee earns total annual compensation of $100,000 or more, which includes at least $455 per week paid on a salary basis;

■ The employee's primary duty includes performing office or nonmanual work; and

■ The employee customarily and regularly performs at least one of the exempt duties or responsibilities of an exempt executive, administrative, or professional employee.

Other Exemptions

The Fair Labor Standards Act also contains other exemptions from coverage, including those for nonemployees such as independent contractors, apprentices, and volunteers. In addition, the FLSA, as well as many state laws, prohibits the use of illegal or oppressive child labor, or the hiring of youths to perform certain specified hazardous occupations. As might be expected, a significant body of law and interpretations thereof has developed over the many years of the FLSA's existence, and the compensation practitioner is well advised to consult with the local office of the U.S. Department of Labor when the more difficult problems of exemption, coverage, contract labor, and child labor do occur.

OTHER PERSONNEL-RELATED LEGISLATION

Although extremely important, the Wage and Hour Law is certainly not the only law with which human resources professionals must be well acquainted. Indeed, they must have a working knowledge of a growing list of employee discrimination, privacy, immigration, benefits, and other personnel-related legislation in order to have any hope or possibility of success in this most important but complex profession.

Below are brief summaries of the more important labor legislation with which human resources practitioners must be familiar, and, depending on their particular responsibilities, may be required to thoroughly understand and interpret. Being familiar with these laws may also help the reader to prepare for and understand future people/employee legislation that will undoubtedly affect the human resources function.

National Labor Relations Act (NLRA), 1935

Often known as the Wagner Act, this legislation basically and essentially gave employees the legal right to join a labor organization of their choice. The law also sets up the National Labor Relations Board (NLRB), to coordinate and administer the provisions of this first major piece of labor legislation.

Innumerable books and articles have been written about the profound impact of the NLRA (or Wagner Act, if you prefer), on labor-management relations in the United States. All human resources specialists, whether or not their company is involved in collective bargaining, should have a working knowledge of this landmark law.

Subsequent labor legislation, such as the 1947 Labor-Management Relations Act (more familiarly known as the Taft-Hartley law), and the Labor-Management Reporting and Disclosure Act of 1959 (Landrum-Griffin law) are also on the list of the should-know-and-be-familiar-with legislation for all human resources practitioners, whether their company is union or nonunion.

Protected Concerted Activity—Section 9(a).

Many personnel/human resources managers find that one of the Wagner Act's most important but least understood provisions is Section 9(a), Representatives and Elections. Most managers are at least vaguely aware that the Wagner Act gave employees the legal right to organize a union, as well as to join one of their choice. At any number of personnel and human resources seminars, however, the collective opinion of the conferees always seems to be that as long as there wasn't a union representing the company, Section 9(a) was not something to get overly excited or concerned about.

What, then, is the problem with Section 9(a) and why is it so important? The answer to that question is simply that Section 9(a) basically deals with the subject of protected concerted activity, meaning that any employee or group of employees has the right to present grievances to their employer whether or not that employee or those employees are represented by a union. Let's look at the text of Section 9(a), Representatives and Elections, as it appears in the National Labor Relations Act:[1]

> Sec. 9(a). Representatives designated or selected for the purpose of collective bargaining by the majority of the employees in a unit appropriate for such purposes shall be the exclusive representatives of all the employees in such unit for the purposes of collective bargaining in respect to rates of pay, wages, hours of employment, or other conditions of employment: *Provided*, that any individual employee or a group of employees shall have the right at any time to present grievances to their employer and to have such grievances adjusted, without the intervention of the bargaining representative, as long as the adjustment is not inconsistent with the terms of a collective-bargaining contract or agreement then in effect: *Provided further*, That the bargaining representative has been given opportunity to be present at such adjustment.

What the above Section 9(a) means and why it is so important is made clear in the following example. If any employees (as few as two, and in some cases even a single employee representing a group of other employees) go to their supervisor or employer and complain about some condition of employment not at odds with the rules and regulations of the union contract (if there is a union in the company), those particular employees are protected under the provisions of current labor law just as though they were actually a legal, bona fide labor organization representing the employees of a particular bargaining unit. These employees also enjoy the same degree of protection under labor laws even if there is no union in the company and the complaining employees are not represented by any union. Then, as you might expect, any employer who fires or unjustly disciplines such employees, risks receiving an unfair labor practice charge. Therefore, it is well to remember: Employees always have the right of representation with or without the services or assistance of a labor organization.

---

1. Section 9(a), Labor-Management Relations Act, 1947, as amended by Public Laws 86-257, 1959, and 93-360, 1974. The Taft-Hartley law amended the National Labor Relations Act, which was subsequently amended by the Labor-Management Reporting and Disclosure Act of 1959, the Landrum-Griffin Act.

Labor Management Relations Act, 1947

This act, more popularly known as the Taft-Hartley law, was passed in 1947 over the veto of President Harry S Truman. While the Wagner Act of 1935 had given employees the right to self-organization and to join a labor union of their choice, this act gave employees the right to not join a labor union. Passed in response to a record number of strikes and labor unrest in 1946, the Taft-Hartley Law (Section 7, Rights of Employees), stated clearly that:

> Employees shall have the right to self-organization, to form, join, or assist labor organizations, to bargain collectively through representatives of their own choosing, and to engage in other concerted activities for the purpose of collective bargaining or other mutual aid or protection, *and shall also have the right to refrain from any or all of such activities* except to the extent that such right may be affected by an agreement requiring membership in a labor organization as a condition of employment as authorized in section 8(a)(3). [Emphasis added.]

The realistic balance of free choice between the Wagner Act's right to join and the Taft-Hartley's right to not join a labor organization had now been struck.

Labor-Management Reporting and Disclosure Act, 1959

The overall purpose and provisions of this law, known popularly as the Landrum-Griffin Act, are to insure that all members of labor unions have the inherent rights of free speech, free assembly, and, perhaps just as important, access to union financial records, which their officers are required to maintain. The law also requires unions to account for all their funds, and sets up rules and regulations for the election and tenure of union officers.

Equal Pay Act, 1963

This act requires that both male and female workers receive equal pay for equal work, that is, for work performed under similar working conditions, and that requires equal skill, effort, and responsibility.

Civil Rights Act, 1964

Title VII of this act, together with Executive Order 11246 forever outlawed employment discrimination in the United States on the basis of race, color, religion, sex, or national origin.

This prohibition applies to all terms and conditions of employment, including hiring, discharge, and promotion. Unlawful discrimination is defined in the act as

1) the intentional discrimination against any member of a protected class, or

2) when an employer's company policies or practices, though neutral in themselves, have an unintentional adverse impact on a protected group or class of employees.

It is most important for human resources professionals to keep in mind the basic truth well known to all equal employment opportunity coordinators and managers, namely, that proclaiming yourself as a truly equal opportunity employer will avail you little if your work force is lacking in or entirely devoid of minority and female operational and especially managerial personnel. The facts and statistics contained in your company's EEO-1 Report and your affirmative action plan, whether voluntary or mandatory, must support your claim as an enthusiastic equal opportunity supporter.

Lilly Ledbetter Fair Pay Act, 2009

This legislation addresses the pay equity concept with particular emphasis on the timing and filing of a charge of discrimination in an equal-pay lawsuit. This law amending the Civil Rights Act of 1964 provides that the 180-day statute of limitations for filing an equal-pay lawsuit regarding pay discrimination resets with each new discriminatory paycheck delivered to the complainant. (Prior to Lilly Ledbetter, the statute of limitations for presenting an equal-pay lawsuit was the date the pay was agreed upon, not the date of the most recent paycheck.)

Civil Rights Act, 1991

In a further strengthening of the country's uncompromising stand on equal opportunity, this latest civil rights legislation permits individuals claiming unlawful, intentional discrimination to bring suit for both compensatory and punitive damages, and may request that their cases be tried before a jury. Also, an employee prevailing on such a discrimination claim may be entitled to back pay, reinstatement to the former job, as well as attorney's fees.

Age Discrimination in Employment Act (ADEA), 1967

This act, passed in 1967 and amended in 1978 and 1986, prohibits employers with over twenty employees from discharging or discriminating in any way against their employees who are forty or older because of their age. The ADEA does not prohibit early-retirement agreements provided it can be shown that the retirements are totally voluntary and that no form of coercion was used to convince employees to sign early retirement agreements.

AFFIRMATIVE ACTION PLANS AND AGREEMENTS

Three major laws require that employers who have contracts or subcontracts with the federal government must take affirmative action and must develop written affirmative action plans whereby the employer commits to employing, training, and advancing individuals in certain protected categories:

1) **Executive Order 11246** requires employers with federal contracts or subcontracts in excess of $10,000 to take affirmative action (using a written plan of action) to hire and promote persons without regard to race, color, religion, sex, or national origin.

2) **The Vocational Rehabilitation Act of 1973** prohibits discrimination by government contractors or subcontractors against handicapped persons. Such contractors are required to take affirmative action to employ and promote the handicapped. Any contractor or subcontractor awarded $2,500 or more in government contracts is subject to this law.

3) **Vietnam Era Veterans' Readjustment Assistance Act of 1974** requires companies holding $10,000 or more in government contracts or subcontracts to take affirmative action to employ and promote qualified, disabled veterans and veterans of the Vietnam era. This law prohibits these employers from discriminating against veterans in all employment matters.

Under all three of the above laws, employers must develop written affirmative action programs if

■ their government contracts or subcontracts total $50,000 or more, and
■ they employ fifty or more employees.

Failure to comply with any of the provisions of these affirmative action plans or programs could result in

■ loss of the government contract, and
■ disbarment from bidding on other government contracts for a period of three years.

SEXUAL HARASSMENT

As discussed in Chapter 8, discrimination in what is probably its most insidious form occurs when an employee of either sex is subjected to unwelcome sexual advances, requests for sexual favors, and other conduct of a verbal or physical sexual nature. In addition, such unwelcome advances or requests are often accompanied by threats of job loss, not being promoted, a hostile work environment, or other unpleasant consequences.

To avoid liability or responsibility for such sexual conduct on the part of its employees, including managers and supervisors, the employer must take definite and immediate steps to fully investigate such conduct as soon as it first becomes apparent, or is known by or called to the employer's attention. Such immediate action, together with an impartial and fair investigation, normally assures protection in most cases from legal liability to the employer. Conversely, no investigation at all or even unwarranted delays in beginning an investigation of sexual harassment complaints or charges, practically guarantees the employer an indefensible legal position.

ADDITIONAL LEGISLATION

Americans with Disabilities Act (1992/1994) (Amended 2009)

This act prohibits discrimination against the disabled by private employers. Employers may not discriminate against individuals with a disability (formerly referred to as handicapped persons), if these individuals are able to perform the essential functions of the specific job held or sought. If the individual's disability impedes or would impede job performance, the employer is required to take steps to reasonably accommodate the individual; however, the employer becomes exempt from this requirement if doing so would impose an undue hardship on the employer.

The Americans with Disabilities Act (ADA) was revised as of January 1, 2009, as the "ADA Amendments Act" (ADAAA.) The ADA, which originally became effective in 1992, has been greatly expanded to include many other disabilities heretofore excluded by law or legal interpretation. For example, the amended law now requires that disabled persons be covered under ADAAA even if their condition could be mitigated by medication, assistance technology and equipment, or learned behavioral adaptations. Such was not the case under the original ADA. In addition, the disability does not have to limit more than one major life activity, which in itself is broadened to include working, communicating, concentrating, thinking, reading, and other activities of central importance. And finally, ADAAA states that the limitation in question need not be significant or severe, but merely a "substantial limitation." However, transitory and minor impairments still do not qualify as disability.

Congress's intent in this legislation was to set the groundwork for a disabled person and the company working together, rather than creating an adversarial climate as so often happens with many, if not most, other labor-oriented laws. Some state legislatures have also passed laws protecting the handicapped and disabled against any form of discrimination.

Occupational Safety and Health Act (OSHA), 1970

The Occupational Safety and Health Act, also called the Williams-Steiger Act, and more commonly known as OSHA, was designed to promote safety and health in the workplace. This law requires virtually every employer in the United States to furnish its employees with a place of employment literally free from any safety hazards that are likely to cause death or serious injury to them. Under the law, OSHA has the authority to levy fines and assessments on employers who do not maintain an environment of safety and protection at their work sites. The law is administered by the Occupational Safety and Health Administration of the U.S. Department of Labor.

Employee Retirement Income Security Act (ERISA), 1974

The ERISA law is probably the most significant and far-reaching piece of pension legislation ever passed by the U.S. Congress. In one sense, ERISA did for retirees and pensioners what the Wagner Act of 1935 did for employees in the 1930s, that is, it protected their rights to a secure retirement just as the Wagner Act protected their rights to join a labor union for a (perceived) more secure working life.

ERISA protects employees' rights not only with regard to retirement plans, but relating to health and welfare plans as well. This is all accomplished and enforced by the federal government requiring that employers have written plan documents, summary plan descriptions to be distributed to employees, and annual reports to the federal government, and that all plan assets be held in trust together with strict fiduciary responsibilities. Substantial penalties may result from employer violations of ERISA regulations, including loss of deferred tax status of the particular plan involved.

It may be of some historical interest to readers to learn that ERISA legislation faced some formidable opposition when it was first proposed. Because all this occurred more than 35 years ago, most human resources practitioners by this time are probably aware that ERISA opponents had their own version of its acronym—"Every Rotten Idea Since Adam!" Their clever humor, however, was not sufficient to prevent the passage of this landmark personnel legislation.

Immigration Reform and Control Act (IRCA), 1986

This law was passed by Congress to eliminate the illegal practice of employers hiring unauthorized alien workers. Employers are required under this law to verify the identity and work status of every new employee the company hires. All employers, regardless of the size of their company, are subject to the provisions of IRCA.

Employers are required to document all employee verifications, and must maintain files of various documents including copies of Social Security cards, work permits, birth certificates, and other acceptable proofs of nationality and work status. All such documents must be kept ready for examination by immigration authorities and agents at any time. If employers knowingly hire unauthorized aliens, they face significant fines and possible imprisonment. Such fines may also be imposed if the I-9 forms, which specify the particular documents the applicant or employee has submitted to the employer as proof of hiring eligibility, are not well documented or maintained (see I-9, Employment Eligibility Verification form illustrated in Chapter 12).

On March 1, 2003, in response to the tragic terrorist attacks of September 11, 2001 in New York City and Washington DC, services formerly provided by the Immigration and Naturalization Service (INS) were transferred to the Department of Homeland Security (DHS) and renamed the Bureau of Citizenship and Immigration Services (BCIS.) Shortly thereafter, the BCIS was renamed the U.S. Citizenship and Immigration Services (USCIS.) In support of the DHS overall mission, the priorities of the USCIS are to implement solutions for improving immigration customer services, continue to eliminate immigrant adjudications backlogs, and to promote national security. The USCIS is responsible for working to fundamentally transform and improve the delivery of immigration and citizenship services. The USCIS operates with 250 local and field offices, and includes 15,000 employees and contractors. Alejandro Mayorkas was sworn in as USCIS director on August 12, 2009.

HR professionals must be very aware of and familiar with the USCIS bureau in order to closely follow the latest and current developments in immigration laws and regulations. For example, the relatively new E-Verify program, which is an Internet-based system operated by the USCIS in partnership with the Social Security Administration (SSA), is currently free to employers and is available in all fifty states. (Thirteen states have passed laws requiring public and/or private employers [including contractors and subcontractors] to use the E-Verify system. Similar legislation is pending in other states as well.) E-Verify provides an automated link to federal databases to help employers determine employment eligibility of new hires and the validity of their Social Security numbers.

As of September 8, 2009, employers with federal contracts or subcontracts that contain the Federal Acquisition Regulation (FAR) E-Verify clause are *required* to use E-Verify to determine the employment eligibility of employees performing direct, substantial work under those federal contracts, as well as the eligibility of new hires organization-wide, regardless of whether they are working on a federal contract.

Consolidated Omnibus Budget Reconciliation Act (COBRA), 1985

Employers with twenty or more employees are legally bound under COBRA to provide their former employees as well as the families of these employees the opportunity to purchase the same health care (medical and dental) group coverage that they had been receiving from their employer and that would normally cease at the time they left the company for any reason, other than gross misconduct. Such reasons, or qualifying events, as they are known, would include termination of employment, reduction of hours of employment, death or divorce of a covered employee, retirement or disability of a covered employee thus entitling the employee to Medicare, and status change of a dependent child to that of nondependent status.

COBRA coverage is limited to 18 months for employees and 36 months for dependents. Employers must give eligible employees written notice of COBRA rights at the time the qualifying event occurs, that is, termination of employment.

On February 17, 2009, President Obama signed into law the American Recovery and Reinvestment Act (ARRA), which establishes a 65 percent government subsidy for eligible workers toward their COBRA coverage for up to 9 months. Workers who were involuntarily terminated between September 1, 2008, and December 31, 2009, with annual incomes of less than $125,000 (single) or $250,000 (couples) are eligible. And although the employee (not the employer) will be responsible for abiding by the salary cap that determines eligibility, the HR staff will, of course, still have responsibility for overall administration of this new COBRA revision. The law also provides that employers will receive a credit against payroll taxes for the cost of the subsidy.

(*Note*: On December 19, 2009, the 9-month COBRA subsidy coverage was extended by six additional months by President Obama for existing COBRA-qualified beneficiaries, and provided new qualified beneficiaries with up to 15 months of the 65 percent subsidy.)

In addition, two laws, the Uniformed Services Employment and Reemployment Rights Act (USERRA) and COBRA also contain special health coverage provisions for people who leave work for military service. These individuals are allowed to continue coverage for themselves and their dependents under an employment-based group health plan. COBRA provides for 18 months of coverage with extensions for certain events; while USERRA provides for 24 months of coverage with costs of such coverage varying depending on the length of military service involved.

The Health Insurance Portability and Accountability Act (HIPAA), 1996

On August 21, 1996, the Health Insurance Portability and Accountability Act was signed into law, the main purpose of which was to protect and insure the health coverage of people who switch from one job to another. In order to achieve this objective, the law limits the use of preexisting health conditions to exclude or delay medical coverage benefits via waiting periods and generally eliminates eligibility restrictions based on health status. In addition, HIPAA also contains provisions to reduce the administrative costs of providing and paying for health care by simplifying the administration of claims payments and by standardizing electronic submissions of financial and administrative health plan information. Also, within these administrative provisions are new privacy and security safeguards, as well as penalties for noncompliance. The Act emphasizes (but does not require) the use of electronic format to maintain or transmit health care information, which in turn leads to HIPAA privacy provisions and definitions of protected and individually identifiable health information.

The Federal Department of Health and Human Services has requested and received extensive feedback, discussion, and comments regarding HIPAA privacy provisions, especially as to patients' access to their own medical records as well as having more control over how their personal information is used. In 2001, the Bush administration announced that it would immediately begin the process of implementing such privacy protections, and the Privacy Rule of the Act became effective as of April 14, 2001. Compliance by all health care organizations—including health care providers, employers, life insurers, and one-physician offices—was required for the Privacy Rule by April 14, 2003, and for HIPAA Electronic Data Interchange by October 16, 2003. The compliance date for HIPAA Security Rules became effective in April 2005.

The Health Insurance Portability and Accountability Act was designed to be the first major step toward health care reform in the United States. A summary of its major provisions follow:

▬ Allows workers to move from one employer to another without fear of losing group health insurance.

▬ Requires health insurance companies that serve small groups (two-fifty employees) to accept every small employer that applies for coverage.

▬ Increases the tax deductibility of medical insurance premiums for the self-employed.

▬ Requires health insurance plans to provide inpatient coverage for a mother and new-born infant after a normal birth, or 96 hours after a cesarean section.

■ Creates medical savings accounts (renamed Archer MSA's in 2001) that can be used to cover qualified medical services. The Archer MSA is a savings account that earns tax-deductible interest for medical purposes. Archer MSA's are often used by small businesses or self-employed individuals as a way to pay for health-care services to employees. An Archer MSA works much like an IRA. The account owner will make contributions and earn interest on the funds. The gains are tax deferred or tax free when withdrawn for medical expenses. If funds are removed for any other purpose, a penalty may be incurred and taxes will usually apply.

Overall, there is no disagreement that HIPAA has resulted in significant and sweeping changes in most transaction and administrative information systems in the entire health care industry and that it will continue to do so.

Human resource professionals must also be especially familiar with all compliance provisions of HIPAA and must work with their own in-house or outside health care administrators to protect the company's interests. It constitutes another complexity added to the HR function that demonstrates HR's increasing importance and value to the organization and its profit objectives.

Uniformed Services Employment and Reemployment Rights Act (USERRA), 1994

The Uniformed Services Employment and Reemployment Rights Act is a federal law intended to ensure that persons who serve or who have served in the Armed Forces, Reserves, National Guard, or other "uniformed services": (1) are not disadvantaged in their civilian careers because of their service; (2) are promptly reemployed in their civilian jobs upon their return from duty; and (3) are not discriminated against in employment based on past, present, or future military service.

Worker Adjustment and Retraining Notification Act (WARN), 1988

This law in general requires employers of 100 or more employees to provide at least 60 days' advance written notice of layoffs and plant closures to affected employees, their union representatives, and local government officials. The advance-notice requirement also applies if a plant closing will affect fifty or more employees, regardless of company size, or if a layoff affects at least one-third of the employees and at least fifty employees. (If 500 or more employees are affected by the layoffs or plant closure, advance notice is required regardless of the one-third provision.)

If the employer does not give the required notice, it may be held liable for all back pay and benefits for the 60-day notice period for affected employees.

Veterans' Rights and Military Service, 1948

The Selective Service Act of 1948 and subsequent legislation requires companies to reemploy employees who are called to or volunteer for military service, whether active or on reserve duty. The simplest guideline to follow in complying with this law would be that the employer must return military service veterans to the job they would have had if it had not been for their military service. Employers must also grant employees leave time for reserve duty, summer camp, and other training, and they may not require employees to use vacation time for these periods of service.

Although such military leaves may be unpaid, many companies offer to make up the difference between the employee's regular rate of pay, and whatever earnings the employee received from military duty. The U.S. Department of Veterans Affairs offers various manuals and other literature detailing all rights and privileges of returning veterans. Human resource professionals will find these manuals to be handy, understandable references concerning veterans' reemployment rights.

Employee Polygraph Protection Act (EPPA), 1988

Some companies in the past have relied heavily on polygraph or lie detector tests to screen employment applicants, and to test employees where questions of theft, embezzlement, or other wrongdoing were involved. Polygraph tests are generally not permitted to be used as evidence in court, and basically have been found to offer no more than psychological value in assisting employers in hiring or in exposing guilty parties in cases of theft.

In 1988 President Ronald Reagan signed the federal Polygraph Act, which prohibits polygraph testing by employers except under somewhat limited and restricted conditions. The conditions must be carefully monitored and controlled. Under this federal law, lie detector tests may not be given to job applicants for employment; they may be used only where there is clear evidence that a theft involving money or property has taken place on the employer's premises or property. In a number of states, polygraph testing is prohibited altogether.

Workers' Compensation Laws

You will even today still hear many people, including supervisors and managers, refer to this well-known worker-protection program as Workmen's Compensation. So it was called in years past, prior to sexual equality laws and language. The substance of this form of insurance has not basically changed since it was first enacted in Maryland in 1902 (even though it was subsequently declared unconstitutional). The first Workmen's Compensation laws to be held constitutional were passed in 1911 by four states—California, New Jersey, Washington, and Wisconsin. Since that time, every state has adopted some type of Workmen's/Workers' Compensation act.[2]

Essentially, an employer is required to carry Workers' Compensation insurance for each of its employees, and to pay premiums to either a state fund or to a private carrier to provide its employees compensation for wages lost as a result of an occupational illness or disease, or an injury occurring while on the job. Workers' Compensation laws also protect the company by making it generally immune from lawsuits by employees for damages resulting from an occupational injury, illness, or disease. Unless the employer's conduct is deemed to be wanton and reckless, even its own negligence is included under the umbrella of Workers' Compensation. Workers' Compensation laws also provide payment for medical treatment, hospitalization, and rehabilitation services for injured or disabled employees.

Unemployment Insurance Laws

This form of insurance protection is a very meaningful program to both employers and employees alike, especially in times of economic recession, consolidations, mergers, and reductions in force. Unemployment insurance laws, governed and controlled by individual state laws, are designed to provide temporary income protection for those workers who find themselves out of work through no fault of their own. However, an employee who quits a job voluntarily and without good cause, who is discharged for misconduct, or who refuses to apply for or accept suitable work may be disqualified by the state from receiving benefits.

Unemployment insurance, contrary to popular notion, is not paid for or provided by the federal or state government; it is paid for by the individual employer on the basis of the company's experience rating, basically determined by the number of unemployment claims paid by the state on behalf of a particular employer during a given period of time.

Currently, unemployment insurance costs (taxes) to employers range from a low of 0.00 percent of payroll in eight states (Colorado, Hawaii, Iowa, Kansas, Missouri, North Carolina, South Dakota, and Washington) to a high of 0.96 percent in Massachusetts.

2. Chruden, Herbert J., and Arthur W. Sherman, Jr. *Personnel Management*, 5th ed. Cincinnati, Ohio: South-Western Publishing, 1976, p. 494.

In June 2009, the United States average cost of legally required insurance benefits for private industry (including Social Security, Medicare, and unemployment insurance) was $2.13 per hour (7.8 percent of total compensation). Weekly unemployment benefits for claimants varied from a minimum of $5 per week in Hawaii to a maximum of $900 per week in Massachusetts. Thus, the fewer discharges and layoffs you have in your company, the lower your experience rating, and the greater the savings in unemployment insurance tax dollars will be.

It must be stated, however, that the unavoidable increase in unemployment insurance recipients in the current recession (2.8 million in May 2008 to 9 million in 2009), and the extension of unemployment benefits from 26 to the current 99 weeks, presents an almost unavoidable fiscal disaster to private businesses and states as well. Improvement will come, but in the meantime the challenges are great.

Fair Credit Reporting Act (FCRA), 1970 (amended 1997)

Employers who require investigative-type consumer reports on current or prospective employees must advise these individuals in writing that information about their character, general reputation, or personal characteristics may be disclosed in such reports. Under the FCRA, the employer must obtain the applicant's written authorization before the background check is conducted. This authorization must be written on a document separate from all other documents such as the employment application. Such notice is not required, however, if reports are to be used for employment purposes, such as a person being considered for a promotion when the individual has not specifically applied for the position in question.

If an applicant is rejected either wholly or in part due to the information contained in a consumer investigative report, the employer must advise the person of this fact and must also supply the name and address of the consumer reporting agency that made the report.

Willful violations of these provisions of the Fair Credit Reporting Act makes the employer liable for actual damages, punitive damages, and attorney's fees, while negligent failure to comply will result in employer liability for actual damages and attorney's fees.

Family and Medical Leave Act (FMLA), 1993 (as amended)

The FMLA requires covered employers to provide up to 12 weeks of unpaid, job-protected leave to eligible employees for certain family and medical reasons. Employees are considered eligible if they have worked for a covered employer for at least one year, and for 1,250 hours over the previous 12 months, and if there are at least fifty employees within 75 miles of the facility involved. Unpaid leaves of absence must be granted for any of the following reasons:

1) To care for the employee's child after birth, or placement for adoption or foster care.
2) To care for the employee's spouse, son or daughter, or parent, who has a serious health condition.
3) For a serious health condition that makes the employee unable to perform the assigned job.

Other benefits and protection of FMLA include the following:

1) For the duration of FMLA leave, the employer must maintain the employee's current health insurance coverage under any existing group health plan.
2) Upon return from FMLA leave, most employees must be restored to their original or equivalent positions with equivalent pay, benefits, and other terms of employment. (Note: Certain highly paid, designated key employees may be refused reinstatement after FMLA leave if they are informed when they apply for FMLA leave that they *are* key employees, if they are notified as to the reasons for denial of reinstatement, and if they are offered a reasonable opportunity to return to work from FMLA after they receive the no-reinstatement notice. (Key employees are defined as those salaried employees who are among the highest paid 10 percent of employees within 75 miles of the work site.)
3) The use of FMLA leave cannot result in the loss of any employment benefit that accrued prior to the start of an employee's leave.

FMLA does not affect any federal or state law prohibiting discrimination, or supersede any state or local law or collective bargaining agreement that provides greater family or medical leave rights. (Effective July 2004, California became the only state with paid family leave.) The U.S. Department of Labor is authorized to investigate and resolve complaints of violations of FMLA, and an eligible employee may bring a civil action against an employer for alleged violations.

In 2008, the FMLA was amended by the National Defense Authorization Act (NDAA) that provided for two new military family leave entitlements. The U.S. Department of Labor's Wage and Hour Division published a final rule under the FMLA that became effective on January 16, 2009. The Military Family Leave Section 585(a) of the NDAA amended the FMLA to provide two new leave entitlements:

1) Military Caregiver Leave (also known as Covered Service Member Leave): Under the first of these new military family leave entitlements, eligible employees who are family members

of covered service members will be able to take up to 26 work weeks of leave in a "single 12-month period" to care for a covered service member with a serious illness or injury incurred in the line of duty while on active duty. Based on a recommendation of the President's Commission on Care for America's Returning Wounded Warriors (the Dole–Shalala Commission), this 26-work-week entitlement is a special provision that extends FMLA job-protected leave beyond the normal 12 weeks of FMLA leave. This provision also extends FMLA protection to additional family members (i.e., next of kin) beyond those who may take FMLA leave for other qualifying reasons.

2) Qualifying Exigency Leave: The second new military leave entitlement helps families of members of the National Guard and Reserves manage their affairs while the member is on active duty in support of a contingency operation. This provision makes the normal 12 weeks of FMLA a job-protected leave available to eligible employees with a covered military member serving in the National Guard or Reserves to use for "any qualifying exigency" arising out of the fact that a covered military member is on active duty or called to active duty status in support of a contingency operation. The Department's final rule defines qualifying exigency by referring to a number of broad categories for which employees can use FMLA leave: (1) short-notice deployment; (2) military events and related activities; (3) children and school activities; (4) financial and legal arrangements; (5) counseling; (6) rest and recuperation; (7) post-deployment activities; and (8) additional activities not encompassed in the other categories, but agreed to by the employer and employee.

The final rule also includes two new DOL certification forms that may be used by employers and employees to facilitate the certification requirements for the use of military family leave.

And finally, although FMLA leave is unpaid, the statute provides that employees may take, or employers may require employees to take, any accrued paid vacation, personal, family, or medical or sick leave, as offered by their employer, concurrently with any FMLA leave. This is called the "substitution of paid leave."

Sarbanes-Oxley Act of 2002 (Post Enron)—Ethical and Legal Issues and Guidelines for Employees

While the Sarbanes-Oxley Act was primarily intended by Congress to immediately address the various scandals and fraudulent accounting schemes by some of the nation's leading corporations such as Enron,

Tyco, WorldCom, Adelphia, and other lesser players, it also contains a number of employment-related provisions that have potentially great significance for managers and supervisors of people, and especially for human resource specialists in a "post-Enron" world. When, as a result of Enron's illegal actions, thousands of its employees lose their jobs, retirement accounts become insolvent, stock prices plummet, and the company files for Chapter 11 bankruptcy protection, all those in the field of managing, advising, and working with employees must become aware of the far-reaching consequences of this new legislation, including the very severe penalties included for violations of its provisions.

Sarbanes-Oxley specifically protects so-called whistleblowers (i.e., employees of public companies who, using lawful procedures, disclose information relating to what appears to them to be fraudulent conduct in their organization). The whistleblower's complaint must be filed with the U.S. Department of Labor and, under certain conditions, could be referred to a federal court if the matter is not resolved within prescribed time limits. Public companies are required to have their audit committees set up procedures to facilitate the confidential, anonymous submission of information by employees relating to questionable accounting or auditing practices. Severe criminal penalties are required for any retaliation or adverse employment action directed against the whistleblower involved.

Another key area of concern to lawmakers was the shredding of documents where there are pending proceedings and subpoenas issued for the destroyed documents, as in the Enron case. The Act strengthens and broadens existing federal statutes, including its new application to an individual acting alone, even if such action occurs before any grand jury subpoena has been issued. Any person or group of persons destroying investigative evidence in such situations is considered to be obstructing justice and risks imprisonment of up to 20 years. HR professionals as well as corporate attorneys should also be aware that such obstruction tactics and penalties *could* also be involved in wage and hour investigations and audits, EEOC administrative charges, and other workplace investigations. In addition, Sarbanes-Oxley also addresses illegal manipulation or fraud with regard to employee pension plans and increases original ERISA monetary penalties and potential prison sentencing by up to 10 years. The Act further imposes more stringent requirements for complying with corporate transparency and reporting corporate financial wrongdoing and threatens stiffer individual penalties for noncompliance with the Act. This latter requirement is aimed at all levels of the executive suite including chief executive officers and chief financial officers, as well as members of in-house and outside corporate counsels. The lines have been drawn, the new law has teeth, and the future path of corporate governance should be a bit straighter as well as narrower.

But again, as we consider all the above rules, regulations, and penalties relating to corporate governance, we cannot help but wonder (and the thought is certainly not original) why it is necessary in a country such as ours that we must legislate honor, honesty, and integrity! (And as if in answer to this question, we are reminded that in 2009, the disclosure of a *$50 billion* "Ponzi" scheme bilking thousands of investors—some, of their life savings—caused absolute astonishment in the financial community, as well as in the public at large, as to how such a crime could have gone undetected for so long a period of time. [See *United States v. Bernard L. Madoff*, 09 Cr. 213 (DC) Plea: Guilty. Sentence: 150 years.] Also, at about the same time, other similar [though less costly] financial scandals surfaced, and the cry for added and more stringent regulation was never louder.)

It can probably be safely assumed that the vast majority of us do not instruct our children in the art of cheating on examinations, copying other students' work product, or executing other nefarious practices; yet, in our company or business, some of us try to illegally circumvent tax laws or inflate profits and balance sheets to lure investor support and raise share prices. And somehow we see no incompatibility in our values and in fact even rationalize that "everybody does it!" Fortunately, in our business culture—and especially post-Enron—we are hearing and reading more of the word "spirituality" in shops, offices, and even perhaps executive suites. Such workplace spirituality is not to be thought synonymous with religion per se but may rather be defined as a growing spirit of trust between employer and worker in establishing a culture of rule keeping rather than one of rule breaking. In most cases, of course, this spiritual culture reflects the attitude and actions of the head of the company whose example, good or bad, employees are inclined to follow. If shabby workmanship, quality, and accounting are tolerated by top management, the work force will react in like manner. But if top management trusts and sincerely listens to its people, permits them to do their jobs and attain their goals as they see fit, and levels with them when things are bad as well as good, then there is still hope for our economic system. The late J. Edward Deming invented and stressed the concept of Quality Circles wherein employees via group action decide which is the best method of producing a product based on their own intimate job knowledge, with little interference from management after goals and parameters have been set. The Quality Circle embodies elements of this workplace spirituality in that employees produce value based on their own knowledge and enthusiasm in getting the job done as it should be done, and especially when they are convinced that their employer considers integrity and ethical dealings as being part and parcel of company policy. These spiritual values will then easily translate into legitimate material values assuring the success of the company and the security of the worker.

Note: At the time of this writing, a public outrage developed against large financial and other corporations that were on the brink of bankruptcy or failure due in part, it was asserted, to their own greed and "innovative" methods of packaging financial instruments that ultimately led to the current global recession. The outcry was further exacerbated when, after receiving government "bailout" funds, it was disclosed that these same companies were still awarding large bonuses and salaries to their employees. The author feels the above developments must be mentioned in order that the reader may have a basic understanding of the economic climate and conditions that existed at the time of this writing.

In addition, the installation in 2009 of a new, Democratic administration and Congress in Washington, DC, must also be taken into account by the HR professional as new and revised personnel legislation will undoubtedly affect human resources operations and in a number of cases has already done so.

Garnishment Laws

Garnishments essentially are court orders requiring an employer to withhold specific amounts of money from an employee's wages for payment of a debt owed by the employee to a third party. The most common garnishment payments involve:

Child support

Bankruptcy proceedings

Unpaid taxes

Garnishment deductions are normally the concern of the payroll department, which in many instances reports to the vice president, director, or manager of human resources. Garnishment orders from courts can become major items of concern for human resources professionals, especially in more difficult economic times. Good times or bad, the volume of such withholding orders continues to grow, especially as more states pass laws to insure stricter enforcement of child support legislation.

The company involved receives no extra compensation or fee for its garnishment work, and in fact, may even be held liable for payment of the subject claim if the garnishment was not legally or properly handled by its employees.

In addition, it is sometimes necessary to assign personnel on a full-time basis to handle just the garnishment work. In spite of these expenses, most human resources professionals would probably agree that these garnishment laws do benefit society in general and taxpayers in particular, and that by and large they do have our support.

EMPLOYMENT-AT-WILL LAWS AND CONCEPTS

The employment-at-will doctrine is basically a carryover from the old English common law that permitted any given employer to discharge an employee at any time, for any reason, or for that matter, for no reason at all. In our modern era, however, this right has been qualified, restricted, limited, and in some instances totally invalidated by the courts, especially state courts. Discharges of employees by companies involving matters of public policy (for instance, employee's refusal to alter company books or records, or to violate other laws or policies affecting the public) are prohibited or ruled against in most courts.

Employment-at-will is a highly complex area of personnel administration. Some courts hold that an employee or supervisory handbook may create an employment contract between employer and employee, and that the employee can only be discharged for violation of the specific reasons listed in the handbook, and for no other reason. Competent labor counsel should be called in to assist the human resources specialist or equal employment opportunity coordinator in adding disclaimer language to personnel handbooks and manuals. The disclaimer should clearly state that the terms and conditions mentioned in such publications are not the only reasons for which an employee may be terminated; and that the handbook or manual involved is not intended to constitute a contract between employer and employee.

Employment Contracts and Noncompetes

It should be clearly understood by the HR professional that simply because we do not acknowledge that our personnel policy manuals and employee handbooks are employment contracts, such contracts are not to be used. And as indicated below, the employment contract is essentially a standard document for most high-level executive positions. It is another HR tool that should be applied and used as circumstances dictate.

Occasionally, a company will have an assignment or project of a limited nature that must be completed within a certain period of time. For example, a company may enter into an employment contract with a college communications or English professor to develop a specific project manual over the three months of summer. The terms of the contract, including compensation, benefits, and other agreed-upon conditions, are all duly spelled out in the employment contract.

Probably the employment contracts most often used are those between companies and executives that are hired by corporations. These contracts normally spell out what is expected of the executive, as well as the perquisites and incentives that may be expected when certain specified goals and objectives are met. Compensation, stock options (where applicable), and medical, retirement, and other employee benefits are included in the contract.

Another type of contract used in business is the traditional noncompete agreement in which employees agree that in the event they leave the company for any reason whatsoever, they will not seek employment with a competitor organization (or start their own competitive company), usually for a specified period of time. Other terms and conditions may also be added to such an agreement, but the noncompetitive business restrictions are the essence of the contract.

Attempts to enforce noncompete agreements through the courts have not always been successful, and they are sometimes regarded more as a deterrent in discouraging former employees from joining competitive firms.

At-Will Statement

One of the best and most effective means of insuring the company's employment-at-will status is to include a statement in the employment application itself that the company in question takes the position that any employment relationship is at-will, that it may be terminated by either party (employer or employee) at any time, and that only the president of the company has the right to make any other arrangements to the contrary. By signing the employment application, the applicant is agreeing to accept employment with this particular company under the at-will concept.

Figure 10-2 below contains a sample statement that might be included on the application for employment form:

FIGURE 10-2
Sample Employment Application Form Statement

In consideration of my employment, I agree to conform to the rules and regulations of (company name). I understand that any employment relationship is at will and may be terminated at any time, with or without cause, and with or without notice, at the option of either the company or myself. I understand that only the president of (company name) has any authority to enter into any agreement for employment for any specified period of time, or to make any agreement contrary to the foregoing.

(Applicant's signature) _____

It is also most important that all managers, supervisors, and interviewers in the company understand that they must not make any oral statement guaranteeing the employee permanent employment or job security. An assurance by a manager or supervisor to the applicant or to an employee, such as "Now if you keep your nose clean and do your job, you've got a job here for life" (or some such guarantee in perhaps even more refined language), has spelled defeat for any number of companies in attempting to defend their at-will positions.

SMOKING RULES, ORDINANCES, AND POLICIES

In recent years, to smoke or not to smoke has become one of those sticky problem situations. Such situations may not have profound consequences for the organization, but they may cause disruption, waste time, and, in some cases, severely impact employees who are just not able to tolerate cigarette smoke, whether primary or secondary. More and more human resources managers and directors are looking to state or local smoking ordinances as the basis for settling those thorny questions of smoker versus nonsmoker rights within their own organization.

Most smoking ordinances originate with state legislatures, and all tend to be local rather than federal in nature. In many states, smoking in public places is restricted, but private employers have the right to designate smoking and nonsmoking areas within their places of business, or even to prohibit all smoking within their buildings and on their premises, including in company vehicles. Some states protect the rights of smokers to smoke or use tobacco products away from company property during nonworking hours.

A trend is also becoming apparent among some companies to increase medical plan contributions for covered employees and spouses who smoke on or off the job. Skyrocketing group medical costs in the past have prompted some employers to increase fees and deductibles, establish caps or dollar limitations on claims, and in some cases to even completely eliminate medical and dental coverage for those employees whose lifestyle choices such as smoking, nonmedical-related obesity, substance abuse, or failure to wear seat belts account for a greatly disproportionate share of group medical and dental claims dollars paid by employers.[4] On the other hand, some state legislatures

---

4. A press release by the Centers for Disease Control and Prevention (CDCP) in November 2008, indicates that although fewer U.S. adults smoke, smoking still causes 443,000 deaths annually and costs $193 billion. An estimated 19.8 percent of U.S. adults (43.4 million people) were current smokers in 2007, down from 20.8 percent in 2006. And based on that rate of decline, it is highly unlikely—if not impossible—that the national health objective of reducing the prevalence of cigarette smoking to 12 percent or lower will be met by 2010.

are now branding such restrictions and practices as discriminatory. The federal Equal Employment Opportunity Commission seems to be taking the same position, primarily basing its stand on the provisions of the Americans with Disabilities Act of 1992, which the EEOC says forbids such policies and practices.

Future laws and regulations dealing with health care reform may eventually result in the elimination of such employer practices, medical restrictions, and claims caps, in addition to mandating other totally new concepts of health care financing and delivery.

LAWS AND REGULATIONS REGARDING ACCESS, DISCLOSURE, AND RETENTION OF PERSONNEL FILES AND RECORDS

Whether computerized or manual personnel files are maintained in your company, you should be aware of some of the legal aspects of personnel file maintenance. First, although there are no federal laws that require private employers to grant employees access to their personnel files,[5] there are some state statutes that do allow it (see Table 10-2).

You will note that a number of states do allow current as well as former employees the right, upon request, to inspect and copy their personnel and/or medical file records, and to include their own written rebuttals of any and all matters that they may wish to contest. With the exception of the states listed in Table 10-2, however, employers in other states will find it to their advantage to take the position that personnel files are company property, and as such are not to be copied or privately inspected by employees or former employees.

Instances may occur where employees make what appears to be genuine, good-faith requests to review the contents of their personnel files when, for example, an employee believes it might contain some detrimental item or statement that might be harmful to the individual's progress or advancement within the company. If, after attempting to assure the employee that the human resources department allows only factual documents and material to be placed in these files (and this certainly should be the case), the person still remains unconvinced and wishes to see the file, it is good practice to review each document together, while keeping the file on your side of the table. If the employee objects to some statement or remark in the file for whatever reason, the person should be given the opportunity to submit a written statement of rebuttal concerning the specific matter or episode involved, and have it included in the file. Most people will accept this

---

5. Federal Occupational Safety and Health Act regulations, however, do require that employees must have access to their medical and (hazardous) exposure records.

compromise concerning inspection of their personnel file as it demonstrates that the company is trying to be fair and that it has nothing to hide.

Personnel Work History Documents

If you have a computerized personnel or human resource records system, you will probably have what is known as a Personnel Work History or some other similar feature in your software, which indicates each and every position ever held by the employee, the departments in which the employee worked, the hourly or salary rates of pay, and a variety of other personnel data items, all of which, of course, can be very helpful if not essential to supervisors and managers of people. The Personnel Work History document is totally factual as to an employee's status and work history with the company, and there is no reason to object to furnishing current (or even former) employees with a copy of this very helpful and complete information. Offering to provide this document, incidentally, will also obviate the need of employees or former employees to peruse their personnel files, for resume purposes, to see what jobs were held, time on each job, rates of pay, and the like.

As to the length of time personnel records must be maintained, federal law requires that employment applications and other personnel information be kept for a period of at least 12 months. Longer retention requirements apply to medical and hazardous exposure records.

The human resources manager or director should also be concerned with the kinds of personnel information and data that should or should not be included in the personnel file. In general, any materials having to do with employee hiring, promotion, training, or discipline (employment applications, resumes, performance appraisals, and disciplinary warnings and notices) may be legitimately included in the personnel file. However, any information relating to medical records, garnishments, affirmative action plans, employee charges, lawsuits, and related legal correspondence should all be maintained separately. Separate retention of medical records is required by law.

TABLE 10-2
State Laws Relating to Access to Personnel Files[6]
(Applies to Private and Public Employers Unless Otherwise Indicated)

Employees (normally including former employees) in

Alaska	may inspect and make copies of personnel files.
California	may gain access to personnel files to check on employee performance and grievances.
Connecticut	may access, modify, and copy personnel files and medical records. (Private employers only)
Delaware	may access personnel files or medical records on request and at reasonable times.
Illinois	may inspect and copy any personnel records used in making employment decisions.
Iowa	may access and be permitted to obtain a copy of any personnel file maintained by employer.
Maine	may review and copy any personnel file kept by an employer concerning the employee within 10 days of delivering a written request for it.
Massachusetts	may inspect, copy, correct, or remove information from personnel file. (Written request to inspect and copy)
Michigan	may review and copy personnel records at reasonable intervals. (Written request to inspect)
Minnesota	may access, correct, and copy personnel records. (Written request to inspect and copy)
Nevada	may access and copy any personnel file on request.
New Hampshire	may access and copy personnel files, and correct or remove information from such files.
Oregon	may be given reasonable opportunity to inspect all personnel records. (May copy records)
Pennsylvania	may submit written request to inspect personnel file on employee's request and at reasonable times.

6. In most states listed, the express purpose of these laws is to give employees (and former employees) the right to inspect personnel files and records used to determine their qualifications for employment, promotion, pay raises, termination, or other disciplinary action. Employee access and inspection is normally limited to these personnel records.

TABLE 10-2 (continued)

Rhode Island	may submit written request to inspect personnel files.
Washington	may access personnel files on request at reasonable times, at least once per year.
Wisconsin	may inspect and copy personnel documents at least twice per calendar year.

It should be noted that as of 2009, only the seventeen states listed above have general access legislation with regard to current and/or former employees having access to their personnel files and records.

SUBSTANCE ABUSE TESTING LAWS AND REGULATIONS

Private employers generally have the legal right to test their employees and job applicants for drugs, alcohol, and other controlled substances. Preemployment drug testing is becoming more and more common in many companies, and testing employees for drugs and alcohol following an industrial accident is also being done by an increasing number of employers. From a legal standpoint, random drug testing is still the riskier aspect of substance abuse screening, although companies in transportation and other safety-critical industries may be required by state or federal law to establish a drug-free environment using such a policy. The bottom line in this complex area of substance abuse testing, however, is that HR professionals must work with their legal department or outside counsel to be aware of the many state laws that deal with substance abuse testing policies and practices in the geographic areas where their companies operate.

Regardless of what other actions you may take in this matter of substance abuse testing, your very first responsibility as the head of the human resources function is to draft a comprehensive yet clear and understandable policy, which must be distributed to every employee in your company. This statement should make it clear to your customers, suppliers, the general public, and especially to your employees, the exact position your company takes on this issue. Your policy should make it crystal clear that the company means what it says: There will be no exceptions to this policy, and an infraction of the rules will bring swift discipline, up to and including termination. Unless your policy is so worded and is in compliance with state and federal law, the policy will not be effective, and your company will be at a great disadvantage in attempting to defend itself against claims and lawsuits from employees, customers, or others alleging violations of civil and constitutional rights. It is strongly recommended, especially in the beginning, to work with qualified legal counsel to draft the necessary policies reflecting your company's approach to this most vital and important subject of substance abuse screening and testing.

GENETIC INFORMATION NONDISCRIMINATION ACT (GINA) 2008
The GINA law essentially strengthens safeguards of the 1996 Health Insurance Portability and Accountability Act (HIPAA) by limiting insurers' ability to use genetic information to raise rates for an entire group. The Act also prohibits group and individual health insurers from using a person's genetic information in determining eligibility or premiums; neither can insurers request or require a person to have a genetic test. Employers cannot use genetic information when making decisions regarding hiring, firing, promotions, and the like; and they cannot request, require, or purchase genetic information about persons or their family members. (See AARP Public Policy Institute Facts Sheet 156, May 2009, for discussion of GINA law.)

THE HUMAN RESOURCES PRACTITIONER AND THE LAW
This is by no means a complete listing of the statutes the human resources professional must be familiar with. Many volumes have been and will yet be written by competent legal experts and others on the various personnel-related statutes and laws. It is merely a brief overview of some of the more important laws one can most often expect to deal with. In reading about the various laws it becomes obvious that not only federal but state laws as well must be a part of the equation in the environment in which the businessperson operates, and the growing list becomes impressive if not awesome.

CHAPTER PERSPECTIVE
This chapter acquainted the reader with the scope and complexity of federal, state, and local laws that relate to the performance of personnel/human resources functions. The purpose of each law and the relevant concepts were explained in the context of compliance.

Chapter 10 also offered practical advice on how to protect your company from lawsuits in some of the areas covered by these laws. The necessity for the human resources practitioner to gain a thorough knowledge of these laws was stressed.

Wage and Hour Compliance

INTRODUCTION AND MAIN POINTS

Chapter 11 is devoted entirely to the examination of the Fair Labor Standards Act, commonly known as the Wage and Hour law, in the context of human resources compliance begun in Chapter 10. The important 80-hours-per-week supervision requirement of the executive exemption category is discussed as it relates to overtime compensation.

While the Wage and Hour law is specific in its requirements and carries economic penalties, it also provides a compromise solution to the problems of excessive overtime through the concept of the Fluctuating Workweek. This option is defined and detailed examples are offered.

The chapter also explores the possible reasons why the Wage and Hour Division of the U.S. Department of Labor, which administers the law, might investigate or audit your company's personnel, wage, and payroll records. Advice on the best response to make to their inquiries and requests is described. Typical Wage and Hour violations, willful violations, Department of Labor enforcement, and proposed FLSA changes and revisions are identified. The special pitfalls and hazards of retail operations regarding compliance with the Wage and Hour law are discussed.

Finally, a Wage and Hour Self-Defense and Preventive Maintenance Program is suggested to avoid many of the aforementioned problems. Five practical preventive measures (PMs) to follow are described.

After reading the material in this chapter:

■ You will understand the importance of complying with the Wage and Hour law.

■ You will be familiar with several of the Act's most important provisions and concepts, including overtime, the 80-hours-per-week supervision requirement for executive exempt status, and the Fluctuating Workweek.

■ You will understand why the Department of Labor might investigate or audit your company.

■ You will understand the problems of retail operations regarding changes in employee exempt/nonexempt status.

■ You will become familiar with five PMs—preventive measures to avoid serious mishaps in compliance.

THE IMPORTANCE OF KNOWING THE LAW

In Chapter 10, we introduced the basic concepts of the Fair Labor Standards Act of 1938, as amended, commonly referred to as the Wage and Hour law. This chapter is devoted entirely to the understanding of this important law. All human resources specialists should be aware that detailed knowledge of and familiarity with this law is probably the most fundamental prerequisite for performing their job responsibilities—and certainly for performing them well. Compensation analysts, in particular, have a key responsibility to insure that the basic provisions of the Wage and Hour law are being adhered to throughout the organization.

THE OVERTIME PROVISION

In addition to its many other provisions, the main focus of the law's compliance centers on the overtime provisions of the act. It is essential that all personnel classified as exempt from the act's overtime and other provisions actually do meet the qualifications for exemption as spelled out in the law (see Chapter 10 for classification criteria of exemptions covered in the Wage and Hour law).

In most retail organizations, and especially in multifacility retail companies, the executive exemption category requiring the store manager, supervisor, or other entitled executive, to supervise a total of at least 80 hours of work done by others per week, is the most common concern of these organizations. The hours-supervised concept must be thoroughly understood by managers in order for it to be properly applied.

The manager or supervisor must also be perfectly clear on the fact that, in the event that a nonexempt employee (that is, one who is not exempt from the provisions of the law), works beyond 40 hours in any given week, premium dollars must be paid for each hour the person works in excess of 40. Let's look at a simple example:

If a nonexempt employee works 45 hours in a particular work week, the person is paid *straight time* for all hours worked (45, for instance), but he or she must also be paid additional *half time* for each and every hour worked over 40 in that work week (such as 5 hours). For instance, if the employee's base rate is $10 per hour, then that employee would receive $10 times 45 (hours), or $450 for the straight-time hours worked; plus $5 times 5 (hours) for the overtime hours worked, for a total of $25. The employee's total gross pay for this work week will then be $450 plus $25, or a total of $475 compensation for this particular workweek.

Some employees and employers prefer to think of overtime hours in terms of paying time and one-half for all hours worked over 40 in a given work week. The result, of course, is the same. Using the example quoted in the previous paragraph:

$$\$10 \text{ per hour} \times 40 \text{ hours} = \$400$$
$$\$15 \text{ per hour (time and one-half)} \times 5 \text{ hours} = \underline{\$\ 75}$$
$$\text{Total} = \$475$$

This overtime-after-40-hours feature of the Wage and Hour law is perhaps the part of the law that is most understood and, at the same time, most misunderstood both by supervisors and employees alike. Many businesses—and not only smaller ones—will openly complain that they simply cannot afford to pay this premium (penalty) one-half time to their employees. "The cost is too prohibitive." "We'll have to lay off some people in order to be able to pay time and one-half overtime to others." "We may even have to go out of business!" The list goes on and on.

The Need for Compliance
The law is specific, its provisions are clear, and the economic penalties levied against the employer normally serve as effective motivators, as well as tangible reminders as to the wisdom of complying with Wage and Hour law provisions in the future.

The plain facts are that if:
■ your company or business comes under the scope of the Wage and Hour law as to gross revenue and other provisions as most companies do, and
■ you do wish to remain in business, and
■ you do not wish to risk severe penalties for violating the Wage and Hour law, then you do not have a choice—you must comply and pay the premium for the overtime hours.

Typical Wage and Hour Law Violations
Some of the tactics used by employers to unlawfully reduce or entirely avoid the payment of overtime include
1) arbitrarily exempting workers from overtime pay. (In some cases company downsizing pushes authority down through the

ranks, making it harder for employers to know which jobs are exempt and which are not exempt.)

2) pressuring employees to do more work to stay competitive, lengthening the work day, and making overtime an even more thorny issue.

3) routinely ignoring overtime rules. Many small companies, especially, to avoid getting caught, do not keep pay records at all or devise false ones.

4) the fact that some larger companies are more likely to issue mandatory overtime pay policies, but then raise productivity targets and look the other way when employees work off the clock to meet those targets.

5) removing substantial duties (purchasing authority, for example) from exempt jobs while still exempting them from overtime.

6) docking exempt salaried workers at any level for missed work time, making those employees ineligible for overtime pay during that particular work week.

7) simply being ignorant of the law, especially in family or closely held smaller companies.

Willful Violations

The Wage and Hour Division has the authority under the law to require offending employers to go back as many as three years in investigating overtime violations if it is determined that the company deliberately refused to pay the time and one-half rate for overtime hours worked. With the exception of these willful violations, Wage and Hour Division investigations involving 2 years of checking for overtime violations are more common in cases where employers acknowledge they misinterpreted the law and agree to cooperate fully with the division in resolving the problems involved.

Department of Labor Enforcement

In 2009 the U.S. Department of Labor announced that in 2007 its Wage and Hour Division collected more than $220 million in back wages. This represents a 22 percent increase over fiscal year 2006 and is the largest amount of back pay awards in the past 10 years. And nearly 95,000 *more* workers (a total of almost 247,000) received back wages in 2007.

The agency completed 30,467 compliance actions in fiscal year 2007, a 4.75 percent decrease from the 31,987 completed actions in fiscal year 2006; and, as has usually been the case in prior years since 2004 (and HR professionals take note), three-quarters of the concluded cases were initiated by a complainant, as opposed to agency audits or actions.

Wage and Hour Division employees recorded close to 900,000 enforcement hours in 2007 and assessed over $10.3 million in civil monetary penalties.

FLSA Revisions and Changes

The Fair Labor Standards Act is an all-encompassing, Depression-era federal law that established the foundation for a number of labor-related issues, most notably the establishment of the foundation for overtime pay. Many employers (as well as HR managers) were not happy with its current provisions and wanted to see it revised.

Probably the two major changes most often suggested by employers are the ability

1) To offer workers compensatory time off in lieu of overtime pay and

2) To extend the period in which overtime is calculated from one or two weeks or even a month, so that, for example, a company could require employees to work overtime in one week and then reduce the second work week by a comparable number of hours, thus legally avoiding the need to pay overtime.

But then the U.S. Department of Labor did issue new major revisions to the white-collar exemption features of the FLSA, effective August 23, 2004. (See detailed discussion of white-collar exemptions in Chapter 10.) These significant modifications to the law included:

■ Salary test increase to $455 per week;

■ Creation of a new exemption for highly compensated individuals ($100,000 per year); and

■ Elimination of the "long test" for determining whether an employee is exempt from overtime; the U.S. Department of Labor has instead made a single test for each of the categories (i.e., employers no longer have to determine whether an exempt employee is devoting more than 20 percent of his or her time performing nonexempt duties).

It must be painfully obvious to employers, however, that the two major changes in the law, which they favor (see above), are still not included in the latest revisions—nor does there seem to be much hope for future FLSA modifications.

LEGAL ALTERNATIVES TO EXCESSIVE OVERTIME

Hiring additional part-time help, restructuring or staggering work schedules, and introducing other innovative time-management measures and scheduling can definitely help to reduce or even eliminate completely the need for working employees overtime.

Compensation department staff should be able to assist management with statistical analyses and studies as to the best methods of controlling overtime expenses, which in some companies are correctly referred to on departmental profit and loss statements (P&Ls) as wasted money! Such remarks on company documents help to serve as effective reminders to supervisors and managers of the need to keep overtime work and hours to an absolute minimum.

Job Sharing

Many companies also have programs that allow two employees to share the same job. This type of situation, for example, is ideal for mothers who can spare only limited amounts of time away from their children. The HR staff works with departmental management to consider possibly dividing an eight-hour job into two four-hour shifts, an ideal arrangement for the two women. On those jobs involving scheduled overtime, such an arrangement could save the company premium wages by splitting the shift between such part-time employees. The resultant overtime savings might then allow the company to offer limited or pro rata benefits to such employees as an incentive to reduce turnover, as well as overtime.

There are many highly qualified and capable people in the job market whose only impediment is that for one valid reason or another, they are just not able to work a full eight-hour job each day of the work week. Any number of smart company CEOs understand this situation well, and they make every effort to arrange hours and shifts to suit the convenience of these part-timers. Far from being considered second-class workers, such companies view them as a valuable and profitable resource, and offer good wages and benefits accordingly.

FLUCTUATING WORKWEEK

One less-well-known provision of the Fair Labor Standards Act, as amended, offers some relief to employers on the overtime pay issue by providing a compromise solution to the need to pay time and one-half for overtime hours. This provision, known as the Fluctuating Workweek, allows companies to set up a weekly paid, nonexempt salary method of compensation so long as certain conditions of employment exist in the job involved. These conditions include the following.

1) An employee's working hours must be such that they normally vary to the extent the employee can almost never be sure of a specific beginning or ending of the daily work shift due to the requirements and necessities of the work.

2) The employee must be made aware that wages will be paid under the Fluctuating Workweek method of payment, must fully understand the provisions of the Fluctuating Workweek, and must agree to compensation under this method of payment.

Although employee hours should still vary in order to use the Fluctuating Workweek payment method, recent discussions with the U.S. Department of Labor indicate that employers may now use the Fluctuating Workweek program without strict adherence to the original notification requirements as stated in item 2) above. However, experience tells us that for reasons of proper communication, employee morale, and fairness, employees should certainly be made aware of the system of compensation under which they are working. It is strongly recommended that human resources or compensation managers verify the requirements with the Labor Department before actually installing a Fluctuating Workweek program in their companies.

The law specifically does require, however, that a person classified on Fluctuating Workweek must receive a guaranteed weekly salary, which in effect compensates the employee for all straight-time hours that may be called for in a given workweek. Although the person is still a nonexempt employee, any amount of work performed during the week (regardless of how little) guarantees payment of the full week's salary to the employee. In return for this somewhat generous guarantee to the worker, the employer is only required to pay half-time to the employee on Fluctuating Workweek for overtime work (for example, for all hours worked over 40 during the work week), rather than the normal time and one-half rate. In addition, the half-time rate under Fluctuating Workweek decreases progressively as the total number of hours worked during the week increases. It must be kept in mind, however, that regardless of the number of overtime hours worked, the half-time rate may not decrease to less than one-half of the current minimum hourly wage.

The following examples should help clarify this somewhat complex provision of the Wage and Hour law:

Example 1:
- Weekly guarantee = $400
- Hours worked this week = 47
- Hourly wage = (based on number of hours worked this week)
- $400 (weekly guarantee) ÷ 47 (hours worked) = $8.50/hour (which becomes the base hourly rate for this work week)
- $1/2 \times \$8.50 = \$4.25$ (the overtime rate for this work week)

Example 1 (continued):
- 4.25×7 (overtime hours) = \$29.75 (overtime)
- \$400 (weekly guarantee) + \$29.75 (overtime) = \$429.75 (total gross pay for this work week)

Example 2:
- Weekly guarantee = \$475
- Hours worked this week = 58.5
- Hourly wage = (based on number of hours worked this week)
- \$475 (weekly guarantee ÷ 58.5 (hours worked) = \$8.12 (base hourly rate for this work week)
- $1/2 \times \$8.12 = \$4.06$ (the overtime rate for this work week)
- $\$4.06 \times 18.5$ overtime hours = \$75.11 (overtime)
- \$475 weekly guarantee + \$75.11 (overtime) = \$550.11 (total gross pay for this work week)

Example 3:
- Weekly guarantee = \$350
- Hours worked this week = 50
- Hourly wage = (based on number of hours worked this week)
- \$350 (weekly guarantee) ÷ 50 (hours worked) = \$7.00/hr. (which would normally become the base hourly rate for this work week. However, since the regular hourly rate falls below the minimum wage of \$7.25/hour, the base hourly rate for this week must be increased to and calculated on the basis of \$7.25/hour)
- $1/2 \times \$7.25$ (minimum wage) = \$3.63 (the overtime rate for this work week)
- \$3.63/hour $\times$ 10 (overtime hours) = \$36.30 (overtime)
- \$350 (weekly guarantee) + \$36.30 (overtime) = \$386.30 (total gross pay for this work week)

The Fluctuating Workweek might be looked at as a payment method half-way (more or less) between the salary exempt and the hourly nonexempt methods. In retail or service industries where working hours and store coverage are apt to fluctuate on a regular or perhaps seasonal basis, the Fluctuating Workweek can be an alternative for the employer who currently pays large amounts of overtime based on the expensive time and one-half rate as opposed to using this system of paying only half-time for all hours worked over 40.

If you do happen to decide to bring the Fluctuating Workweek into your organization, be prepared for possible complaints from employees who will tell anyone who'll listen, "I only get half-time for my overtime hours while my friends and neighbors are all paid time-and-one-half for theirs!" Or perhaps, "My company is really cheap and doesn't care about its employees," and other similarly uncomplimentary remarks. As with most other aspects of business, taking the time to communicate with your employees to explain the pros and cons of the Fluctuating Workweek is vital, and would certainly be in your best interests to do so.

One company's unique experience with the Fluctuating Workweek involved installing a pilot program in one of its largest field districts. After careful monitoring of the program, the company discovered that many of their field service representatives who had been on a standard 60-hour work week for quite some time and were thus paid time-and-one-half for 20 overtime hours each week, were now beginning to report an average of some 45 hours worked each week. The astonishing thing was that they were actually accomplishing all or most of their regular work in 45 hours instead of their former standard 60-hour work week. This indicated that, at least in part, the knowledge that they were receiving only half-time instead of their former time-and-one-half rate for overtime hours convinced them to get their work done as soon as possible. They were also acutely aware that working the additional overtime hours decreased their basic hourly as well as overtime rate of pay. The additional 15 hours of free time for themselves and their families was undoubtedly their main incentive.

Whatever their individual motivation, the fact remained that these employees were getting more (or at least as much) work done in 45 hours on Fluctuating Workweek as they had formerly done in 60 hours. In this situation, the employee as well as the company benefited. Under the proper conditions, you might try this program at your company on an experimental basis, always with the option of returning to more conventional compensation methods if, for whatever reason, the trial run does not prove successful.

The Fluctuating Workweek method of payment may be used in all states except California (and Canada as well). California and Canada may not legally use Fluctuating Workweek due to preempting state (or provincial) legislation. In all other states, however, it can be and is used; and though you may run the risk of employee displeasure and grumbling if it isn't properly understood, in the long run it is a most economical way for the company to keep the number one expense item—personnel costs—under control.

DEPARTMENT OF LABOR INVESTIGATIONS AND AUDITS

Don't be shocked or surprised if you receive a call one day from one of your field offices or retail stores stating that an investigator from the U.S. Department of Labor is there asking to see personnel records, pay logs, time cards, and other such data. The DOL has probably called upon you for one of two reasons: Either this is simply a routine, unscheduled wage and hour compliance audit, or, as is more likely the case, the DOL received a complaint that one of your employees was classified in the company's records as an exempt employee when actually the individual believed this not to be the case due to the preponderance of nonexempt work done in the normal course of the job. Because, in all likelihood, this person had worked a considerable number of overtime hours without additional compensation and this practice had allegedly been going on for some time, the DOL was informed of these facts, and the department's Wage and Hour Division is now asking the employer involved the very same questions.

If the claimant was an exempt manager or supervisor, that person may even be claiming that at least 80 hours of work by their subordinates had not been supervised by the claimant, and that the claimant should have indeed been properly classified as nonexempt. Therefore, all hours worked over 40 in each work week should be paid as overtime hours.

There are other reasons, such as methods and timeliness of wage payments, that employees contact the Department of Labor, but statistics show that exempt/nonexempt questions, especially those related to the payment of overtime, are the main reasons for a visit to your company by a wage and hour representative. In any event, you are now involved in a full-scale wage and hour investigation.

Cooperation

Your course at this point is clear: You have absolutely no choice; you must cooperate fully (we might as well add cheerfully and without hesitation) in providing the DOL agent with the information, records, files, logs, or whatever other data the investigator requests. The above approach is highly recommended since you will probably fare better by demonstrating an attitude of cooperation and cheerfulness in providing whatever data or documents the DOL requests. Also remember that, regardless of your attitude, it is usually not wise to volunteer any documents or items of information that are not officially requested. Neither you nor any member of your staff are legally obligated to volunteer information or to guide the investigator in any way.

If the DOL agent asks that you arrange interviews with current employees, provide names and last-known addresses and perhaps phone numbers of former employees, by all means do so. The DOL has the legal right to talk with your current and former personnel to determine if they perhaps have now or have had in the past the same type of complaints as those presently under investigation by the DOL. Also be aware that the Department of Labor has the right to subpoena whatever records and information are relevant to the investigation.

The importance of cooperation on the part of the employer with the DOL cannot be stressed too strongly. This is a most essential element in dealing with them, as it is with any federal, state, or local enforcement or regulatory agency. Whether the subject is discrimination, compensation, or any other area of personnel relations, cooperation eventually wins the day. Government employees have a job to do just as you have in the private sector. If you interact willingly with them and help make their investigation as professional and orderly as possible, you will be the winner in the end, whether or not wage and hour violations have occurred.

Keep in mind that you and your local manager or supervisor represent your company or organization, and your job is to do whatever is legally and ethically permissible to successfully defend your employer and to effectively and economically resolve the issues under investigation. Don't forget that if you sincerely believe the information requested is not relevant to the case or situation in question, then by all means politely but firmly make the point in writing to the agent or agency involved. You may want to consult with your legal advisor for a second opinion on this point, but in any event, stand your ground when you're convinced your position is sound.

On the other side of the coin, if a mistake has been made by a supervisor or someone in a management capacity regarding how an employee was compensated under the Wage and Hour law, have it resolved as quickly as possible and try to negotiate the best deal you can. This is where your cooperation and positive attitude toward the investigation will normally work to your advantage. Make sure that whatever dollar settlements are agreed upon for the employee (or former employee) involved are made promptly, and that proper releases are signed by them. It is also the responsibility of the human resources department to make certain that supervisors and managers who were the focus of the wage and hour investigation fully understand the problems that may have surfaced, the seriousness of any errors made, and, most important, that they learn from their experience.

The Department of Labor can be a most helpful source of guidance and counsel before problem situations are officially brought to their attention, and their staff in any local or regional office is neither unreasonable nor hostile either when seeking their advice or in the course of an investigation. They do their job thoroughly and objectively as the law requires, but they are generally understanding, cooperative, and fair.

RETAIL OPERATION PITFALLS AND HAZARDS

One of the key requirements for supervisors and managers to meet the executive exemption test under the Wage and Hour law (see Chapter 10 for criteria) is that they must supervise the work of two or more full-time employees, each working a total of at least 40 hours per week, or supervise or direct any number of part-time employees (or a combination of both full-time and part-time people) whose combined hours total at least 80 per week. Simply stated, in order for supervisory employees to qualify for the executive exemption, they must supervise or direct a total of at least 80 hours of time worked by their employees in a given work week.

If they do not supervise at least 80 hours of work on a regular week-by-week basis, the employer has no choice but to classify these supervisory employees to nonexempt status and must pay them on an hourly rate basis, with time and one-half for all hours they work over 40 in any work week. (The only other choice the employer has is to use the Fluctuating Workweek method of payment described earlier in this chapter, assuming the supervisor's or manager's hours of work are subject to daily fluctuation.)

In the retail business especially, it is certainly to the company's advantage to have store managers, for example, paid as exempt employees, thus eliminating the necessity of paying premium overtime dollars for the long hours usually associated with these kinds of occupations. In economic hard times, we normally find an increase in wage and hour claims due to companies cutting back on numbers of employees and asking (read *requiring*) exempt managers and supervisors to put in additional hours to make up for the reduction in nonexempt personnel hours. Often, no corresponding increase in salary is made for these individuals and, all things considered, the likelihood increases of their claiming to be in a nonexempt status and thereby entitled to overtime after 40 hours.

If a number of supervisors make this claim, and they are successful in convincing the U.S. Department of Labor that such practices are widespread throughout the organization, the company could be facing a massive, full-scale wage and hour investigation in a given district or even in the entire company. Size does not matter in these cases; the economic consequences are potentially most unpleasant if your company is found to be guilty of such violations.

WAGE AND HOUR SELF-DEFENSE AND PREVENTIVE MAINTENANCE PROGRAM

No guarantee exists that you will always receive a clean bill of wage and hour health throughout your company even if you make the most conscientious efforts to insure compliance. The larger your company, and the more outlets or facilities you have, the greater the possibility of wage and hour problems occurring. Some defenses, however, can at least insure against some possibly widespread, undetected, serious violations. These defenses are called preventive measures, and it is suggested that you consider having your human resources compensation group initiate these PMs with your field, office, and headquarters groups as applicable. For example, you could establish one or more of the following preventive measures.

PM-1: Company Internal Audit (CIA) Checkups

This CIA PM would require the help and assistance of the company's own internal audit department to check on the validity of the exempt status (in particular, the executive exemption) of the various store managers in the field. While it is certainly true that the internal audit department has its hands full with its own responsibility of checking financial and cash management methods and procedures at company retail stores and locations, internal auditors can be of tremendous help to human resources as they travel from company location to location keeping a watchful eye out for potential wage and hour problems. Even if they only observed and raised questions when exempt salary managers seem to have no other subordinate help in their stores, for example, such information would surely be of interest to the compensation staff of human resources.

Another CIA PM in which internal audit can be helpful would be in noting whether or not minimum wage, disability, discrimination, and other legally required posters or notices are displayed on the bulletin boards of company stores and branch locations they routinely visit. In addition to checking for these government notices, internal auditors can provide invaluable help to the HR staff by checking on the prominent display of company policy bulletins and statements dealing with sexual harassment, substance abuse, drug testing, and, assuming you are a nonunion company, the president's statement with respect to your reasons for not turning to an outside party (such as a union) to help management run its organization.

As mentioned previously, the internal audit staff may have about all it can handle in traveling long distances and performing its normal auditing functions on a close time schedule without the added responsibility of performing some human resources work as well. Nevertheless, the staff will normally cooperate and make the effort to spend the few extra minutes to check bulletin boards for posting of appropriate notices and documents. Think about the strategy best suited to your company in handling these challenging opportunities, and work with the internal audit manager to obtain his or her cooperation.

While the name internal audit manager may evoke an image of a large company, no company is too small to have an internal audit function, even if it is simply an added responsibility of a staff member who handles a variety of other duties. An investment in self-audit and policing practices in any company usually pays off handsomely in long-term dividends, regardless of the type of operation being audited.

PM-2: Human Resources Department Random Checkups

This preventive-measure procedure could be a random check of selected stores' or other locations' payroll logs and records, personnel status reports, and other personnel data by the human resources compensation group to detect possible minimum wage, overtime, exemption, and wage payment method violations. This PM-2, while similar to the PM-1, would entail a more in-depth check and analysis of wage and hour compliance and could pay valuable dividends in terms of uncovering violations while still in the early stages. The fact that branch and store managers know they are under such random surveillance also goes a long way toward keeping major infractions to a minimum.

PM-2s could be conducted by wage analysts over the phone, by computer network, in writing, or in person, or a combination of these things, depending on the size of your company and the geographic dispersion of your various facilities. A good computer network with proper software should enable the analyst to monitor these activities for each company department or entity. All things considered, nothing works better than a regular or occasional personal visit (or the prospect thereof) to the store or other company facility to keep these critical wage and hour elements under control and in balance.

Many companies find, to their later financial sorrow and loss, that if employee records, especially those dealing with time worked, are not kept accurately and up to date, the Department of Labor will rely on the employee's own records, estimates, or even memory of overtime hours worked and not paid for, as well as for other types of wage and hour violations. Back pay assessments and penalties against the company could be made for the last two or even three years, depending on how willful or deliberate the DOL determines the company has been in evading the law and attempting to avoid these legally required payments. This is why, as in the case of diseases of the human body, good preventive maintenance and early detection of problems can prevent major difficulties, work disruptions, and serious monetary losses at some future date.

PM-3: Human Resources Department Regular Audits

Even the most basic personal computer software available today has the ability to provide a printout or table (or both), showing the employment status of each employee in the company by department, shop, store, or other facility grouping. This tool, sometimes referred to among other titles as a Personnel Status Report (PSR), may include:

Employee's name
Hire date
Company identification number
Job title
Job code number
Rate of pay
Whether salary (exempt) or hourly (nonexempt)
Whether full time, part time, or temporary
Date and amount of last wage or salary increase

The PSR should be run and issued to supervisors and managers either weekly or monthly (the latter reduces paperwork and seems to work out better), and chances are they will find it a great help in administering the compensation, promotion, appraisal, and other employee personnel functions as well. With this information at hand, and being provided to them on a regular basis, managers will have little need or occasion to maintain their own unofficial personnel files on their employees, a practice that could sometimes be quite embarrassing if not actually dangerous when damaging handwritten remarks or notes are made a part of field or noncentralized personnel files.

One unique advantage the Personnel Status Report has for human resources compensation professionals from a wage and hour exemption standpoint is that it gives them an overall, always up-to-date means of identifying and monitoring the number of employees each manager supervises at each company location. The PSR is normally sorted in company and/or location order, and it then becomes a simple matter of scanning the PSR and noting those locations where exempt supervisors or managers appear to not be supervising a sufficient number of subordinate working hours to justify the Fair Labor Standards Act executive exemption.

If an exempt supervisor or manager supervises other exempt personnel, a credit of 40 hours per week is given for each exempt subordinate (as well as for each full-time hourly (nonexempt) person working at least 40 hours per week). In addition, as covered earlier, if a particular location also has part-time, hourly paid employees, the exempt manager or supervisor may take credit for supervising whatever hours these part-time employees work. In other words, if the exempt supervisor or manager supervises any combination of hours of exempt, full-time hourly, or part-time hourly jobs that results in a total of at least 80 hours supervised per week, then for each such week, the manager in question meets the 80 hours of supervision per week wage and hour test and may be considered to have met the executive exemption. If the manager's salary also meets the wage and hour salary test, the manager would then be considered exempt.

When the human resources compensation staff reviews the PSR on a consistent basis, it will be able to easily recognize the first warning signs that an exempt manager has dropped below the 80 hours of supervision required for exemption. The manager's supervisor must then be immediately contacted and instructed to change the status of the manager to either nonexempt (hourly) or to Fluctuating Workweek (weekly paid) for that particular week, and continuing until such time as the manager is again supervising any combination of 80 hours of work in a given work week. It must be emphasized that the 80 hours of supervision requirement for exemption applies week by week only. We may not take a monthly, annual, or other time-frame average, as the law is quite specific in requiring 80 hours of supervision each and every week to meet the exemption test.

With the understanding and cooperation of higher level management to whom exempt supervisors and managers report, the human resources compensation analyst can almost guarantee immunity from wage and hour violations regarding the amount of hours supervised by exempt managers simply by doing the following:

▬ conscientiously auditing each current Personnel Status Report, showing all personnel the manager supervises;

▬ spot checking these employees' time logs; and

▬ alerting the proper officials when exempt managers' status must be changed to nonexempt in order to conform to the law.

This is truly preventive maintenance in action, and is well worth whatever resources must be allocated or redirected from other areas within the human resources department in order to accomplish this objective.

PM-4: Child Labor Violations Checkups
The Wage and Hour law also provides penalties for modern-day abuses of child labor, a practice extremely prevalent in the early part of this century and before. The law establishes minimum hiring ages, maximum number of hours that may be worked, and also when hours

may be worked by children when school is in session. Also specified in the law are the types of hazardous tools and equipment children are prohibited from using or operating, as well as the type of hazardous operations around which they may not work.

The human resources professional must be especially mindful of and pay close attention to a child-labor PM program. It may be the one about which the practitioner may mistakenly feel the most confident, while in reality it may be the very program in need of attention. Without a planned (manual or computerized) applicant tracking system, and frankly a visual spot check every now and then as well, minors will slip by and be hired under legal age limits, or, if legally hired, may be working around hazardous equipment, materials, or operations, working too many hours when school is in session, or other potential child labor violations.

These days, with sophisticated computers and software, we should have no trouble whatever monitoring PM-4. However, other responsibilities abound, and it may at times be rather easy to convince one's self that this aspect of the complex human resources job is being looked after by your competent supervisors and managers who interview, hire, and/or supervise people—including minors—at the various office and field locations. You must also remember that although this is normally the case, human resources staff personnel are ultimately responsible for protecting the corporation from this and other serious and potentially costly employee relations problems by being alert and sounding the alarm as soon as they first develop.

In addition to your more standard safeguards, make an occasional spot check a normal part of your Child Labor PM-4. You may be pleasantly (or unpleasantly) surprised at the results of such an inspection. In any event, current problems will be easier to correct, and you will come to learn through habit and practice that there is no substitute for early detection as the secret to a healthy, thriving personnel relations program.

PM-5: Personnel Action Changes Monitoring and Checkups

When the status of an employee changes for any reason, the document used to make such a change may be called an Employee Status Change Form, a Personnel Action Form, or some other such title. Whatever you choose to call it, you will want to complete a status change for each of the following events.

New hire
Termination
Promotion
Demotion
Transfer

Disciplinary action
Change of marital status
Address change
Phone number change
Leave of absence
Return from leave of absence

Include any other event that may, and likely will, occur to your personnel at some point in time. Whether you use the latest computer network software to input these status changes, or whether you operate with manual forms and input as some companies still do, you once again have a golden opportunity to utilize your preventive-measure techniques by having your compensation group monitor all such changes, and especially all proposed changes.

Probably the most effective way of monitoring personnel actions and changes is to assign the function to a central location such as the corporate or divisional human resources staff, thus insuring compliance with state and federal wage and hour laws and other regulations relating to personnel matters. The responsibility of the human resources central staff would be to check such employee status changes for

1) validity of proposed administrative, executive, or professional exemptions.
2) possible child labor violations relating to age, hours of work, and working conditions.
3) the purpose of ensuring payment of minimum hourly and salary wages.
4) any other aspects of Fair Labor Standards Act compliance.

THE AUDIT FUNCTION

The audit function that is normally the responsibility of the human resources compensation professionals can also be useful in detecting other potential HR problems such as compliance with the Immigration Reform and Control Act of 1986. Compensation staff must insure that the proper I-9 paperwork is complete and that the forms are kept in separate file locations (not in the personnel files) and organized so that citizenship and immigration agents may conveniently inspect them. Compensation can also check for equality of pay rates for male and female workers doing the same jobs, assuming equality of job performance. For that matter, such an audit can be of invaluable help to human resources in monitoring the provisions of all personnel-related laws and regulations summarized in Chapter 10 of this book.

Occasionally, these PM audits of personnel files will reveal comments on the Personnel Action Form from a manager or supervisor such as:

This employee is being terminated (or demoted, transferred, or other) due to a physical disability that prevents this employee from performing all aspects of the job.

Or:

This employee is being terminated (or demoted, transferred, disciplined, or other) on suspicion of having stolen XX dollars (or items of company equipment) from the employer.

To the more-experienced personnel or human resources professional, these two examples of remarks found on Personnel Action Forms may seem a bit bizarre if not unbelievable. However, these well-intentioned supervisors and managers thought they were doing the right thing but did not realize the problems they were creating by such wording, and the position in which they placed their company from the standpoint of legal liability.

Other examples of dangerous remarks on the Personnel Action Form consist of references to race, sex, or age, character assassination, and unsupported accusations of all sorts that, if entered as a permanent record in the individual's personnel file, could be most detrimental to the company's position in the event of discrimination charges or other legal action taken against the company. It must be remembered that anything that becomes a permanent part of an employee's written work record or history will probably be subject to being subpoenaed by the courts in any future legal proceedings.

Another benefit of the compensation audit is that it permits the auditing or checking for required approval signatures on forms or paperwork relating to hiring, discharge, promotions, wage changes, leaves of absence, severance pay allowances, and discretionary bonus payments. It is also important for compensation analysts to monitor personnel action changes coming in over a computer network to insure the integrity and validity of signatures and assigned security codes authorized for processing such actions. Those companies currently employing manual methods and systems must, of course, still check for authorized approval signatures, as well as for accuracy and completeness before entering them into their official human resources files and systems.

Sometimes it is recommended to human resources that in order to facilitate the processing of these Personnel Action (Change of Status) Forms, it might be well to forego the auditing procedure on these recommended actions. This same argument is also made regarding the checking of employment applications, W-4 withholding forms, I-9 immigration forms, and a variety of other new-hire paperwork that cannot be sent over a computer network and must therefore be manually forwarded to human resources for handling. When such paperwork is incomplete, illegible, or in some cases, missing altogether, it is literally the duty of the human resources' staff to follow up with company presidents and managers to correct such problems and counsel them on proper data-handling methods in the future.

Although these audit functions sometimes can be time consuming and tedious, they are absolutely vital to a well-organized, efficient personnel records system that will stand you in good stead, especially when the U.S. Department of Labor, immigration compliance officers, and possibly other government investigators come to call. The audit function, including the review and checking of exemptions, proposed wages, job titles, written comments, and other information on the Personnel Action Form, is a most important ingredient of the compensation analyst's job, and can be effectively done only by and in the human resources department.

PAYROLL FUNCTION

The basic audit function is not the responsibility of the payroll department staff, for example, as their function is one of production (of paychecks) rather than analysis, and they are charged with implementing the wage policies and procedures as established by the human resources compensation group. A timely, correct paycheck (including direct deposit and paycard) is the all-important end result of a cooperative effort between payroll and the human resources compensation staff. Probably nothing can be more traumatic or cause more confusion and complaint than a paycheck error, with the possible exception of a misdirected or missing paycheck, or one that is delayed beyond the normal distribution or delivery date. Thus, payroll department personnel do have a critical responsibility to ensure that payroll and paycheck problems are held to an absolute minimum. However, human resources and payroll people must also understand the need for mutual cooperation while attending to their own individual responsibilities. New businesses as well as companies that have been around for many years all understand the importance of producing balance sheets, profit-and-loss statements, annual reports, and similar items, but they must also be keenly aware that the company's most important, most untouchable document it produces is the weekly, biweekly, or monthly employee paycheck, direct deposit check, or paycard. Incidentally, in order to avoid some of the occasional conflicts between human resources and payroll, and for general efficiency purposes, many companies combine these two functions under the manager, director, or vice president of human resources in order to assure the smooth coordination and operation of these most vital areas.

CHAPTER PERSPECTIVE

This chapter examined the Wage and Hour law and the problems that can arise out of improper compliance or noncompliance with its specific provisions. Typical wage and hour violations, willful violations, Department of Labor enforcement, and proposed FLSA changes and revisions were all discussed in some detail. Special attention was given to the problems of retail operations. It focused on the overtime compensation provision, the necessity for correctly categorizing exempt executive employees, and the Fluctuating Workweek concept. How best to respond to Department of Labor investigations or audits was discussed. Several practical preventive measures to monitor possible problem areas were prescribed.

Personnel Policies and the Personnel Policies Manual (PPM)

INTRODUCTION AND MAIN POINTS

This chapter is about formalizing personnel policies and compiling them into a Personnel Policies Manual (PPM). First, the need for formalizing such policies is discussed. Second, guidelines for constructing a PPM for your company are given, with special attention to the table of contents, the subject index, and the cover. The inclusion of important personnel policy statements in the introductory part of the manual is recommended. These position statements are on the topics of:

Individual department policies
Corporate commitment
Employment-at-will
Equal employment opportunity
Unions
Substance abuse

Sample personnel forms most often used in the human resources function should also be included in your Personnel Policies Manual. This chapter gives twelve examples of customized forms, statements, and agreements, and why and how to use them. These forms cover the following topics:

Application for employment
Confidential reference inquiry
Educational reference inquiry
I-9 (Immigration forms)
Employment eligibility verification
Personal progress interview, appearance, and property return
Warning notice
Voluntary resignation
Exit interview
No solicitation, No distribution, Posting rules
Gambling on company property
Letters of recommendation or reference letters

After reading the material in this chapter:

■ You will understand why it is important to formalize your personnel policies in writing and to compile a Personnel Policies Manual.

■ You will have a good idea of how to go about constructing your Personnel Policies Manual.

■ You will be aware of the importance of including a position statement in the introduction.

■ You will know which sample forms should be included so that managers, supervisors, and HR practitioners will have them as handy reference tools.

THE NEED FOR FORMALIZING PERSONNEL POLICIES

Regardless of the size of your company, one of the principal and key duties of the human resources department (or the person who handles the human resources function) has to be the origination, development, maintenance, and ultimately the publication of all of your approved and official personnel policies. Smaller firms might sometimes feel that the formalizing and publication of their personnel policies is not absolutely necessary inasmuch as their employees already know these policies in a general way, and their supervisors and managers don't want to be fenced in by formal policy statements and inflexible work rules. Some companies might even take the position that if they have no Personnel Policies Manual, no employee handbook, and no published individual personnel policies of any kind, their employees will be unable to challenge the actions or decisions of management or supervisors by pointing out the written provisions of any given personnel policy.

Unfortunately, this head-in-the-sand attitude will create far more problems than it avoids—for companies of any size. In this current era of discrimination complaints and governmental laws, rules, and regulations, the very nature and complexity of operating a modern business enterprise makes it absolutely necessary that every company have a set of specific, clearly written and understandable personnel policies detailing exactly what the company's stand is on any given personnel matter.

If your organization is currently relatively small, you will probably find that, as your company expands and your population grows, your supervisors and managers will soon be requesting, if not insisting, that management establish formal personnel policies where none now exist, and that such policies be written and published, preferably in manual form. Most experienced managers seem to instinctively know that a clear, well-written, and complete PPM, when properly followed and applied, can be one of the most important tools that makes their primary responsibility of getting work done through people much easier.

The lack of a published PPM does not, of course, result in chaos or inertia within a company. However, it could also be argued that the company does not necessarily need a marketing plan, an advertising budget, or viable computer software and hardware, unless the life expectancy of your company is not important to you and your company's stockholders. An effective PPM falls into this order of importance.

In the fortunate circumstance that you have been able to convince your management that putting together a PPM is a wise thing to do, you might ask:

- Where do you start?
- How specifically do you go about creating such a document?

You may or may not be aware that there are many consulting firms, lawyers, and others who will provide you with professional advice and counsel about what such a manual should contain. Many will also offer examples as well as samples of the ideal policies manual for your use in constructing your own. While a number of these services do have merit, you should always keep in mind that you and your associates in ABC Company can normally produce a more-than-adequate PPM simply by compiling all your existing personnel policies into one written format. Then it is highly recommended that you include some very specific statements or disclaimers in your manual in order to protect your company as much as possible against certain charges or complaints such as discrimination or wrongful termination. These measures can also serve to alert everyone inside as well as outside the organization that your company is a nonunion one, assuming that is the case, and that you intend to remain so.

HOW TO CONSTRUCT A PERSONNEL POLICIES MANUAL

You can and should construct your policies manual in the format that best fits your organization's needs and that will be relatively effective in explaining company policy and withstanding employee complaints and the legal challenges that most HR practitioners must inevitably face. The occasion could be an attorney demand letter on behalf of one of your employees (or former employees), or perhaps having to read one of the policies in your manual to a jury when you are defending your position in the courtroom.

While formalizing a policies manual along the following guidelines is no warranty or guarantee of immunity, it will help you to understand what normally goes into the making of a good PPM.

1) Whether you have few or many personnel policies in your company, be sure each of them is included in your manual, which should be revised as policies are added or changed. If each of your policies is spelled out in clear, concise language, there

will be no excuse for supervisors and managers to make up their own policies, regardless of their personal feelings or opinions to the contrary.

2) Establish a table of contents and group your personnel policies under general headings for related policies. For example, you might show a general category of EMPLOYEE BENEFITS. Under this title, you would list all of the various benefits your company offers, benefit eligibility rules, dates of eligibility, and all information related to your company's benefits.

A TABLE OF CONTENTS

Examples of other possible general categories in a PPM's table of contents are set forth in Figure 12-1 below.

FIGURE 12-1
Suggested PPM Table of Contents

The Figure 12-1 example is only a partial listing of what you might want to include in your PPM's table of contents. Depending on the number of policies in the manual, you will want to build on your original listing and amend the table from time to time, as policies are added or changed.

A SUBJECT INDEX

In the back of your policies manual, you will want to include a detailed subject index in alphabetical order indicating the subjects covered and the corresponding page number locations. If in doubt, you will find that over-indexing your subjects is far better than too few subject listings. Your supervisors and managers will thank you if you break your subjects down into as many subcategories as possible.

THE PPM COVER

One word on the overall appearance of your PPM: For aesthetic purposes as well as for readiness of identification and reference, you may want your art department or an outside illustrator to design an attractive cover for it. The cover design may incorporate a picture or drawing of your principal products, or, because it is essentially a human resource product, you may want some design relating to the people perspective as you may envision it, keeping in mind that human resources professionals serve and give helping hands to employees, customers, and others. Whatever your situation, when you have a published, well-written PPM, you have the opportunity of using your talents and imagination as well as those of your staff to create an appropriate and meaningful cover design related to the HR mission statement. Don't attempt a work of art, but have fun and take pride in creating an attractive yet very necessary publication.

POSITION STATEMENTS

Another real advantage of publishing a PPM is that it gives the company an excellent forum for stating its views, philosophies, and objectives in writing, so that everyone (including the courts and plaintiffs' lawyers) may know its official position on a variety of personnel relations subjects. The following possible topics for official position statements do not necessarily appear in the sequence you may choose for your own PPM.

1) On an introductory page of the manual, you might wish to make it very clear that, on occasion, various divisions or departments of your company might find it necessary to issue individual personnel rules or procedures relating to, for example, dress code, personal appearance, tardiness, unexcused absences, or payroll

deductions for cash shortages or missing goods or equipment. These separate local policies or procedures may be necessary, as situations can vary from facility to facility. For example, some employees may deal directly with retail customers, while others will work entirely in office, shop, or warehouse areas, with little if any contact with the customer.

However, your introductory statement might also caution supervisors and managers that, due to the sensitive and potentially discriminatory nature of these individual rules, they should first be referred to the human resources staff before they are published or actually put into effect.

2) Many companies and businesses have a long-standing corporate culture or objective that might also be given prominence on an introductory page of the manual. Your statement might read somewhat like the example in Figure 12-2 below:

FIGURE 12-2
PPM Introductory Page Statement

ABC COMPANY
Our Sales and Service Commitment to Our Customers

ABC Company was founded on a commitment to always provide the best quality product and service to its customers at the lowest possible cost. This original commitment has become a part of ABC's corporate culture, and will continue to be, so long as our customers permit us to serve them.

Although such a company statement of purpose may seem innocuous and even unnecessary, it could serve as a general guideline or Rosetta Stone, if you will, for all of your supervisors in dealing with customers, as well as in managing their employees.

3) It is also very important that your policy manual (as well as any type of employee handbook) contain an at-will employment statement. Such a statement should be placed either on the inside front cover or the first page of your manual, and to be sure of getting the necessary attention, it should be printed in bold or all capital type. Displaying your at-will statement in this conspicuous manner helps to strengthen the company's position that it does not hire prospective employees under any contract of employment. You should also be sure that your statement makes it clear that the personnel policies listed in the manual are to be used only as guidelines by company supervisors and managers who handle personnel matters.

A sample at-will statement is presented in Figure 12-3 below:

FIGURE 12-3
At-Will Personnel Policy Statement

ABC COMPANY
AT-WILL/PERSONNEL POLICY STATEMENT

The contents of this manual set forth general statements of policy that are to be used as guidelines by management when handling personnel matters. As such, these policy statements do not constitute promises of specific treatment to employees and, depending upon the circumstances of a given situation, management's actions may vary from the written policies. THE CONTENTS OF THIS MANUAL DO NOT CONSTITUTE THE TERMS OF A CONTRACT OF EMPLOYMENT.

This manual shall not be construed as a guarantee of continued employment, but rather employment with ABC Company is on an at-will basis. This means that the employment relationship may be terminated at any time, with or without cause, with or without notice, by either the employee or the ABC Company for any reason not expressly prohibited by law. Any oral or written representations to the contrary are invalid and shall not be relied upon by any prospective, past, or present employee.

The personnel policies contained in this manual were written by ABC Company. The manual itself replaces all previous manuals, directives, bulletins, newsletters, pamphlets, and other corporate materials containing statements of personnel policies by ABC Company or its affiliated companies. These policies may be changed and others may be added from time to time.

Albert B. Collins
President and CEO
ABC Company

You will notice that the president and chief executive officer of the company is signing this statement, inasmuch as it serves as the primary shield in protecting and defending the entire company against charges of wrongful termination, especially those based on claims of implied contract and employment guarantees.

4) It would probably be prudent to have another page of your introduction devoted to an equal employment opportunity policy statement, such as the one shown in Chapter 8 of this book.

The importance of this policy statement also requires that it too be signed by the president and chief executive officer of the company.

5) If you are a nonunion company and have a strong commitment to remaining that way, you would be well advised to publish your company's position on the subject of unionization in order to make sure your employees know exactly where your company does stand. Again, you will find no better place to take your stand and make your statement than in the front or introductory section of your PPM.

The following suggested statement is not designed nor intended to be antiunion; it simply communicates the concept that, since in the past, the ABC Company and its employees have always been able to deal with each other on a reasonable and respectful basis, the company sees no reason now to change that relationship by having an outside third party allegedly help run their business. With that thought in mind, we might word our statement something similar to Figure 12-4 below.

FIGURE 12-4

Example of Company's Position on Unions

ABC COMPANY
WHAT ABOUT UNIONS?

ABC Company attempts to provide a good environment for all our employees both as to working conditions and in the personal team relationships between management and all of our people. In other words, you can talk to us, we can talk to you, and with your help, we hope to keep it that way. Each employee is treated as an individual and is an important participant in the operation of our company

In today's uncertain world, there are many pressures and anxieties. We strive to keep our company free from any artificially created tensions and work interruptions that often arise when a union is on the scene. Indeed, there are many other companies where employees have chosen not to have a union and we think it a commendable choice.

ABC strongly believes that individual consideration in employee-supervisor relationships provides the best climate for maximum development, teamwork, and the attainment of employee goals and those of the company. We absolutely do not believe that union representation of our employees would be in the best interests of either the employee or the company.

FIGURE 12-4 (continued)

We believe that a union would be of no advantage to any of us here, nor to our customers, nor to the business growth that we all depend on for our livelihood. We sincerely believe that any outside third party could seriously impair the relationship between the company and the employees, and that it could retard the growth of our company and the progress of ABC employees.

We also believe that we have enthusiastically accepted our responsibility to provide our employees with good working conditions, good wages, good benefits, fair treatment, and the personal respect that rightfully belongs to our people. All these things are already a part of our employees' jobs with ABC and certainly do not need to be purchased from an outside third party.

We are fully aware that all ABC employees want to express their problems, comments, and suggestions to us so that we can all better understand each other. Our employees already have that opportunity here at ABC. This can be and has been done without having a union involved in the communication between the employee and the company. Here you, as an employee, speak up for yourself at all levels of management. We will continue to listen, and to do our best to give you a responsible reply. You should understand that if your supervisor cannot resolve your problems, you are expected to see me!

Albert B. Collins
President and CEO
ABC Company

In addition to including this policy statement on unions in your PPM, it would also be an excellent idea to have it posted at all company locations and facilities in a conspicuous place so that there can be absolutely no doubt about the position your company takes on unionization.

Similarly, the union policy statement belongs in any sort of employee handbook or manual you might publish and distribute to new and current employees as well, so that the new employee, in particular, will find it unnecessary to ask about a union.

6) You may wish to include one other general aspect of personnel and employment relations in the introductory portion of your manual—the matter of substance abuse and the company's attitude toward it. It is, of course, impractical to try to highlight

each of your personnel policies in the introduction, especially when the policy itself is spelled out in detail in the text of your manual. There are, however, certain policies that are and can be so vital to the company's operation that it is probably prudent and wise to emphasize and highlight them in the beginning of the manual, as well. The subject of substance abuse is one of these. Figure 12-5 below is a suggested statement, again signed by the company president.

FIGURE 12-5

Example of Substance Abuse Policy Statement

ABC COMPANY
SUBSTANCE ABUSE POLICY STATEMENT

Contained in this PPM is a clear, comprehensive, and unequivocal policy and program for dealing with the subject of illegal drugs and alcohol in the work environment. Although the specifics of our program are quite well documented herein, I believe it is my responsibility to officially state the company's overall position regarding this critical matter:

It is certainly no secret that substance abuse, which includes the use of illegal drugs and the abuse of alcohol and prescription drugs, is one of our nation's most serious problems. Substance abuse reduces productivity, increases accident and illness rates, and is a main cause of embezzlement and theft. It increases medical and hospitalization costs, and is often a crime. We at ABC Company are quite proud of the fact that we owe our success to safety-conscious, clear-thinking, innovative, and productive employees—and we intend to keep it that way! We also take the position that our customers and employees, as well as ABC shareholders, are entitled to protection from the high costs of lost productivity, increased medical expenses, and unsafe conditions caused by the influence of illegal drugs and the abuse of alcohol and prescription drugs.

Our substance abuse policy makes it very clear that the possession, sale, or use of illegal drugs, alcohol, or the abuse of prescription drugs by our employees in the work environment is unacceptable and against corporate policy. Likewise, the impairment of employees caused by the possession, sale, or use of illegal drugs, alcohol, or abused prescription drugs is also unacceptable and against corporate policy. In the work environment, as a condition of continued employment, our employees are

---

FIGURE 12-5 (continued)

required to be free of any measurable amounts of illegal drugs, alcohol, or abused prescription drugs. If any supervisor or manager has an employee with a problem with drugs or alcohol—or if an employee requests help in this regard—the supervisor or manager is urged to contact our human resources department so the person may be referred to an outside agency for professional help. All inquiries or requests will be kept confidential to the utmost extent possible, with the understanding that drug-screening lab reports and other related documents may be used as admissible evidence in unemployment and workers' compensation benefit determinations, administrative hearings, civil actions, or other legal proceedings.

Our company policy regarding substance abuse is intended to be supportive rather than punitive. We are concerned about coworkers who abuse drugs or alcohol, and we hope that we do not lose a single person as a result of this program. Every one of us is an important member of the team, and the successful implementation of our substance abuse program will guarantee a safe and drug-free environment for us all.

Albert B. Collins
President and CEO
ABC Company

PERSONNEL/EMPLOYMENT FORMS, STATEMENTS, AGREEMENTS

For the convenience of your managers and supervisors, who will hopefully refer to their policies manual at all times when necessary, it is expedient to include in the manual references to (and reproductions of) some of the personnel forms they will more frequently be apt to use. The Bureau of National Affairs, Inc. offers a wide variety of sample forms, notices, and posters covering practically any procedural or policy phase of personnel management, based on the actual policies of many companies, plants, and businesses. These can all be very helpful to a start-up as well as existing human resources department, and I recommend a careful examination of them by any interested human resources manager.

As you can imagine, it would be impractical and unwise to try to include each and every such form or statement in your PPM; however, a few of the most essential and commonly used ones should be considered for inclusion. Figures 12-6 to 12-10 are examples of the forms you might find most helpful in human resources management.

FIGURE 12-6
Application For Employment Form

ABC CO. APPLICATION FOR EMPLOYMENT   ❑ FULL-TIME   ❑ PART-TIME   ❑ TEMPORARY

ABC IS AN EQUAL OPPORTUNITY EMPLOYER. ALL QUALIFIED APPLICANTS WILL BE CONSIDERED WITHOUT REGARD TO RACE, RELIGION, COLOR, SEX, NATIONAL ORIGIN, AGE OR DISABILITY.

IMPORTANT: THIS APPLICATION **MUST BE FILLED OUT COMPLETELY**, EVEN IF YOU HAVE SUPPLIED A RESUME. PLEASE PRINT LEGIBLY.

DATE	POSITION DESIRED				PHONE NO. (AREA CODE)
LAST NAME	FIRST	MIDDLE	MESSAGE PHONE		
PRESENT ADDRESS		CITY, STATE, ZIP			HOW LONG?
PREVIOUS ADDRESS		CITY, STATE, ZIP			HOW LONG?

POSITION DESIRED	DATE YOU CAN START	SALARY REQUIREMENTS

ARE YOU EMPLOYED NOW? ❑ YES ❑ NO	IF SO MAY WE INQUIRE OF YOUR PRESENT EMPLOYER? ❑ YES ❑ NO

EVER APPLIED TO THIS COMPANY BEFORE? ❑ YES ❑ NO	WHERE?	WHEN?
EVER WORKED FOR THIS COMPANY BEFORE? ❑ YES ❑ NO	WHERE?	WHEN?

REASON FOR LEAVING

NAME OF LAST SUPERVISOR AT THIS COMPANY

WHO REFERRED YOU TO THIS COMPANY?
    ❑ EMPLOYMENT AGENCY   ❑ NEWSPAPER ADVERTISING   ❑ FRIEND
    ❑ STATE EMPLOYMENT OFFICE   ❑ COLLEGE PLACEMENT SERVICE   ❑ WALK IN   ❑ OTHER

EDUCATIONAL INFORMATION

CIRCLE LAST GRADE COMPLETED IN ELEMENTARY OR HIGH SCHOOL 1 2 3 4 5 6 7 8 9 10 11 12 ❑ GED		NAME AND LOCATION (CITY AND STATE) OF LAST HIGH SCHOOL		

NAME AND ADDRESS OF SCHOOL	GRAD-UATED	TYPE OF DEGREE	CURRICULUM		GRADE AVERAGE
COLLEGE OR UNIVERSITY	❑ YES		MAJOR		
ADDRESS, CITY, STATE	❑ NO		MINOR		
COLLEGE OR UNIVERSITY	❑ YES		MAJOR		
ADDRESS, CITY, STATE	❑ NO		MINOR		
GRADUATE SCHOOL	❑ YES		MAJOR		
ADDRESS, CITY, STATE	❑ NO		MINOR		
OTHER TRAINING (TRADE, BUSINESS OR CORRESPONDENCE SCHOOL)	❑ YES ❑ NO				

SECURITY INFORMATION

IF YOU ARE OFFERED EMPLOYMENT, CAN YOU SUBMIT VERIFICATION OF YOUR LEGAL RIGHT TO WORK IN THE UNITED STATES?
    ❑ YES ❑ NO

HAVE YOU EVER BEEN CONVICTED—OTHER THAN MINOR TRAFFIC VIOLATIONS, FOR WHICH A PARDON WAS NOT GRANTED?
IF YES, EXPLAIN. (CONVICTION WILL NOT AUTOMATICALLY BAR EMPLOYMENT.)
    ❑ YES ❑ NO

CLERICAL/SHOP SKILLS

SHORTHAND	TYPING	10-KEY		NAME OFFICE MACHINES AND/OR SHOP MACHINES YOU CAN SET UP AND OPERATE
WPM	WPM	BY SIGHT	BY TOUCH	

PC SKILLS AND WORD PROCESSING EXPERIENCE (LIST SOFTWARE YOU ARE SKILLED ON)

REFERENCES

YOU MUST GIVE THE NAMES OF THREE PERSONS WHOM YOU HAVE KNOWN AT LEAST ONE YEAR. PLEASE EXCLUDE RELATIVES AND FORMER EMPLOYERS.

NAME	ADDRESS	PHONE	OCCUPATION	YRS. KNOWN
NAME	ADDRESS	PHONE	OCCUPATION	YRS. KNOWN
NAME	ADDRESS	PHONE	OCCUPATION	YRS. KNOWN

SEE REVERSE

FIGURE 12-6 (continued)

U.S. MILITARY STATUS

BRANCH	RANK

DESCRIPTION OF RELEVANT SKILLS ACQUIRED DURING U.S. MILITARY SERVICE:

WHAT SPECIAL OR PERSONAL FACTS SHOULD THE COMPANY KNOW ABOUT YOU?
(exclude any that would indicate race, color, religion, national origin, sex, age or disability & ancestry)

SPECIAL TRAINING

SPECIAL SKILLS

RECORD OF EMPLOYMENT: FILL IN COMPLETELY, BEGINNING WITH PRESENT OR LAST POSITION.

NAME OF PRESENT OR LAST EMPLOYER		TYPE OF BUSINESS OR COMPANY PRODUCT	
COMPLETE ADDRESS (INCLUDE STREET, CITY, STATE, ZIP)	PHONE NO. ( )	STARTING DATE (MO/YR)	LEAVING DATE (MO/YR)
NAME OF SUPERVISOR	SUPERVISOR'S TITLE	STARTING PAY	FINAL PAY
YOUR JOB TITLE (PRESENT OR LAST)	REASON FOR LEAVING		

DESCRIPTION OF WORK AND RESPONSIBILITIES

NAME OF NEXT PREVIOUS EMPLOYER		TYPE OF BUSINESS OR COMPANY PRODUCT	
COMPLETE ADDRESS (INCLUDE STREET, CITY, STATE, ZIP)	PHONE NO. ( )	STARTING DATE (MO/YR)	LEAVING DATE (MO/YR)
NAME OF SUPERVISOR	SUPERVISOR'S TITLE	STARTING PAY	FINAL PAY
YOUR JOB TITLE	REASON FOR LEAVING		

DESCRIPTION OF WORK AND RESPONSIBILITIES

NAME OF NEXT PREVIOUS EMPLOYER		TYPE OF BUSINESS OR COMPANY PRODUCT	
COMPLETE ADDRESS (INCLUDE STREET, CITY, STATE, ZIP)	PHONE NO. ( )	STARTING DATE (MO/YR)	LEAVING DATE (MO/YR)
NAME OF SUPERVISOR	SUPERVISOR'S TITLE	STARTING PAY	FINAL PAY
YOUR JOB TITLE	REASON FOR LEAVING		

DESCRIPTION OF WORK AND RESPONSIBILITIES

PLEASE EXPLAIN ANY EXTENDED PERIOD OF UNEMPLOYMENT

CONDITIONS OF EMPLOYMENT: I understand that false statements or omissions on this application or resume may result in dismissal at any time. **I agree to a urinalysis drug screening, if required.** I understand and agree that all information furnished on this application may be verified by ABC or its authorized representative. I hereby authorize all individuals and organizations named or referred to in this application and any law enforcement organization or credit bureau to give ABC all information, relative to such verification and hereby release such individuals, organizations, and ABC from any and all liability for any claim or damage resulting therefrom.

In consideration of my employment, I agree to conform to the rules and regulations of ABC. I understand that any employment relationship is at will and may be terminated at any time, with or without cause, and with or without notice, at the option of either the Company or myself. I understand that only the President of ABC has any authority to enter into any agreement for employment for any specified period of time, or to make any agreement contrary to the foregoing.

APPLICANT'S SIGNATURE: X_____

NOTE: If the job you are hired for requires a driver's license, you must furnish a copy of your driving record from the State Motor Vehicle Department.

Interviewer's Notes:

FIGURE 12-7

Suggested Confidential Reference Inquiry

ABC COMPANY
CONFIDENTIAL REFERENCE INQUIRY

(Employee Please Complete This Section)

Dear Sir or Madam:

I have made application to ABC Company for employment. I request and authorize you to release all information requested below by ABC, including that concerning my employment record, character, habits and abilities, and reasons for leaving your employment. The following data may help in identifying me and my employment record:

Name While in Your Employment _____
Social Security No. _____
Dates of Employment: From _____ To _____
Position Held _____
Department _____
Immediate Supervisor _____
Rate of Pay: $ _____ Per _____
Reason for Leaving:

_____
_____
_____
_____

Signature _____ Date _____

(Past Employer Please Complete This Section)

Dear Sir or Madam:

We are asking your assistance in making an employment decision and would like to reassure you that all information provided on the form will be held in strictest confidence. An immediate reply will be appreciated. Please don't hesitate to contact me if I can reciprocate in providing you with information regarding former ABC employees.

Thank You,

_____
Mary Cameron
Human Resources Manager

FIGURE 12-7 (continued)

Dates of Employment: From _____ To _____
Rate of Pay: $ _____ Per _____
Position Held   _____
Department   _____

	EXCELLENT	GOOD	FAIR	POOR	COMMENTS
Quality of Work					
Dependability					
Cooperation					
Attitude					
Attendance					

Reason For Leaving:

_____

Would You Reemploy?
Other Remarks:

_____
_____
_____
_____

Signature: _____ Title: _____
Phone No.: _____ Date: _____

FIGURE 12-8

Example of Educational Reference Inquiry

ABC COMPANY
EDUCATIONAL REFERENCE INQUIRY

(Employee Please Complete This Section)

Dear Sir or Madam:

I have applied for employment with ABC Company. I hereby
authorize all individuals and organizations named or referred to
in this request to give ABC all information relative to such
verification and hereby release such individuals or organizations
and ABC from any and all liability for any claim or damage
resulting therefrom.

Applicant's Signature _____ Date _____

FIGURE 12-8 (continued)

The following information has been provided by the above-signed applicant. Would you please verify this data by a check mark in the spaces provided, indicate any discrepancies in the comments section below, and sign the completed form. We sincerely thank you in advance for your cooperation.

Sincerely,

_____

Mary Cameron
Human Resources Manager

Applicant's Name: _____

VERIFY(✓)

Social Security Number: _____

Date of Birth: _____

College or University: _____

Graduate School: _____

Other (Vocational, Trade or Correspondence): _____

Dates of Attendance: From _____ To _____

Degree or Courses Completed: _____

Major: _____

Minor _____

Credits Completed: _____ Grade Point Avg.: _____

College or University Official: _____

(Signature)

Date: _____

Comments: _____

_____

_____

_____

FIGURE 12-9
Employment Eligibility Verification Form

OMB No. 1615-0047; Expires 08/31/12

Department of Homeland Security
U.S. Citizenship and Immigration Services

**Form I-9, Employment
Eligibility Verification**

Read instructions carefully before completing this form. The instructions must be available during completion of this form.

ANTI-DISCRIMINATION NOTICE: It is illegal to discriminate against work-authorized individuals. Employers CANNOT specify which document(s) they will accept from an employee. The refusal to hire an individual because the documents have a future expiration date may also constitute illegal discrimination.

Section 1. Employee Information and Verification *(To be completed and signed by employee at the time employment begins.)*

Print Name: Last	First	Middle Initial	Maiden Name

Address *(Street Name and Number)*		Apt. #	Date of Birth *(month/day/year)*

City	State	Zip Code	Social Security #

I am aware that federal law provides for imprisonment and/or fines for false statements or use of false documents in connection with the completion of this form.

I attest, under penalty of perjury, that I am (check one of the following):

☐ A citizen of the United States
☐ A noncitizen national of the United States (see instructions)
☐ A lawful permanent resident (Alien #)
☐ An alien authorized to work (Alien # or Admission #) _____
until (expiration date, if applicable - *month/day/year*)

Employee's Signature	Date *(month/day/year)*

Preparer and/or Translator Certification *(To be completed and signed if Section 1 is prepared by a person other than the employee.)* I attest, under penalty of perjury, that I have assisted in the completion of this form and that to the best of my knowledge the information is true and correct.

Preparer's/Translator's Signature	Print Name

Address *(Street Name and Number, City, State, Zip Code)*	Date *(month/day/year)*

Section 2. Employer Review and Verification *(To be completed and signed by employer. Examine one document from List A OR examine one document from List B and one from List C, as listed on the reverse of this form, and record the title, number, and expiration date, if any, of the document(s).)*

	List A	OR	List B	AND	List C
Document title:					
Issuing authority:					
Document #:					
Expiration Date *(if any)*:					
Document #:					
Expiration Date *(if any)*:					

CERTIFICATION: I attest, under penalty of perjury, that I have examined the document(s) presented by the above-named employee, that the above-listed document(s) appear to be genuine and to relate to the employee named, that the employee began employment on *(month/day/year)* _____ and that to the best of my knowledge the employee is authorized to work in the United States. (State employment agencies may omit the date the employee began employment.)

Signature of Employer or Authorized Representative	Print Name	Title

Business or Organization Name and Address *(Street Name and Number, City, State, Zip Code)*	Date *(month/day/year)*

Section 3. Updating and Reverification *(To be completed and signed by employer.)*

A. New Name *(if applicable)*	B. Date of Rehire *(month/day/year)* *(if applicable)*

C. If employee's previous grant of work authorization has expired, provide the information below for the document that establishes current employment authorization.

Document Title:	Document #:	Expiration Date *(if any)*:

I attest, under penalty of perjury, that to the best of my knowledge, this employee is authorized to work in the United States, and if the employee presented document(s), the document(s) I have examined appear to be genuine and to relate to the individual.

Signature of Employer or Authorized Representative	Date *(month/day/year)*

Form I-9 (Rev. 08/07/09) Y Page 4

FIGURE 12-10
Suggested Personal Progress Interview Form

ABC COMPANY
PERSONAL PROGRESS INTERVIEW

This form is to be completed by company managers and
supervisors together with each full-time, part-time and
temporary member of their organization. THE PRIMARY
PURPOSE OF THIS INTERVIEW IS TO ESTABLISH OPEN
COMMUNICATION BETWEEN MANAGERS OR
SUPERVISORS AND THEIR EMPLOYEES. A completed
copy of this form should be sent to the human resources
department for the employee's personnel file.

Employee Name: _____

Employee No. _____

Job Title: _____

Company/Dept. Name: _____

Company/Dept. No.: _____ Time on Job _____

Hire Date _____

We need and would appreciate your comments on the following:
(Please tell it in your own words as you see it.)

What do you like most about your job?

_____

_____

_____

_____

What do you like least about your job?

_____

_____

_____

_____

What changes, in areas outside of your control, could be made
to improve your job?

_____

_____

_____

_____

FIGURE 12-10 (continued)

How would YOU rate your own overall job performance in the following areas:

(Check one: 5 = most effective; 1 = least effective)

	1	2	3	4	5
INITIATIVE					
PRODUCTIVITY					
JUDGMENT					
EFFORT					
TEAMWORK					
SAFETY					
JOB KNOWLEDGE					
FOLLOWS DIRECTIONS					
CUSTOMER SERVICE					
TELEPHONE SKILLS					
ATTENDANCE					

Do you feel ready for more responsibility? If so, what type?

_____

_____

_____

Where do you see yourself in 1, 5, or 10 years? (Answer as you wish.)

_____

_____

_____

Have you successfully met your job-related goals over the past 6 months?
Yes: _____ No: _____
Specifically, what have you done?

_____

_____

Let's set some goals for your job for the next 6 months:

_____

_____

_____

FIGURE 12-10 (continued)

What changes would you suggest to help make our crew function better overall?

_____

_____

_____

Is there any way that I, personally, can help you to be more productive?

_____

_____

_____

Any additional comments?

_____

_____

_____

Manager/Supervisor's Signature _____

Title _____ Date _____

The Personal Progress Interview

The personal progress interview form (PPI) is one of the more important tools in the overall human resources inventory. The personal progress interview serves as a half-way or balance point between the use of complex performance appraisal systems (sometimes stereotyped and time consuming), and having no appraisal program at all. Used conscientiously at regular, predetermined intervals, this PPI form creates an environment of what might be called comfortable communication between supervisors and employees. It asks employees what they like most as well as least about the job, what improvements and changes could we (you and I) make to it, and if the employees are ready for more responsibility. Supervisors and employees then together set goals and review progress on the job-related goals previously set six months (or other period of time) ago. In order to completely avoid eliminating the appraisal function, employees are asked to rate their own overall job performance in specific areas.

You may find that the use of this form can result in some surprising and valuable information about which the supervisor was totally unaware. Many if not most employees will often not confide in their boss, or let them know when something important is bothering them. The PPI interview process sets the stage for some amazing discoveries by simply asking employees in so many words, "say, Mary (or

Dave), how's everything going, and just what do you think about your job?" You may learn that morale in the department, shop, or plant is not quite as good as you thought it was. Or, as a nonunion employer, you might also hear that one or more people are occasionally making comments in the lunchroom about "how great this place would be if we just had a union around here!"

One of the best motivators in personnel relations is recognition or attention to employees, even if it's just taking the time to ask them what they think. Use of the personal progress interview process fills this need, while at the same time demonstrating to employees that perhaps the company does genuinely value the opinion of their most important asset. Once again, it follows the general theme of this book that if you value your employees and help them to be more productive and successful, you yourself will become successful. The employee, you, and the company will all be winners. To do this, supervisors, managers, and the human resources department *must communicate* with employees. HR professionals must know employees' needs, wants, and desires, and help them attain their goals. The personal progress interview is an effective way of helping them to do this.

Proper and conscientious use of this personal progress interview form will replace the drudgery, procrastination, and general unpopularity of filling out performance appraisal forms (whether supervisory or self-appraisal) with an enthusiastic and positive response from both the employee and the supervisor/manager.

OTHER FORMS

Personal Appearance, and Return of Company Property

As a matter of convenience, the policy issues of employee personal appearance and the proper return of company property may be combined into a single form as illustrated in Figure 12-11 below. Appearance standards are most important to companies and industries, especially those involved in retail sales operations. Studies and experience time and again indicate that the buying public in general expects to be served by employees of neat and clean appearance; and the courts, in general, support reasonable appearance standards required by companies and businesses.

It is also prudent that companies require the agreement of newly-hired employees that they will return all company property at the time of termination of employment, including uniforms, keys, tools, manuals, ID cards, and so on, and that if all such property is not returned, the employer is authorized (where permitted by state law) to deduct the cost of said items from the employees' paychecks.

FIGURE 12-11

Sample of Appearance and Property Return Agreement Form

ABC COMPANY
APPEARANCE AND PROPERTY RETURN AGREEMENT

I understand that it is my responsibility to, at all times, keep my personal appearance at a level that is acceptable to our ABC Company customers. And I also understand that appearance standards are determined by the company on the basis of its public image and customer reaction. If a uniform is required to be worn at the company facility at which I work, I agree to appear in that uniform during all working hours. The company will provide me with whatever uniform is to be worn, and I will be responsible for the cleaning, pressing, and maintaining of those items furnished by the company as well as any furnished by myself. All items of uniform furnished by the company are the property of ABC, and must be returned if I leave the company. If I do not return any uniform items, I authorize my employer to deduct their replacement cost from my final paycheck, where permitted by state law.

I further agree that, if I leave the company, I will return all equipment, keys, tools, ID cards, manuals, etc., which are the property of ABC. If I do not return ALL items that are the property of the ABC Company, I authorize my employer to deduct the replacement cost of said items from my final paycheck, where permitted by state law.

Number of Uniforms Returned: _____

Employee's Signature: _____Date: _____

Number of Uniforms Returned: _____

Supervisor's Signature _____Date: _____

Warning Notices

One of the most important functions of managers and supervisors is the documenting of work performance—good and bad—of the employees they direct or supervise. Specific, written documentation is and probably always will be the number one defense when a company finds itself in a court of law trying to explain the reasons it terminated a particular employee who has brought suit for wrongful termination. For example, when a company can clearly demonstrate that, prior to termination, a worker was given written warning notices detailing the infraction(s) involved, and stating that similar violations in the future could result in further discipline, up to and including termination— "Case dismissed!" would not be an unlikely verdict! Figure 12-12 is an example of an effective warning notice form.

FIGURE 12-12
Sample Warning Notice Form

ABC COMPANY
WARNING NOTICE

Name of Employee Receiving Warning: _____

Job Title:_____ Employee No.: _____

Date Warning Issued to Employee: _____

Name of Supervisor Issuing Warning: _____

Job Title: _____

Department Number and Name: _____

THE INTENT OF THIS NOTICE IS TO INFORM YOU THAT YOUR PERFORMANCE HAS NOT BEEN SATISFACTORY FOR THE REASONS INDICATED BELOW, AND TO PROVIDE YOU WITH AN OPPORTUNITY TO COOPERATE WITH YOUR SUPERVISOR IN ATTEMPTING TO CORRECT THIS SITUATION. HOWEVER, IF THIS MATTER IS NOT CORRECTED WITHIN (30, 60, 90 DAYS OR specify), YOU WILL BE SUBJECT TO FURTHER DISCIPLINARY ACTION, UP TO AND INCLUDING TERMINATION.

Details of Situation (Be sure to include dates of specific incidents):
_____
_____
_____
_____
_____

X_____   _____
   Employee's Signature   Supervisor's Signature
Date: _____   Date: _____

Note To Employee:
Signing this form does not indicate agreement with the above statements. It simply verifies that you have been informed of the above action, and that you have received a copy of this warning notice.

Names of Witnesses, if any:
Witness #1: _____
Job Title: _____
Witness #2: _____
Job Title: _____

Voluntary Resignation

Where at all possible, it is always a good idea to have terminating employees sign a voluntary resignation form when they leave the company of their own accord. In a subsequent charge, complaint or court action, it may be your primary defense in showing that the employees did leave voluntarily, and that they voluntarily signed a resignation form on the date indicated. See Figure 12-13 below for an example of a voluntary resignation form.

FIGURE 12-13

Sample Voluntary Resignation Form

ABC COMPANY
VOLUNTARY RESIGNATION

This completed form should be attached to the final paperwork for an employee who resigns voluntarily, and should be then forwarded to the human resources department for processing.

I, _____, SSN _____,
hereby resign my position as _____
                                          (Job Title)
from _____ Effective _____
        (Company/Dept. No.)

My reason(s) for voluntarily resigning my job is (are):
(Please check all reasons that apply):
_____ Relocation
_____ Illness
_____ To seek other employment
_____ Have obtained other employment
_____ To return to school
_____ Personal/family business
_____ Dissatisfied with pay, hours of work, working conditions,
        type of work (Please comment briefly in comments
        section below.)
_____ Retiring
_____ Other reasons

Comments: _____
_____
_____
_____

Amount of notice being given:
_____ days   _____ weeks   _____ none
                          Signature: _____
                          Date Signed: _____

Exit Interview

Another excellent tool of personnel management and one that supplements the Voluntary Resignation form is the exit interview process, including the exit interview form, an example of which is given in Figure 12-14 below. The exit interview process assists the human resources practitioner in determining patterns or trends of events occurring within a company or department, and will often reveal critical problems with supervision, or with work rules, wages, or working conditions that do not surface while the person is still employed.

It is also important that the respective supervisor and manager of the terminating employee be provided with a copy of the exit interview form in order to offer an opportunity to correct some particular condition or situation about which they may not have been aware.

A personal exit interview between the terminating employee and the supervisor and/or manager, or with a member of the human resources staff, is usually the most productive method of obtaining information from the employee. Many times, employees will tell you more than you ask if they feel the interviewer is a good listener and is genuinely interested in what they have to say.

Where the personal interview procedure is not practicable, the next best method is to mail an exit interview form to all employees who leave your organization—full-time, part-time, and even temporary—and ask if they would take the time to complete and return the form. You might be surprised at the percentage of returns you can get for your efforts. To insure a maximum response, set up the form in a folded card format with postage prepaid, and preaddressed to your human resources department. Most people will find this method convenient. Others will wish to say more and will return the form in a separate envelope, sometimes with attachments and occasionally even photographs of company property or equipment if related to their discharge or resignation.

At the same time, the reader should also be cautioned about drawing hasty conclusions or opinions based solely on exit interview statements. Occasionally, the information or feedback from the terminating employee is inaccurate, sometimes exaggerated, or just plain wrong, due to the person's lack of experience or time on the job, or failure to see the total picture.

Nevertheless, your employment relations manager, EEO coordinator, or some personnel staff member should take the time to carefully read each of the exit forms. Your HR department will then have taken the first steps toward monitoring employee morale and be in a better position to anticipate, correct, and prevent problems before they become serious. In addition, every now and then someone will return a form that has some good things to say about the company and its supervisors. That's good information, too, and you wouldn't want to miss it.

FIGURE 12-14

Sample Exit Interview Form

ABC COMPANY
EXIT INTERVIEW FORM

Name _____

Social Security Number_____

Co./Dept. No. _____ Department Name _____

Job Title _____

Length of Service: Years _____ Months _____

Employment Status: ❑ Full-Time ❑ Part-Time ❑ Temp.

Paid By: ❑ Hour ❑ Weekly ❑ Monthly

What Was Your Main Reason(s) for Leaving ABC?
(Check all that apply.)

❑ Relocation ❑ Benefits
❑ Working Environment ❑ Supervision
❑ Layoff ❑ Terminated for Cause
❑ Training ❑ Pay
❑ Return to School ❑ Hours
❑ Career Change ❑ No Advancement

Other Reason(s) (please specify):

_____

_____

_____

How would you rate ABC on the following items?
(Check one box for each item)

	EXCELLENT	GOOD	FAIR	POOR	COMMENTS
Supervision	❑	❑	❑	❑	
Training	❑	❑	❑	❑	
Advancement Opportunities	❑	❑	❑	❑	
Communication/ Feedback	❑	❑	❑	❑	
Your Treatment as an Individual	❑	❑	❑	❑	
Company Benefits	❑	❑	❑	❑	
Rate of Pay	❑	❑	❑	❑	

FIGURE 12-14 (continued)

Was there anything in particular you especially liked about
your work experience at ABC?

_____

_____

_____

Was there anything in particular you especially did not like
about your work experience at ABC?

_____

_____

_____

How could your own job have been improved upon?

_____

_____

_____

Additional Comments:

_____

_____

_____

Signature_____ Date _____

We sincerely thank you for taking the time to complete this exit
interview form. We will do our best to see that your thoughts
and observations are put to use by the ABC organization.
Once again, thank you very much.

ABC Human Resources Department

Solicitation, Distribution, Posting

In the event yours happens to be a nonunion company, you might find
the following form or statement in Figure 12-15 to be a valuable tool in
helping you to remain that way. In actuality, the form has a two-fold
purpose, in that it creates a workable system for internal posting, and
it prevents your being deluged with requests to post notices of outside
meetings, social events, and charitable causes on your bulletin boards.
The wording of the statement also has the general approval of the
National Labor Relations Board as it relates to the posting of (or
refusal by the company to post) union organizing information and
material. The statement follows.

FIGURE 12-15
Sample No Solicitation, No Distribution—Posting Rules Form

ABC COMPANY
NO SOLICITATION—NO DISTRIBUTION—POSTING RULES

In order to prevent disruption of operations, interferences with work, as well as inconvenience to employees, the following policies apply to all facilities of the ABC Company:

1. Solicitation by employees for any purpose is not permitted during working hours.

2. Distribution of literature of any kind by employees (other than company literature) is not permitted in working areas at any time.

3. Distribution of literature and/or solicitation for any purpose by nonemployees on company premises is not permitted at any time.

Posting on Company Bulletin Boards

All materials for posting on company bulletin boards or on company property will be screened and must be approved for posting by the store manager, or by the general manager or plant manager of the facility involved. At company headquarters, the ABC human resources department must approve all materials for posting on ABC Company bulletin boards. All materials will be initialed and dated, and will be posted for a period not to exceed two weeks, with the exception of job postings.

Materials advertising non-ABC Company products or services will not be posted. Sideline business advertisements for household cleaning or personal care products (perfumes and toiletries, dinner and tableware items, for example) will be denied posting rights. Solicitation by employees or outside persons for these and other similar products is also prohibited.

All company presidents and managers should see that NO SOLICITATION—NO DISTRIBUTION signs are posted at all entrances to each company facility.

Gambling on Company Property

In addition to the aforementioned items that should not be allowed or permitted on company property, it would probably be well to include a specific notice or statement in the PPM dealing with the subject of gambling. See sample statement in Figure 12-16.

FIGURE 12-16
Sample Gambling on Company Property Notice

ABC COMPANY
GAMBLING ON COMPANY PROPERTY

Gambling in any form on company property is strictly prohibited. All forms of betting, including lotteries, football, baseball, and other types of sports pools, card playing for money, or any other type of gaming activity in which money is involved, are not appropriate in a business environment, and are not permitted on company time and on company premises.

Letters of Recommendation/Reference
Many times, in a well-meaning attempt to help a terminated employee secure work in another organization, company presidents, managers, or supervisors will write glowing letters of recommendation or reference relating to the person's employment with their company. If it should so happen that the terminated employee later decides to bring charges or suit against the former employer for discrimination or wrongful termination, the company finds itself in the somewhat embarrassing position of having highly recommended and praised—in writing—the abilities and talents of someone who had perhaps been previously fired from the job due to incompetency or other problems. Legal counsel generally recommends the wiser course to be for the company to have a policy that no such letters of praise be written, using the suggested language in Figure 12-17 below.

FIGURE 12-17
Sample Statement Regarding Requests for Letters of Recommendation/Reference

---

ABC COMPANY
POLICY STATEMENT REGARDING REQUESTS FOR
LETTERS OF RECOMMENDATION/REFERENCE

ABC Company does not provide letters of recommendation; however, if requested in writing, ABC will provide a statement outlining dates of employment and positions held by former employees.

This is the only information that will be provided in response to reference requests from prospective employers.

FIGURE 12-17 (continued)

All requests for information on past employees should be directed to the ABC human resources department. Managers and supervisors are especially cautioned not to provide letters of recommendation or to give out any information whatever, either in person or over the telephone, regarding the employment of former employees. Refer all such requests to human resources.

The forms and statements shown above in their entirety may be thought of as customized forms to be used by the individual employer as necessary. Their suggested content should be especially helpful to supervisors and managers, as well as to the human resources staff. Keep in mind also, that if you do choose to follow their format in your company, you should regularly review and make changes in them from time to time as business conditions change or new labor laws are passed.

There is available a vast number of other personnel forms that most businesses and employers will have occasion to use at some time or other. Basically these others are all standard forms, that may be obtained through various management services companies or stationery suppliers.

CHAPTER PERSPECTIVE

In this chapter the importance of formalizing personnel policies and compiling them into a Personnel Policies Manual was discussed. Guidelines for constructing a PPM for your company were given. The important personnel policy statements that should appear in the introductory part of the manual were delineated. Also highly recommended was the inclusion of sample personnel forms to be used as reference tools by managers, supervisors, and HR staff. Examples of customized forms were presented and their use explained.

Lifestyles and Medical Cost Containment

INTRODUCTION AND MAIN POINTS

This chapter highlights the problems surrounding the rising cost of group medical insurance coverage to business. The effect of lifestyles on employees' health has brought several issues under scrutiny by employers. These issues include:

Substance abuse

Failure to wear seat belts

Smoking or other use of tobacco

Body weight

Aerobic exercise

Cholesterol levels

Physical examinations

Participation in high-risk sports

The rising costs of insuring those persons with unhealthy or high-risk lifestyles has caused many employers to limit or deny employees group medical insurance to them or to require that they pay higher premiums for same. These measures have been unpopular, and many people oppose them. Other problems of the current system such as preexisting conditions and the ineffectiveness of COBRA, a stop-gap program, are also discussed.

In this important arena of health care, the human resources department must heed the call to contain costs from the management of the company and communicate changes in plan coverage to employees.

The need for changes to the system is demonstrated, but the wholesale dismantling of our current high-quality health care delivery system is viewed as the wrong direction for the country to follow.

After you have read the materials in this chapter:

■ You will be aware that the problems surrounding the rising costs for group medical insurance coverage are serious ones.

■ You will know what several of the lifestyle issues are as they relate to health insurance coverage of employees.

■■ You will know about several plans of employers who wish to contain the costs of their medical insurance coverage by limiting or denying coverage to those with unhealthy or high-risk lifestyles.

■■ You will be aware of other health care system problems such as preexisting conditions and the inadequacy of COBRA.

■■ You will know why the current system is in need of change, but not of dismantling.

THE RISING COSTS OF GROUP MEDICAL INSURANCE

As discussed in a previous chapter on employee benefits (Chapter 9), medical care insurance coverage is probably the most important of all employee benefits from the employee's point of view. The rising costs of medical insurance and claims paid by employers, even though currently rising at a slower pace, all give rise to justifiable concern among business and government leaders, and the general public as well. Solutions and ideas are being offered from many sources, including both state and federal agencies, but medical costs continue to edge upward in company benefits budgets.

LIMITING OR DENYING COVERAGE

One step more and more companies are taking in their continuing battle against ever-escalating medical costs is to limit or even deny altogether group medical coverage to employees who choose to follow unhealthy or riskier lifestyles than those of their fellow employees. For example, in some companies, covered employees and their spouses and dependents who are proven guilty of alcohol, drug, or controlled substance (prescription drug) abuse when involved in a motor vehicle accident in which a covered person was the driver are also denied coverage. In other instances, employees, covered spouses, and dependents involved in motor vehicle accidents while not wearing an available seat belt are also not eligible for company medical benefits coverage.

Companies are also beginning to examine other areas of lifestyle selection that impact on the health of employees and their spouses and, therefore, affect group coverage rates. Interest has been focused on:

■■ employees who smoke or use tobacco in any form;

■■ employees whose body weight is not within specified weight tables;

■■ employees who do no aerobic exercise, such as walking at least 30 minutes a day, three days a week;

■■ employees whose blood cholesterol levels substantially exceed recommended limits;

■■ employees who do not receive periodic physical examinations;

■■ employees who engage in other high-risk lifestyles or activities, such as:

Sky diving
Motorcycling
Mountain climbing
Auto and boat racing
Piloting private airplanes
Bungee cord jumping.

To encourage the practice of regular physical examinations, some companies pay the full cost of exams for employee and spouse without the necessity of meeting annual deductibles.

RESTRICTED LIFESTYLE VERSUS HIGH MEDICAL COSTS

The clamor persists, and will probably become more and more vocal, that companies do not have the right to restrict, control, or interfere with an individual citizen's lifestyle, either on, or (especially) off, the job. However, more employers seem to be accepting the challenge and will continue to run the risk of bad publicity, irate stockholders, legal challenges, or threatened boycotts, in order to keep medical cost increases in line. It is hoped that, in the long run, such measures will help the company avoid benefit cutbacks, at best, and bankruptcy, at worst. You can expect to see more and more managements insisting that if their employees and their spouses choose riskier or, at least, unhealthy lifestyles, these people will be required to pay an increasing amount of corporate health care costs.

Human resources directors and managers continually find themselves solidly in the center of the fray: On the one hand their top management or board of directors insists they control medical costs, and on the other, company employees or union representatives point to the continual erosion of employee benefits as their members share more of the medical plan costs, or benefits are reduced or selectively eliminated.

COBRA

While the Consolidated Omnibus Budget Reconciliation Act of 1985 (COBRA) allows former employees to purchase medical insurance from their employers for up to 18 months (36 months for dependents), the cost of such coverage can often be prohibitive for persons who have just lost their job, their sole source of income. So, on February 17, 2009, President Obama signed into law the American Recovery and Reinvestment Act (ARRA), which established a 65 percent government subsidy for eligible workers toward their COBRA coverage for up to 9 months; and on December 19, 2009, the 9-month COBRA subsidy coverage was extended by 6 additional months by President Obama, both for existing COBRA-qualified beneficiaries and for newly qualified beneficiaries, with up to 15 months of the 65 percent subsidy. (See Chapter 10 for a detailed discussion of COBRA subsidy eligibility and military service coverage.)

THE FUTURE OF U.S. HEALTH CARE

Despite the fact that the quality of U.S. health care is unexcelled in any other country, no logical or caring person will dispute the fact that problems do exist within our health care system. Many people have no health care, often because they cannot afford it. In other cases, they *can* afford it but prefer not to pay premiums, opting to spend out-of-pocket for doctor/hospital charges if and when they or their dependents become ill. In addition, not all employers offer group health insurance coverage to their employees, or offer it only to the employees but not their dependents.

To this end, on March 23, 2010, while this third edition of "Human Resources" was almost concluded, President Barack Obama signed into law the "Patient Protection and Affordable Care Act," probably the most expansive piece of social legislation enacted in decades. This comprehensive health care insurance law was passed by the 111th U.S. Congress to provide access to health insurance for *all* Americans by the year 2014.

In addition, the legislation contains a number of insurance market reforms as to mandatory coverage, costs, coverage limitations, profits, and other aspects of the health insurance industry. Individuals will be required to buy health insurance, subsidized according to income, or face an annual fine. Employers of 50 or more employees will be required to offer quality health care insurance coverage. Insurance companies may no longer deny children coverage based on a preexisting condition. Starting in 2014, insurance companies cannot deny coverage to *anyone* with preexisting conditions. These are only some of the highlights of the new law and all HR professionals should immediately begin to research and understand the various new rules and regulations as they apply to their own companies.

Opponents of this legislation point out that this unprecedented liberalization of coverage of our health care system will be so costly that even a wealthy nation such as ours will not be able to afford it. They contend that the burden on current and especially future taxpayers will be awesome if not impossible. Proponents vigorously dispute this opinion and in fact see the Act as a cost-saving measure over the course of the years. Obviously, only time will provide the true answer. But health care reform is now the law of the land and human resources practitioners will be at the forefront of its administration in the corporate world.

CHAPTER PERSPECTIVE

This chapter focused on the problems of continuing to provide employees with their number one benefit—health insurance coverage. In an effort to contain the rising costs of insurance, employers have had to limit or deny group medical insurance to employees with unhealthy or high-risk lifestyles, or require them to pay higher premiums. Lifestyle issues discussed included substance abuse, failure to wear seat belts, smoking or other use of tobacco, body weight, aerobic exercise, cholesterol levels, physical examinations, and participation in high-risk sports. Controversy has arisen over these unpopular measures.

The role of the human resources department in managing this most important employee benefit program is discussed.

The chapter also dealt with other problems of the current health insurance system and discussed the just-enacted health-care insurance law, which will extend health insurance access to all Americans by the year 2014, and contains a number of insurance market reforms.

Diversity in the Work Force

INTRODUCTION AND MAIN POINTS

This chapter tackles the meaning of one famous buzzword—diversity—and what its implementation in the work force can mean to human resources professionals, management, supervision, and the community. Diversity is defined, and specific examples of diversity in the workplace are discussed.

An historical perspective on diversity in America's cultural and political roots, as well as diversity's impact after the initial Civil Rights Act, is offered.

What attitude and steps human resources professionals should take to accommodate these changes is discussed.

After you have read the material in this chapter:

━ You will understand what diversity means as applied to the work force.

━ You will know that diversity is not something new to this country.

━ You will know how human resources professionals should best respond to increased diversity in the work force.

BUZZWORDS

Buzzwords are those catchy words and clever-sounding phrases that often seem to spring literally from nowhere, capture the attention of human resources managers and management consultants, and, as a result of constant repetition, eventually become a part of our everyday business management vocabulary. (*Note*: Definitions will be found in the Glossary at the end of this book.) Some familiar examples will serve to illustrate the point.

Management by Objectives (MBO)
Total Quality Management (TQM)
Management by Walking Around (MBWA)
Employee Empowerment
Reengineering
Benchmarking
Broadbanding

Teaming
Downsizing
Rightsizing
Outsourcing
Restructuring
Multiculturalism
Information Superhighway
Globalization
Managing Diversity
Human Engineering
Ergonomics
Human Capital

Such words normally have a rather limited life span due to the fact that their exact meaning is sometimes unclear, ill-defined, or at best, debatable. Sooner or later, it no longer appears in management memos, college textbooks, or graduation speeches, and is eventually replaced by one or more newly created terms patiently awaiting their own introduction into management books, tapes, and seminars.

DIVERSITY DEFINED

There is one such word, however, that will probably outlast the rest of its listed colleagues by many years. That item is the last one mentioned, *Managing Diversity*. Let's officially define this particular term:

Merriam-Webster's Collegiate Dictionary (11th edition) defines the word *diverse* as

"**1.** differing from one another: UNLIKE

"**2.** composed of distinct or unlike elements or qualities..."

We can all probably agree that the definition of diverse describes the human condition very well. The diversity in races, colors, creeds, religious preferences, national origins, and a host of other differences and diversities the world over is self-evident.

DIVERSITY LEGISLATED

With the advent of a multitude of local, state, and federal laws protecting the rights of peoples and groups, the business community (voluntarily or otherwise) now employs literally millions of women and minorities. Thus, American industry has become the microcosm or empirical laboratory where diversity will be tested to see if it will work; that is, to determine if this diversity of colors, feelings, opinions, and choices can work together permanently, progressively, productively, and, ultimately, profitably. Eventually, it might even prove to be the experimental evidence we've been looking for to determine just how we can and must all work together as human beings on a universal or global basis. A simpler way of saying it might be that business and industry will now be the proving ground to demonstrate just how we can work together as employees, neighbors, and perhaps even as nations.

AN HISTORICAL PERSPECTIVE ON DIVERSITY IN THE UNITED STATES

Many historians, observers, and other students of history who study the American experiment of government going back some 200 and more years ago conclude that the political success of the early colonies rested largely on the fact that these early citizens had come to the new world specifically hoping to find a land where diversity of opinion and interest, as well as of nationality, culture, and religion were tolerated. As described in their political documents, this new country would be a place where they could enjoy the freedom and the right to be able to say, do, write, and think as they wished, within a government of laws that they themselves chose to establish. They knew that if they were not able to manage this diversity of interests, their experiment would fail—and they were not about to let that happen. Freedom was the bottom line of their great experiment, and the return on their investment and sacrifice has prospered ever since.

AN ANALOGY WITH BUSINESS TODAY

We are all flooded with expert opinions that, as more and more women, minorities, and people with different lifestyles and sexual preferences enter our work force, the diversity of their viewpoints, interests, needs, and cultures will create monumental complexities for supervisors and managers, the likes of which we have never seen.

Magazine Publishers of America reports that, according to the U.S. Department of Labor, the number of African Americans, Asian Americans, American Indians, and Hispanics working in the United States represented just 7.6 percent of the work force over 50 years ago. In the year 2007, based on U.S. Department of Labor EEO-1 reports, that number stood at 34.25 percent and the U.S. Census Bureau has estimated that the total minority population in the United States will comprise 50 percent of our total population by the year 2050. It should be evident to all CEOs and HR professionals alike that these are serious considerations and that the company that has not prepared for this event may very well find itself included in other statistical data reporting the number of businesses, large and small, that failed to survive.

Similar to professionals in other disciplines, most human resources professionals wonder and speculate about what the business environment will really be in the future if, as predicted, minority employment continues to increase while fewer nonminorities enter the work force. The answer to this is simply that there will be a need for substantive changes in some company policies, programs, and procedures to accommodate this influx. However, there should really be no reason for major readjustments or for reengineering (see the buzzword list on pages 251 and 252) the total infrastructure of the business to the point that it will be unrecognizable from the way business was formerly conducted.

The Civil Rights Act of 1964, together with succeeding amendments and other new civil rights legislation, set the stage and established the blueprint to guide employers in the hiring and promotion of minorities and women in the workplace. It can be no coincidence that those business organizations that cooperated and complied with civil rights laws should discover the many advantages of employing these groups, and that they were by and large successful. Similarly, there is no reason now to believe that those organizations that accept the principles of diversity management will not be equally successful.

From a practical and realistic view, most company presidents and managers have had the challenge of managing diverse groups of employees for a number of years. For instance, homosexuals have been acknowledged as comprising a certain percentage of the work force in the past, and from this point on into the future it will become a matter of reality and fact that these and others we may think of as belonging to diverse groups will be entering American business in ever-increasing numbers. We may speculate as to what the exact percentage of increase may be, but the projected demographic statistics of U.S. population figures should provide us with some reliable evidence as to the mathematical probabilities of diversity employment.

Whatever the exact percentages may be, it is certain that supervisors will be required to devote an increasing amount of their time to the management and direction of these diverse newcomers. Individual opinions notwithstanding, the point must be acknowledged and understood by every supervisor and manager, and particularly every human resources manager—that full-scale diversity management is already here today, and that it will not go away! These changes will not take place without a challenge; however, the companies that are prepared to step up to the challenge and look at it as an opportunity, will be the winners from a competitive as well as a societal standpoint. In any event, companies will need all the help they can get in order to prepare their own supervisors, managers, and general employee population to properly play their individual roles.

DIVERSITY AND THE HR FUNCTION

The stage is now set for human resources specialists and professionals, who had better be prepared to add another key function to their job description: namely, advising and counseling line managers, office and staff supervisors, and probably most of all, the top management of the organization, about the proper, the legal, and the best way of coping with this new challenge of managing diversity.

For the experienced human resources professional, it should not really be necessary to retrain or go back to school in order to successfully handle this subject. Savvy and competent human resources practitioners will take the pragmatic approach to the matter by

- displaying a large amount of patience;
- proactively implementing meaningful orientation and training classes for members of these diverse groups;
- providing whatever other assistance may be necessary to make them productive; and,
- from a moral as well as good-business point of view, making them feel welcome and wanted.

DIVERSITY AND SUPERVISION

It will be supervision's most important responsibility to make it clear to all current employees (both nondiverse and diverse) that everyone without exception will work together cooperatively and productively. Worker harmony and teamwork are absolute essentials for successful diversity management, and hostile personal feelings toward other workers must be left outside before employees (and especially supervisors and managers) come into their office, store, shop, factory, warehouse, or laboratory. Failure to do so must be dealt with in the same way as any other disciplinary problem.

One of the cardinal principles of personnel management is that nothing must be permitted to disrupt or adversely affect the operation of the work group. Management and supervision have not only the right, but the duty, to resolve the matter and restore harmony, even if that means the termination of the employee creating the problem. For example, there have been cases where employees have complained to their bosses about the personal appearance or personal hygiene (such as failure to bathe regularly) of another employee. Since these lifestyles were sufficiently offensive to disrupt the operation of the work group, the offenders were advised by supervision to either change their personal habits or seek employment elsewhere. Such disciplinary measures under these circumstances are generally supported by the courts.

DIVERSITY AND THE ROLE OF THE HUMAN RESOURCES EXECUTIVE

Although the tone must be unmistakably set by the CEO of the company, diversity management and its successful implementation throughout the corporation should generally be the direct responsibility of the head human resources professional. The wise and perceptive human resources manager, director, or vice president will readily understand how diverse populations can present not only meaningful challenges but also major opportunities—realistically, even profitable opportunities—for bringing new ideas and viewpoints into the company. In addition, the company will be thought of in the community and by the public in general, as one of those good neighbors we spoke of earlier.

There can be no better advertising campaign for an organization than the reputation of being a company that willingly, even enthusiastically, hires, trains, and promotes minorities, women, and all other members of diverse groups into its work force. All progressive and proactive companies know that the age of diversity has already arrived—that the future is not just coming, but the future is *now*!

HOW CORPORATE AMERICA VIEWS DIVERSITY

In 2006, the Ethnic Majority reported that a number of large, well-known companies recognizing both moral responsibility and business opportunities for diversity-sensitive employers have established corporate diversity Web sites to emphasize their commitment. These companies include Aetna, AT&T, Booz Allen Hamilton, General Mills, General Motors, Hewlett-Packard, IBM, Lucent Technologies, Nissan, PricewaterhouseCoopers, Toyota, and Waste Management.

Cultural diversity in the workplace utilizes our country's skills to its fullest, and contributes to our overall prosperity. Realistically, as a nation, we must admit that this hasn't yet happened; and though there are many good signs, progress is slow. And, yes, we and the whole world are currently experiencing a very severe and difficult economic recession, but the economy will rebound and the savvy companies such as those mentioned above will likely still do their utmost to acquire and maintain a diverse cultural workforce.

As the human resources general, rapid implementation of the diversity concept in your own organization should be one of your prime targets and strategies.

CHAPTER PERSPECTIVE

This chapter discussed the meaning of *diversity* in the work force and its implications for the business world. Diversity was defined, and an historical perspective on diversity in America, both at its inception as a nation and after the first Civil Rights Act, was presented. Guidance for human resources, as well as other areas of a business organization, was provided regarding the best attitude and appropriate steps to be taken to accommodate these changes. Finally, it was pointed out that twelve well-known, large American corporations have established corporate diversity Web sites to emphasize their commitment to the overall goal of establishing true cultural diversity in the American workforce.

Other Issues and Challenges in Human Resources

INTRODUCTION AND MAIN POINTS

This chapter deals with some specific issues and challenges in the area of human resources for which no clear-cut solutions have yet been found. The HR practitioner is being alerted to the fact that these are some of the issues for which there is probably no consensus about the ideal way in which they should be handled. They are examples of problems that fall into the general category of consideration on a case-by-case basis. The pros and cons of each issue are explored. Issues include:

Smoking in the workplace
Hiring smokers
HR systems of software and hardware
Merit pay versus new pay methods
Disaster recovery plans
Telecommuting
Cell phones in the workplace
Preemployment testing
Personnel policy exceptions
Attitude surveys
Liability for employees driving company vehicles
Ergonomics

After you read the material in the chapter:

■ You will know that there is no consensus about smoking, as various laws prohibit smoking and others protect the rights of the smoker.

■ You will know that there are four approaches to dealing with HR data management: manually, mainframe computer systems, personal computer systems, or outsourcing.

■ You will learn effective methods of handling disaster recovery plans, telecommuting, and cell phones in the workplace.

■ You will have an overview of various compensation arrangements: automatic progression pay systems, merit pay and pay-for-performance systems, and new pay methods.

■■■ You will have insight into the application of preemployment testing criteria after having read an excerpt from the *Griggs v. Duke Power* decision (see pages 268 and 269).

■■■ You will understand the importance of adhering to personnel policies and not making exceptions, to safeguard the company as well as your own credibility.

■■■ You will understand the value of attitude testing but realize that such testing should not be used casually.

■■■ You will learn how to protect the company from liability suits arising out of employees driving company vehicles.

■■■ You will understand the value of ergonomics in the workplace.

■■■ You will have a better insight about whether to disclose problems of former employees relating to violence, dishonesty, and performance when job reference inquiries are received from other companies.

SMOKING IN THE WORKPLACE

As discussed in Chapter 10, the subject of smoking in the workplace is still controversial and will probably continue to be for some time. Keeping in mind the health, comfort, and safety of the company's most important asset as well as those other valuable people, your customers, you might think about recommending to your top management that all company facilities, including stores and all customer areas, be smoke-free, and that employees be allowed to smoke outside of company premises if desired. This type of a smoking policy is already in effect in many companies, and all indications are that others are preparing to follow suit.

Recent survey data on the harmful effects of even secondary smoke should also alert companies without smoking policies about the potential liabilities of not addressing this very critical personnel issue. Look for the federal government, based on recommendations by the surgeon general, to come out with increasing legislation designed to curb the use of cigarettes and tobacco in any form in private business as well as in public places. In a number of city councils and state legislatures as well, smokers are finding less and less support. As early as 1995, for example, California passed legislation that imposed a virtual statewide ban on smoking in the workplace. (As of January 2010, twenty-five states had enacted statewide smoking bans on all enclosed places, including bars and restuarants. Other states ban smoking in most enclosed places, except adult venues such as bars and casinos, if the owners choose.)

HIRING SMOKERS

The subject of hiring smokers, of course, then becomes an integral part of the overall smoking question, and it too is anything but clear-cut. The human resources employment staff, as well as operating supervisors and managers, are all well aware that many highly qualified and capable applicants are smokers, and that by having a no-smoker hiring policy, you are probably passing up a certain amount of talent that your company might happen to need at the time. It becomes difficult, if not impossible, however, to explain that we support a smoke-free environment for our company (assuming that is the case) while we hire smokers because of their special talents.

Over the past several years there has been a dramatic increase in the number of state statutes regulating smoking in the workplace.

Some of the provisions of these workplace smoking laws include
- written and/or posted smoking policy or rules;
- posting of signs;
- specifying smoke-free and smoking-permitted areas;
- reasonable accommodation for smokers;
- penalties and/or civil remedies for noncompliance;
- requiring the control of smoke with existing physical barriers and ventilation systems.

On the other hand, Topix reports that as of August 2007, twenty-nine states have passed smoking legislation protecting the rights of smokers. Smokers' rights laws (often included in a state's fair employment practice statute) generally prohibit employers from discriminating against workers in the areas of hiring, promotion, or medical benefits insurance coverage on the basis of use or nonuse of tobacco.

It is suggested that you work closely with your legal department or local counsel in your state to assist you in coping with this vexing personnel challenge of smoking in the workplace.

SYSTEMS SOFTWARE AND HARDWARE, MAINFRAME, MICROPROCESSOR, OR OUTSOURCING

It is strongly recommended that your department have state-of-the-art information systems software and hardware that allow for current operations as well as future growth. Smaller companies and those with limited resources may find they cannot afford the cost of these computer installations, and that is understandable. However, as we enter the age of information and the Internet's prevalence (see Chapter 16) and with the ever more rapid gathering, processing, and analysis of data, these are among the most necessary costs of doing business, and employers must recognize them as such. A listing of human resources system software vendors along with their products and services can be found in Chapter 5.

Personal computers including laptops are by far the first choice of a majority of organizations for almost all their business applications. In some cases, huge sums of money have been spent on converting to personal computers as companies rely on the perceived long-term, economic advantages of abandoning less volatile and more expensive mainframe operations. Should you decide to change, however, don't make the switch to total PC applications too quickly; if you are experiencing no major problems, mainframe processing may be more than adequate for your company at the present time. Have your information systems experts and others analyze your needs from a cost/value perspective, then make your decision. The decision as to the adequacy—current and future—of your human resources information system must be a priority.

Outsourcing should be investigated as an alternative. Many companies have decided that outsourcing some or much of their human resources electronic record-keeping functions (benefits, retirement plans, and others) to outside professional companies, reduces or completely eliminates the need for high-powered and expensive HR information systems. It might be the smart way to handle your processing needs, as more and more corporations are doing. Others, for various reasons, prefer the do-it-yourself, in-house system, but outsourcing should at least be kept in mind as another option.

DISASTER RECOVERY PLANS

Regardless of the type or design of the human resources information system you may have now or in the future, provision must be made for a disaster recovery plan. In the event that human resource operations are disrupted for any reason (i.e., natural disasters such as fire, flood, earthquake or terrorist or other man-made catastrophes), a contingency plan for off-site storage of data must be in place so that operations may be resumed as quickly as possible. It would be unthinkable to lose HR or other company records because duplicate data files and important documents had not been kept.

In the past, some companies may have had second thoughts about disaster recovery programs because of the added expense of duplicating files, leasing space or storage facilities, and so forth. However, as a case in point, most financial companies affected by the September 11, 2001, World Trade Center attack were able to almost immediately resume operations because of good backup procedures. Their experience has served to alert and convince many companies of the necessity of duplicate secured data, regardless of cost. For firms involved with e-commerce, for example, Web servers and necessary data bases as well as Web-based programs must be readily and rapidly available to reduce the interruption of business and insure business continuity and security.

From the standpoint of designing recovery plans, companies must assess the vulnerability of their own operation to determine their individual company needs. Where necessary, consideration should even be given to the need for a second site to continue operations if the original site is unserviceable. A company's need may call for leased space in a building site capable of holding computer equipment. If disaster strikes, a previously arranged agreement with a so-called crate-and-ship vendor can insure that the hardware and software are shipped to the new site within 24 hours. A business may also choose to build its own off-site, completely equipped, and fully functioning disaster operation recovery center, or it may employ a vendor who provides such services. The solution for some companies may be as simple as making duplicate computer files, transferring the data to tape on off hours and storing these tapes in secure vaults on or off company premises.

Whatever system is chosen, all companies must understand that when operations are interrupted for any reason, an effective disaster recovery plan is a necessity to resume business safely and efficiently. And of this fact, the author is quite sure human resource professionals will need no persuasion

NEW ROLE OF THE VIRTUAL OFFICE AND TELECOMMUTING

A still relatively new trend in employee relations is the concept of the "virtual" office, in which workers *virtually* take their offices with them while working at home or some other location. The virtual office then, by definition, is "wherever the worker happens to be performing work for the organization." The overall work operation in the virtual office is referred to as telecommuting, which in turn owes its existence and popularity to the integration of computer and telecommunications technology. Telecommuting may be done at home, at a company store or field location, at a customer's location, on the road, or at a combination of these locations so long as the personal office (read "computer") is on the desk or in the briefcase.

Even though the telecommuting idea has been around for some 35 years, it may still be thought of as "relatively" new, at least to some companies and employees. Over 33 million workers in the United States each year telecommute from home at least some of the time, and their numbers are growing. Telecommuters probably average 40 hours per month away from the office, thus reflecting the change in our economy from production to service, from industrial to knowledge-based. But, many more millions of other workers do not telecommute either through lack of opportunity, need, or interest. We will examine below the pros and cons of the telecommuting concept, its many potential benefits to companies, workers, and the community, as well as the role of the human resources professional in establishing and monitoring such programs for efficiency, effectiveness, and, of course, their compliance with Wage and Hour and other related employment laws and regulations.

Potential Benefits of Telecommuting/Virtual Office Programs

Employers, the individual, and the community at large may all realize potential benefits from telecommuting/virtual office programs in the following ways:

Employers. Employer savings are most apparent in office overhead and premises costs such as for heat, lighting, air conditioning, maintenance, equipment, and overall costs of office space per se. With the elimination of travel time and office environment interruptions, the telecommuter's productivity normally increases, probably in the range of 10 percent to 40 percent, and significant productivity gains have been reported by telecommuters and their managers. In the event of family relocations, telecommuters and their skills can still be retained by the company. Work disruptions such as transportation strikes, severe weather conditions, or natural disasters pose no problem for telecommuters because their work and contribution to the company continue unchanged.

The Individual. Reduction of travel time and costs ranks as the primary motivation for persons interested in telecommuting. In addition, job opportunities are greatly expanded since distance and travel time to and from work are no longer considerations. Because of the flexibility of work hours, the telecommuter finds it easier to handle personal family matters such as caring for small children, doing errands, and keeping medical appointments, while performing job duties on a time schedule that is personally convenient.

The Community. The most obvious benefits of telecommuting for the community are a decrease in traffic congestion and the related reductions in air pollution and conservation of fuel and energy. Another easily overlooked benefit to certain members of the community relates to the opportunities telecommuting provides for disabled persons who may have difficulty in traveling or in performing work in a normal nine-to-five day; parents with small children; those responsible for caring for elderly or sick relatives; or those with a variety of other personal situations requiring special attention. We should point out here that unique accommodations may be necessary on the part of employers to make these things a reality, but the community itself must also be proactive in working with and encouraging companies and organizations to provide such opportunities to its citizens.

Drawbacks

Acknowledging the fact that the perfect employment or managerial program has yet to be developed, we list below some potential drawbacks of the virtual office/telecommuting program.

As with any other project, for the telecommuting/virtual office concept to work properly, all aspects of it must be conscientiously analyzed and a specific list of pros and cons drawn up and considered. It does not lend itself to every business situation, but given the right circumstances and a thoughtful application, the program can yield benefits for all parties. Nevertheless, home-based telecommuting does not support the wishes, desires, or capabilities of every worker. Some employees can only work in an atmosphere of fixed hours and managerial direction; such an environment, for example, might best suit the needs of young workers just coming into the work force. For others, the "social" aspect of interrelating with other workers may be important. For older employees the mindset of "going to the office or to the shop" may be a difficult hurdle to overcome, and they may not be as work effective in a "home alone" setting.

Then again, some (perhaps many) homes do not lend themselves to serious concentration and error-free work where such distractions as small children, blaring television sets and loud music, or discussions in the next apartment are commonplace.

From an employer viewpoint, a company's culture or its management approach may not be adaptive to flexible work performance methods. Some managers do not wish to be involved in "remote management," while others lack the confidence that a home-based staff would perform at the same quality levels as directly supervised workers.

It should also be noted that there are some workplace tasks that are probably best accomplished by the interactive-team approach: for example, design work, customer service activities, sales strategies, and other types of group creative effort. Many varieties of clerical activity may also thrive best in a closely controlled setting.

Security

The ease and popularity of telecommuting is in part due to the proliferation of broadband Internet connections such as cable modems and digital subscriber lines (DSL). But specifically because of these innovations, a potential security problem arises—one that many companies fail to consider adequately before they hand their telecommuters a laptop and a password to access their corporate network from home.

The problem (like so many we face in our IT culture) develops when clever hackers are able to attack an unsecured home computer and tap into a company's internal network, thus giving them access to whatever confidential data was authorized for the telecommuter. Utilizing appropriate software and hardware anitvirus and firewall methods is essential to shield the company from such security breaches, but as always the expense of implementing such solutions is a key cost/value decision that must enter into the company's telecommuting program picture.

But before the verdict of "telecommuting just isn't for us" is handed down from top management, it bears repeating that notwithstanding the above drawbacks, a good telecommuting/virtual office program is always possible with the proper thought, preparation, resource commitment, and support of everyone involved.

Legal Aspects of Telecommuting

Telecommuting in its simplest form might be defined as "bringing your work home with you." But when work is brought home, businesses must be aware that, by and large, traditional state and federal employment laws are no less applicable to the "virtual office" than to the traditional office. In fact, telecommuting can be even more of a compliance challenge because of its unique nature and concept if, as already noted, careful thought and planning is not done before the program is implemented.

For example, as covered in Chapter 11, applicable wage and hour laws of the federal Fair Labor Standards Act and comparable state statutes require that individuals not exempt from the provisions of these laws must be paid one and one-half times their regular rate of pay for all hours worked in excess of 40 in any given work week. (Again, Chapter 11 also reminds us that "time worked" includes all hours an employee is required to be on duty, as well as all time during which an employee is permitted or suffered to work whether or not the person is requested to do so.) FLSA also requires that employers keep records of time worked by such nonexempt employees, including total hours worked in each pay period.

As the popular expression suggests, it doesn't take the intelligence of a "rocket scientist" to determine that the challenges of monitoring the worker's home or virtual office for compliance with the above-mentioned laws pose a much greater complexity than in the regular office environment.

The solution to this dilemma might lie in the company having a written agreement with the home-based employee that specifies the hours the person is to work and also requires the advance approval for any contemplated overtime. Another legal approach might be to approve telecommuting operations only for those employees who are exempt from federal and state overtime laws.

HR professionals will also immediately recognize the dangers of discriminatory selection (or retaliatory nonselection) of persons for participating in telecommuting privileges. Those charged with selection of personnel must not create the impression that members of a protected class have been denied participation in the program because of race, color, creed, sex, age, and so forth. In like fashion, if an employee has previously complained about discrimination or harassment and is denied a telecommuting request, a creditable claim of retaliation may shortly be delivered to the HR manager's desk.

One area employers and HR people must be especially aware of in their telecommuting programs is that of disability discrimination. In fact, if and when a disabled person can no longer work in a normal office environment, permitting such an employee to work at home would probably be considered a "reasonable accommodation" as such term is defined in the Americans with Disabilities Act (ADA) and various state laws. However, federal ADA law, it should be noted, does not specifically list telecommuting as a reasonable accommodation, while the U.S. Equal Employment Opportunity Commission states that it is a reasonable accommodation so long as the disabled person can perform the principal functions of the job, and the accommodation would not cause the employer undue hardship. The courts generally agree with the EEOC, but as with some other areas of employment law, court decisions are by no means consistent.

With reference to the disabled employee being able to perform the essential functions of the job at home, once again if the employer is opposed to such an arrangement, having an up-to-date, clear, and comprehensive job description (as pointed out in Chapter 5) is the employer's first line of defense in refusing a home office arrangement, especially when it clearly lists certain duties and responsibilities that cannot in any way be performed at home by any employee, whether disabled or nondisabled.

From the standpoint of health and safety, the U.S. Occupational Safety and Health Administration distinguishes between home offices of telecommuters and those involving home manufacturing operations, and its rules regarding inspections and reporting will still apply to the latter but not to home office environments. Employers, however, should still be aware of the conditions of the home offices to insure their safety and reduce the possibility of workers' compensation claims being filed. Since the telecommuter works as well as lives at home, it may sometimes be difficult to determine or prove that an injury was actually sustained in the course of employment. Again, the only reasonable safeguard in dealing with this and other aspects of telecommuting is a written agreement or contract between the parties specifying all the necessary provisions.

In conclusion, we come back to our original premise that a telecommuting/virtual office program can be a vital, cost-effective component of any company's labor force, so long as it is properly designed and all operational, security, and legal compliance issues are monitored and maintained.

CELL PHONES IN THE WORKPLACE

There can be little doubt in our current information technology revolution that cellular phones are here to stay. Cell phones grow smaller in size while increasing in range, efficiency, and convenience, and it is difficult today to find someone who doesn't own one. This universal attachment to the cell phone, however, has caused unforeseen problems in any number of workplaces on account of irritating ringing and distracting conversations, all of which frequently adversely affect work operations and productivity. So the first impulse of the HR professional might be to have a regulation or policy to control the use of cell phones in the workplace. And depending on the individual company situation such a policy might be in order. Be advised, however, that there is far from universal agreement as to what provisions such a policy should contain, with the possible exception that it is becoming increasingly clear to company managers and owners that the outright prohibition of cell phones in the workplace is impracticable and unworkable. Setting up a policy of "no cell phones in the workplace" might sound like the easy solution, but policing it borders on the impossible. Where companies have found it necessary to establish a cell phone policy, instead of outright banning, they have required that these and all other communication devices be placed on silent mode, that calls are limited to essential matters or emergencies, that time limits (e.g., one or two minutes) must be observed, and that employees are at least *discouraged* from bringing cell phones to work.

Personnel policies regarding the use of cell phones while driving company vehicles usually are more definite in that they strictly prohibit cellular phone usage when conducting company business, and that if cell phone usage is necessary, the employee must stop and park the vehicle in a safe place until the call is completed. (Some states have or are considering adopting laws to prohibit use of cell phones while driving.) In addition, it might be wise to include in this policy, if applicable, a statement to the effect that all calls of a personal nature are only to be made on breaks, and that this applies to the use of personal cell phones as well as company phones. It might also be appropriate from a courtesy standpoint to add that "While interacting with customers or in meetings, cell phones and pager ringers must be turned off."

MERIT PAY VERSUS NEW PAY

If you have attended conferences or personnel seminars on the subject of merit pay, you have probably been exposed to various statements and speeches by personnel consultants and other experts urging you to consider abandoning the traditional merit pay and pay-for-performance systems in favor of the so-called new pay methods of compensating employees.

Such new pay methods may include:

■ *Team-based pay strategies*, wherein all team members share in increased compensation rewards based on achievements of the team rather than individual goals.

■ *Annual or one-time bonus awards* that are proposed on the theory that a bonus for achievement rewards the employee with the whole loaf rather than getting only a slice of the total annual increase amount each payday. The larger reward on a one-time basis theoretically is more meaningful and increases employee motivation for improved job performance.

■ *Competency-based reward systems*, which recommend that the competency requirements of either the person or the job be used as the fundamental basis for defining value. The knowledge, skills, and abilities of the individual, regardless of job or position assignment, it is claimed, will determine the pay decision. Alternatively, the competency requirements for the successful performance of the individual job or position itself might be used in setting up a competency-based pay system. However, it should be noted that not many companies currently use competency exclusively in making pay decisions, because other factors (such as job performance and results) are also taken into consideration.

A number of these different compensation arrangements have existed and been advocated for a number of years. While some companies have tried new pay, it has not yet exactly revolutionized the payment of wages and salaries in the business community, and it does not appear to be doing so any time in the near future.

Any number of meaningful improvements in our compensation systems have been proposed and adopted in recent years, and the change/improvement process should continue. However, there should be tangible, demonstrable improvements when proposed changes directly and radically affect an employee's paycheck, even those concerning the method of wage payments. There are few items in the business world that are as highly sensitive and jealously guarded as the American worker's paycheck.

Over the past 5 to 10 years, merit pay itself has been making inroads in the compensation structures of many large as well as small companies. The old automatic progression pay systems, often the favorite of the unions, seems to have lost much of its luster and steam as employers increasingly look more for performance results than length of service. If your organization still has any vestige of automatic wage increases in your compensation program, do whatever you can to change it to a merit structure. Merit pay is here to stay!

PREEMPLOYMENT TESTING

Even among people not associated with the human resources field, the subject of preemployment testing can usually generate a good deal of interest and discussion, at times including heated debate. The testing controversy is not new; it has been going on for many years.

Legal Points

Preemployment testing has been the target of civil rights legislation almost since the enactment of Title VII in 1964, and it probably reached its apex with the precedent *Griggs v. Duke Power Company* decision by the U.S. Supreme Court in 1971 (401 U.S. 424, 3 FEP 175). In this case, the company had established requirements that, as a condition of employment in or transfer to certain operating departments in which only whites were employed, a high school education and passing of two general intelligence/aptitude tests, were required. The question at issue was whether an employer is prohibited by the Civil Rights Act of 1964, Title VII from instituting these requirements when neither one is shown to be significantly related to successful job performance. Both requirements operate to disqualify black applicants at a substantially higher rate than white applicants, and the jobs in question formerly had been filled only by white employees as part of a long-standing practice of giving hiring preference to whites.

A company official testified that the high school diploma and intelligence test requirements were established by the company with the intent of generally improving the overall quality of the work force. The evidence, however, showed that employees who had not completed high school or taken the tests continued to perform satisfactorily and make progress in the departments where high school and test requirements existed.

In reversing the judgment of the Court of Appeals, Mr. Chief Justice Burger, who delivered the opinion of the Supreme Court, held that

> Good intent or absence of discriminatory intent does not redeem employment procedures or testing mechanisms that operate as 'built-in headwinds' for minority groups and are unrelated to measuring job capability...

and that

> Nothing in the (Civil Rights) Act precludes the use of testing or measuring procedures; obviously they are useful. What Congress has forbidden is giving these devices and mechanisms controlling force unless they are demonstrably a reasonable measure of job performance. Congress has not commanded that the less qualified be preferred over the better qualified simply because of minority origins. Far from disparaging job qualifications as such, Congress has made such qualifications the controlling factor, so that race, religion, nationality, and sex become irrelevant. What Congress has commanded is that any test used must measure the person for the job and not the person in the abstract...

After *Griggs*, various court decisions as well as EEOC and other federal agency guidelines on employee selection procedures eventually began to present major problems for employers as well as the compliance agencies as to the proper and legal methods of employment testing. Thus, in 1978, the EEOC, together with other federal agencies jointly adopted a set of guidelines known as Uniform Guidelines on Employee Selection Procedures, to meet the need for clarification. These guidelines incorporate a single set of principles designed to assist employers, labor organizations, employment agencies, and licensing and certification boards to comply with requirements of federal law prohibiting employment practices that discriminate on grounds of race, color, religion, sex, or national origin. These guidelines are available from the EEOC and other sources, and HR professionals should be thoroughly familiar with them.

Practical Points

In addition to its legal aspects, let's discuss some of the practical or objective points of preemployment testing. From the standpoint of using employment tests as a means of selecting the best applicant for a job opening, such tests are not the key predictors of success in hiring that some interviewers may claim them to be. The subject of testing is broad enough in its own right that numerous books have been written, seminars held, judicial rulings made, and courses offered, thus, it will not be our purpose here to try and convince anyone one way or the other. If you have been in the personnel or human resources field for any length of time, you've probably already formed your own opinion about the value of testing.

Certain types of testing, including clerical, typing, mechanical aptitude, and basic mathematics can be useful to the interviewer when hiring for jobs in which these particular skills are required. However, these or any of the many other employment tests currently in use are simply more evidence that may indicate whether or not this candidate should be offered the opportunity to join the company. You would, of course, be remiss if you did not take into consideration the applicant's experience, education, personality, appearance, interview results, previous track record with other companies, and a host of other (including legal) factors that must necessarily play a part in the overall selection process. To ignore any of these latter qualities and to base one's hiring decision simply on test cut-off scores (whether validated or not) does a grave injustice to the applicant, and can involve the company in serious legal problems, as well.

PERSONNEL POLICY EXCEPTIONS

Chapter 12 dealt with the subject of personnel policies and the policy manual, and you were urged to have specific, written, and well-communicated personnel policies in your organization. Recalling the old adage that "rules were made to be broken," you will inevitably, sooner or later, face the situation where a manager, supervisor, foreman, or employees themselves, will request that for a good and sufficient reason, an exception should be made for a particular employee with regard to some specific personnel policy. You will probably be told that Mary White or Jim Smith is one of the best workers this manager or supervisor has ever had, who never misses or is late for work, and is really very deserving of being granted an exception to policy.

It is not the intent here to belittle such a request, for in many cases it is most natural, even recommended, that the personnel manager fully appreciate an employee's plight and have empathy for his or her problem. This is especially true when the policy exception involves some aspect of medical plan coverage where denial of the request could possibly result in severe financial hardship to the employee and his or her family. It would probably be the most natural thing in the world for the personnel manager to be inclined to approve the exception request in an effort to help a loyal, deserving, and perhaps long-service employee. Even though it would be a nice gesture and undoubtedly very much appreciated by the employee and his or her family, there are also good business reasons why approving the exception might not be the right decision:

1) Any policy exception you make or are contemplating making must be done with the full realization that, even though you will benefit this particular deserving employee, you are in all probability being unfair to other employees who may be in a similar situation, and for whom no exception request was made or even considered. If granted, you may be establishing a very embarrassing precedent when someone wants to know why you made the exception for Sally or Bill "and you won't do the same for me!"

2) If the exception request involves the company's medical or retirement benefits policies, you might want to check to be sure that its approval would not be considered a violation of the Employee Retirement Income Security Act, to which most companies are subject. If it can be shown that there was indeed some violation of ERISA laws, the entire qualification status of your retirement benefit plan, for example, could be in jeopardy, with the possible loss of its pre-tax-deferred contribution feature that participants enjoy.

Therefore, be very careful of the normal inclination to help a deserving employee by approving an exception to a company policy. In the long run, you will make your own job a lot easier while at the same time protecting the company by not granting such policy exception requests. Making your calls or decisions in this manner is not the way personnel or human resources managers win popularity contests, but it is a way of living up to the responsibilities of the job, while making it just that much easier to not grant future exception requests.

ATTITUDE SURVEYS

For any number of years, managers have been advised by consultants and other experts that, if they want to get in touch with the true feelings of their employees, they should send out attitude surveys so the employees can tell you how they really feel on any number of work-related issues. Quite often we think we know the likes and dislikes of employees, but just as often are surprised when we don't. The attitude survey, frequently done anonymously in order to encourage participation, can be very effective in discovering what people really want, or what they like or dislike.

However, it is well to exercise some caution in using this tool. When you ask employees to tell you candidly just how they believe a particular problem can be corrected, what new or revised procedure they'd like to see in place, or what new benefit they think should be added to the benefit program, you'd better be prepared to do (or at least come close to) what they are asking you to do! If they recommend or ask for something via the attitude survey—and for whatever reason (often financial) you are not in a position to grant it—you've then got a bigger problem than if you had never asked people what they liked or disliked, or wanted or didn't want, in the first place. Attitude surveys can be effective, provided you limit them to those particular benefits or problems that, if necessary, you are prepared to grant or resolve, respectively.

LIABILITY

Employees Driving Company Vehicles

If your company happens to be one in which your employees are required to drive company cars, trucks, or any other type of vehicle requiring a current, valid driver's license, you will want to install a fail-safe system to ensure that none of your employees will ever step into a company vehicle without being in possession of that current, valid driver's license.

When these employees are first hired, their job offer should be contingent on their presenting you with an up-to-date motor vehicle driving record report, and a current, valid driver's license for the state in which the person will be (or may be) driving. The new hire would then be required to fill out a standard driver questionnaire form, which should include questions such as:

■ Has your operator's license/registration ever been suspended or revoked?

■ Have you ever had a conviction involving drugs, alcohol, reckless driving, homicide, manslaughter, or assault arising out of the operation of a motor vehicle?

■ Have you been involved in any motor vehicle accidents in the last five years?

■ Have you received any driving citations (other than parking or those listed above) in the past five years?

In addition to the above questions, applicants should agree to sign a statement included as part of the driver questionnaire that they will only operate company vehicles:

- when in full possession of their faculties;
- when the vehicle is in safe mechanical condition;
- in accordance with all traffic laws, signals, and markings; and
- in a courteous manner at all times.

An additional statement on the questionnaire authorizes any state motor vehicle department to disclose information regarding the applicant's driving record. The applicant certifies that the answers given are true and further agrees that any falsification of information requested on the questionnaire form is cause for dismissal. The applicant then signs the questionnaire, which is subsequently included in the individual's personnel file.

It is also very important to establish a procedure whereby, on at least an annual basis (or perhaps even every six months), each employee updates and signs another driver questionnaire form. In this way, the driving records of all employees are monitored, preferably by human resources, on a continuing basis for serious traffic violations—including DWIs—and especially for suspended or revoked licenses.

By setting up this type of driver questionnaire program, your company may be protecting itself from the liability of millions of dollars in jury verdicts in the event one of your employees with a suspended or revoked driver's license is involved in a serious or fatal traffic accident. Whatever the cost of administration, such a program is probably one of the best investments your company can make.

Also, in addition to the above, the Governors Highway Safety Association reports that six states (California, Connecticut, New Jersey, New York, Oregon, and Washington), the District of Columbia, and the Virgin Islands now prohibit all drivers from talking on handheld cell phones while driving. Also, nineteen states, the District of Columbia, and Guam ban text messaging for all drivers. HR professionals should review their state and local laws regarding these issues and adapt their company policies accordingly.

ERGONOMICS AND THE WORKPLACE

Whether the term is *carpal tunnel syndrome*, *repetitive stress injury*, or *musculoskeletal disorder*, American employers are experiencing a phenomenal growth of this general class of health problem among their employees. The cause of this malady has been pretty much identified, while the solution, as in many situations, is somewhat more complex and challenging.

The increase in carpal tunnel syndrome cases and associated ills parallels the tremendous growth of personal computers both at work and at home. Most current estimates indicate that 76 percent of American's own home computers and 68 percent have one at their desk at work. The very nature of computer operations requiring repetitive hand and wrist motions for extended periods of time can result in numbness, swelling, weakness, and burning pain in the hands, wrists, and fingers. Such injuries involving repetitive stress and overexertion by people operating computers can account for more than 60 percent of all job-related illnesses and is now the nation's largest workplace health problem. Treatment for carpal tunnel and other related injuries may involve physical therapy and exercise regimes; in some cases, surgery may be required.

To protect employees while at the same time combating this menace to every company's workers' compensation and medical and disability benefit programs, the applied science of ergonomics has been developed. Ergonomics, sometimes called human engineering, is concerned with designing and arranging things people use so that the people and things interact most efficiently and safely. The key to successful ergonomic applications is to keep the physical requirements of the job (i.e., lifting, bending, reaching, twisting, pushing, pulling, carrying) within the physical limitations of the employees performing the job. (Here again, as stressed in Chapter 5, an up-to-date job description can be of great help in protecting both the employee and the company when it clearly spells out a job's minimal physical and mental requirements.)

A number of companies are proactively setting up ergonomic training programs to assist their employees in taking an active role in the prevention of repetitive stress injuries. Creating ergonomic work stations and instituting regular stretch and relaxation breaks and exercises are recommended by fitness experts and specialists as a means of getting employees and companies involved in preventing such injuries. There are also state-mandated regulations requiring businesses to institute ergonomic training programs if they experience recurring claims involving stress injuries.

Stress-related injuries represent another aspect of human resources involvement that, depending on the size and product of the company, may require specialized knowledge and attention on the part of the HR professional to protect the company and reduce costs. The duties and knowledge requirements of the HR man or woman never seem to decrease in proportion to technological advancements and improvements—if anything, the opposite is true.

JOB REFERENCES

Perhaps one of the most problematic issues personnel and HR managers face today is the almost no-win situation of giving job references to other companies that are considering their former employees for hire. Surveys usually indicate that most HR managers, convinced of the possibility of lawsuits or other legal actions against their company, refuse to provide information about former employees. These and most other HR professionals still abide by the safe approach of disclosing only name, rank and serial number information when asked about the performance, reliability, character, honesty, and such, of an exemployee who was perhaps discharged three weeks previously for theft, or an act of violence against a supervisor or fellow employee.

Despite these majority feelings against full disclosure of problems involving a former employee, however, the tide of opinion, both managerial as well as legal, does seem to be turning. This change of attitude or policy is coming about as more companies are finding that in the process of not disclosing a more serious character or personality flaw of one of their former employees, the boomerang effect takes over, and the company is now being sued for what the employee did not disclose to the new employer. Once again, HR faces the typical no-win situation, with possible defamation lawsuits if you do disclose, and negligence or other types of lawsuits if you don't.

Employment lawyers are more likely to advise their corporate HR clients to change the no-comment approach to reference inquiries to one of objective disclosure of violent behavior incidents or other safety-sensitive problems of those they formerly employed. If, in the opinion of the HR manager, the incident or problem is of a sufficiently serious nature, the wiser course would be to provide detailed disclosure to the prospective employer. As with all important matters handled in the HR function, the unbiased facts and reasons for disclosure should be documented to protect the company against potential defamation lawsuits from the exemployee.

In support of this legal advice, HR managers argue that when the situation is reversed and they are attempting to hire a former employee of another company, it's logical for them to also want to know everything they can about the person under consideration. They also contend that from the employees' standpoint, full disclosure is always welcomed by those who want their new employer to be aware of their prior good performance and track record.

Release Forms

Another way companies can further protect themselves from liability is to have departing employees sign release forms stating that they will not sue their former employers over job reference inquiries. On the premise that people (and especially exemployees) are not always inclined to do or give something for nothing, some companies now offer employees who resign or are terminated a stipulated amount of severance allowance, ranging from an extra two weeks' to a month's pay, for example, if, without coercion, they will sign an agreement that they will not bring job-reference or wrongful termination litigation against their former company. Although the validity of these release agreements has been upheld in some courts, there is, as yet, no specific blanket form that might guarantee immunity in each case in question.

State Laws

In addition, a number of states have passed laws protecting employers who provide truthful information from defamation and other claims. However, even though these laws do not provide complete protection to employers, and some require job applicants to sign statements authorizing reference inquiries, some observers worry that companies may take advantage of the opportunity to retaliate against former personnel, especially when they leave for a better job opportunity.

From this discussion, one may conclude that the little-or-no-information job reference policy is changing slowly, but that the dilemma will probably persist for quite some time.

CHAPTER PERSPECTIVE

This chapter discussed the intricacies of several controversial issues or unresolved problems in the area of human resources. Readers are made aware of the following issues or problem areas and gained some perspective on possible resolutions.

■ Where should your HR department stand on smoking and hiring smokers?

■ Should your department continue to handle its data management manually, with mainframe systems or PC systems, or outsource the task?

■ Should your compensation group modify its pay arrangements to new pay methods?

■ Have you established a practicable, workable disaster recovery plan for vital personnel records and other data?

■ Have you considered the advantages of the virtual office program and telecommuting for appropriate employees in your company?

■ Should you consider establishing a cell-phones-in-the-workplace policy that will work for the employees as well as the company?

■ Would your proposed preemployment test pass muster under the law?

▬ Should you make an exception to the personnel policies spelled out in the PPM to a deserving employee, especially one having to do with health care?

▬ Should you take an attitude survey and then file the results away indefinitely for lack of funds?

▬ Can you find a way to not only hire good, qualified drivers to drive company vehicles but also to monitor any changes in their status?

▬ Should you institute a program to prevent repetitive stress injuries?

▬ Should you disclose instances of violence, theft, poor performance, or other problems of former employees applying for jobs with other companies?

Human Resources and the Internet

INTRODUCTION AND MAIN POINTS

Chapter 14 illustrated some seventeen different examples of familiar buzzwords that catch the attention and fancy of business professionals, including personnel/HR managers and management consultants. One word purposely omitted from this buzzword list of business vocabulary is Internet, which, in its meteoric rise in general popularity and acceptance, did not even pause long enough at the buzzword category to be considered a serious contender for mention or inclusion on that list. The Internet, with its universal interest, value, affordability, and appeal for all types of businesses, groups, and individuals, has already reached the point of induction into the Business and Personal Essentials Hall of Fame. Other inductees that you will recognize as already enjoying this honor include the computer, the copier, the stapler, and—who could ever forget?—the familiar paper clip that first appeared on the office desk about 1919. Since data gathering and disseminating responsibilities are hallmarks of the human resources profession, each practitioner should be on the cutting edge of utilizing this most powerful business tool to its full advantage.

After studying the material in this chapter:

■ You will learn the background of the Internet itself. This brief history is included here in order to give you a better understanding of the potential of this powerful new tool.

■ You will understand the relationship and value of the Internet to the human resources operation.

■ You will be shown how the Internet can operate as an essential tool in the retrieval and distribution of information and data used in the day-to-day HR function.

■ You will be pointed in the right direction toward exploring on your own the almost endless possibilities of discovering personnel/human resources information that might be exactly suited to your own company's needs and requirements.

■ You will understand the advantages of vendor management systems and e-procurement in hiring contingent workers.

■ You will be shown the potential value of electronic e-learning training systems.

■ You will learn more about search engines and how to use them.

■ You will be shown and most likely convinced of the unbelievable potential for companies large and small that advertise their products and services on the Internet. Human resources practitioners can play a key role in convincing top management of the wisdom of using this medium to advertise employment opportunities and to recruit for their greatest asset: employees, system members, associates, human resources, human capital—in other words, people.

THE PHENOMENON KNOWN AS THE INTERNET

For those few people (maybe one or two!) not totally familiar (or perhaps not at all familiar) with the Internet, some introductory background remarks are in order:

1) The Internet can be thought of as an electronic pipeline or information superhighway made up of millions of so-called *nodes*, a node being defined as an individual computer, personal or otherwise, which is connected to a network.

2) The Internet as an entity is really thousands of networks connected to a vast global network. This Internet pipeline/superhighway circles the earth, with data and information of practically every kind flowing through it (or on it), picking up and dispensing its informational contents to corporations, universities, government agencies, and individuals in almost every location on earth.

3) In addition to being a practically unlimited yet easily accessible source of knowledge and information, the Internet is still one thing more. It is the means or the vehicle by which people can communicate with other people at any time, about any subject, anywhere on the face of the earth. Probably never since the invention of the printing press has there been such a revolution in the way that people are able to communicate with each other. Through its unique characteristics and availability to practically everyone, thoughts and ideas constantly flow back and forth over the Internet between individuals and groups of people in all walks of life. The Internet potential for problem solving, peaceful dispute resolutions, scientific advancement, and especially for understanding among and between persons, communities, and nations is actually unlimited.

These comments are not meant to be predictive since any number of other proposals or ideas related to the welfare and benefit of human beings have in the past proven unsuccessful, and in many instances can now only be classified as fads, their good intentions notwithstanding. But today few people (perhaps those one or two again) are of the opinion that the Internet will also turn out to be such a fad; however, with its growing enthusiasm and accessibility to people and organizations all over the world and its phenomenal growth and development, the Internet is no passing fancy and the future is bright and brilliant.

A better understanding of the background and history of the Internet might help us make our own judgments as to its potential.

INTERNET BACKGROUND AND HISTORY

Perhaps the last object or force one might associate with the origin of the Internet would be nuclear energy, and although it was designed for use with electronic rather than nuclear power, there remains a historical relationship between the Internet and the atom that makes for one of those serendipitous events so common in the history of scientific research, invention, and discovery.

Need for Maintaining Communication

At the time of the Cold War with the Soviet Union, the Pentagon in Washington had initiated every manner of contingency they believed could occur in the event of an all-out nuclear war with Russia. One primary concern was the necessity for maintaining military as well as civilian communication facilities in the event the nation was bombarded with awesome atomic or hydrogen weapons that would certainly destroy existing hardware and equipment, military command centers, and switching stations and related wiring, no matter how well-armored or protected. Additionally, the central communication nerve centers were thought to be primary targets for incoming ballistic missiles.

The assignment of finding an answer to this seemingly impossible problem was given to the Rand Corporation, a prestigious think tank of the scientific community. Toward the goal of having some form of instant network linking cities, states, and military facilities following a nuclear attack, Rand—with particular credit to their Paul Baran—designed such a program in 1964. It would be a totally decentralized network with each station (node) completely autonomous and operating effectively when the normal communication was in chaos.

Each node in Rand's solution would be equal in rank to every other node and have its own capability of sending, receiving, and passing on messages, and the delivery system itself would be practically indestructible. Evolution then followed from military communication to scientific and academic usage as newer and faster computers and links were developed. As all such entities began to talk to each other over "internetworks," the Internet was the inevitable result.

It didn't take long for marketing and commercial interests to realize the commercial value of this new medium, and we now find the home pages of virtually all businesses on the Web. With as much public interest as the Internet has generated, money is being made in Internet sales and marketing, with plenty of opportunity for all interested commercial parties. (And why should any company *not* be interested?)

With the advent of "social networking" sites, such as Facebook, MySpace, and Twitter, technical barriers to an individual's presence on the Web have disappeared, and millions of people regularly present many aspects of their lives to the world in this manner.

Truly, for both businesses and individuals, Internet access has developed into a necessity, just as the telephone once did.

Fueled by the prospect of freedom of access to almost unlimited knowledge and the ability to speak and contribute one's own thoughts and ideas freely and with little restraint, the Internet's pace of growth into the future can only be described as a spectacular feeding frenzy. So long as the Internet continues to belong to everyone and to no one at the same time, there is literally no end in sight!

SOME INTERNET BASICS

In the first edition of this book published in 1997, somewhat detailed explanations were given as to how the average household user could join the relatively new worldwide Internet club. It discussed the need for a computer, a telephone line, and a modem which, together with a service provider, would then allow one to access the World Wide Web. It discussed and explained search engines, hypertext linkages, Web browsers, and a PC mouse, as well as the different types of charges and fees involved for those interested in becoming Internet subscribers.

At the time of the publication date of the second edition of *Human Resources* (2004), the many millions of "veteran" Internet users had to be reasonably familiar with the above terms and their meanings; and it is probably safe to say that in the year of publication of this third edition (2010) there are still many millions of people in the world who, for whatever reason, are not yet Internet users but who will sooner or later have the opportunity to use it. For this latter group (as was done did in the second edition) I list below some capsulized explanations of the basic elements of the Internet.

Hookups. Any individual—company president/owner, butcher, baker, candlestick maker, or HR professional—can become a member of this worldwide knowledge college. Actually, it's relatively simple, and though there is some expense involved, as you might expect, all you need for a basic hookup is a computer, telephone line, and a modem. While it's still perfectly possible to access the Internet through your home telephone line using a modem (acronym for *mo*dulator *dem*odulator), today more than half of household Internet users have dedicated high-speed, or "broadband," connections through their local phone company, cable company, or other provider. The term *modem* is often still used to refer to the small box such a company installs in your home—such as a DSL (digital subscriber line) modem or cable modem—that will connect (directly or wirelessly) to your home desktop or laptop computer.

Service Providers. You will order your broadband service from—or connect your dial-up modem to—a service provider, one of a number of such companies that own and control the "doorways" to the Internet to request admittance and membership. A relatively modest installation and monthly fee are required to enter this interesting and almost unbelievable world of cyberspace, but whether it is used for personal or business reasons—or both—you will have the pleasure of looking forward to an incredible journey!

Because the Internet is not actually located any place on earth, it is necessary to go to different computer systems (addresses) to access the services you want; however, one of the most important advantages of Internet service providers is that they offer subscribers direct access to the World Wide Web (the Web), a term that will be discussed later in this chapter.

Search Engines. If you have no original address for your subject, you have the option of searching the World Wide Web with a search engine, a computer program that searches through large amounts of text or other data to find material on the Web. Examples of some of the better-known search engines include. Google (the hands-down leader), Yahoo, and Microsoft's new Bing, as well as Ask and AOL. Searching simply requires entering your topic of interest or a key word, and an index page of links (hypertext linkages) is created by the search engine which matches or satisfies your request. Your Web browser (software used to explore the Web) should have a feature that points you to your search engine.

The hypertext linkages referred to above and offered by Internet service providers are highlighted words, phrases, or pictures in the text that the user simply points to or clicks on with the PC mouse in order to jump automatically to another related area in the same document, to another document at the same site, or to another site altogether. Thus, no additional addresses are necessary in searching for a particular subject once the viewer has arrived at the first port of call.

Online service provider companies are a typical business organization with a CEO, board of directors, and stockholders. They are subject to all established laws and regulations and have their privately owned physical plants or infrastructures. As already mentioned, the Internet itself is not in a specific location, and no one really owns it. Internet providers simply provide doorways that give organizations and people access to dedicated communication lines used to transmit data.

Usage and the Law. Once inside the Internet system, the user is free to request or contribute data on just about any subject imaginable, including all types of personnel/human resource subjects and information (as discussed below), and much more. But as with any organization, company, or group, certain reasonable rules and regulations must be followed, violations of which—including attempted pornographic and illegal activities—can result in loss of Internet service and, where warranted, prosecution. Because of the millions of individuals and businesses in the United States alone that participate in online services, a completely new body of law has evolved, one that will undoubtedly continue to grow as Internet technology develops.

HUMAN RESOURCES PROFESSIONALS AND THE INTERNET

One of the more challenging problems in writing about how human resources professionals can use this almost limitless knowledge found on the Internet is the fact that, just like the universe, the world of the Internet is also constantly changing. If the author points out some specific locations (addresses) where helpful personnel or human resources data are to be found on the Internet, it is not only possible but likely that before this information even reaches the reader, things will have changed, and what was unheard of today may be valid tomorrow. It has been said of the development of the Internet that because it is created by people, it has all the characteristics of a living organism. Each day something new is born. Each day something grows. And each day some part of the Internet dies.

Therefore, in the interests of keeping its readers as up-to-date as possible, this book will concentrate on the more established organizations and institutions where such human resources information resides and can be accessed by the user. The assumption may then be made that the continued existence of these organizations on the Internet and for some time into the future will likely be more assured. You will be given as much detail as possible so you can obtain the particular type of information and answers you may need to do your HR job.

FACETS OF THE INTERNET

The Home Page (Web Site)

You will see the term *home page* referred to frequently in this chapter, and you should know that a home page is simply the first or primary screen (page) of that particular organization's total presence on the Internet. It may consist of, for example, the company's logo, mission statement, general information about the company, and listings of everything it offers to Internet browsers, surfers, or just plain viewers.

Each company, individual, corporation, college, government bureau, or any other organization you will find on the Internet has a home page, and each home page will be the same size as your PC screen, regardless of whether you are as large as IBM or as small as The Little Acorn restaurant. In addition, by advertising on the Internet, and using a bit of creative artistry and imagination, the home pages of many millions of small companies can be considered their storefront as seen by viewers literally worldwide. This exposure results in an incredible bargain to the advertiser, especially considering that the cost of setting up a business home page is relatively modest.

And what better place to advertise a company's job openings, employee benefits, its history, mission statement, and whatever else might seem appropriate than on its own Web site! See discussion of "Employment Opportunities Posted on a Company's Web Site" in Chapter 7.

The World Wide Web

Before launching into the more likely organizations and sites that will provide valuable input for human resources professionals, we must spend a few minutes identifying and defining one of the most vital terms and functions on the Internet. You will constantly read and hear it referred to in the Internet community as the Web, short for the World Wide Web.

You will probably hear this name identified in a number of ways, including

■■■ the graphical and interactive area of the Internet;

■■■ the whole gamut of resources that can be accessed using the various related computer tools provided;

■■■ the universe of hypertext servers (computers or software packages) that allow text, graphics, sound files, video clips, and other Internet elements to be mixed together. These hypertext servers provide and serve the hypertext linkages described earlier in this chapter.

RECRUITING SOURCES

It is no great secret to most HR managers and professionals (and especially to employment managers and recruiters) that the cost of newspaper, magazine, and trade journal advertising can range anywhere from expensive to outrageous! At the same time, the mandate from their own managers (and/or CEOs) is always to find well-qualified applicants in the least amount of time and at the lowest possible cost.

Well, HR employment and other practitioners take heart. Help has arrived, as many thousands of companies have already found out. Job recruiting is experiencing an absolute boom on the Internet and the Web, and the number of people logging onto the Internet to list or find jobs is expected to continue to increase far into the future. Employers are posting job and position openings on their own home pages or with one of the many job-posting sites currently available. Job seekers can also post their own resumes on Web sites such as Monster.com (an online recruitment center for job seekers and employers alike) in order to ensure a wide coverage of employers looking to fill available job openings.

Many companies think that, from the standpoint of economy and effectiveness, posting job openings on their own home page results in an added benefit of product promotion and company awareness by those reading and/or responding to their listings of job opportunities. Many organizations, however, in addition to or in lieu of home page recruiting, still prefer to list their job openings with commercial job-posting sites. The best of both worlds resides with those employers who list their job opportunities with these job-posting sites and, in addition, have hotlinks back to their own Web sites or home pages.

There are literally thousands of employment-related sites on the World Wide Web, among which CareerBuilder, Yahoo! HotJobs, and Monster.com are the best known. For HR job openings, SHRM's HRJobs is a comprehensive source. It is also generally felt that since attrition is known to be somewhat high among these thousands of sites, the individual corporation's own Web site will always be a viable as well as reliable option.

Software programs currently exist and are constantly being further refined and developed to enable companies to track applicants, organize data, and transfer information from resumes into an applicant data base file, using e-mail, fax, or scanning. Any local Internet access provider will be able to assist a company or individual job applicant by answering questions and providing information about the services of employment-related sites on the World Wide Web.

Vendor Management Systems and e-Procurement

This book has repeatedly stressed the importance and absolute value of employees—sometimes referred to as human resources, and more recently human capital—to the success of any business organization. It has also stressed that labor expense ranks number one on any business balance sheet and that the need for effective and efficient recruitment, usage, and measurement of this resource cannot be overstated. One of the increasingly popular means of satisfying work force requirements to meet a company's specific needs relating to this important commodity is the use of contingent or temporary staff workers by more and more organizations.

Software systems and programs have been in place for a number of years for the optimum procurement and inventory requirements of industrial goods and materials, and some vendors of these programs have now turned their attention to the procurement and automation of services, including recruitment, management, and administrative processing of contingent or temporary workers. Such vendor management systems are designed for companies to work with contingent work force suppliers to gear up or gear down worker volume as needs change; acquire unique or special talent for one-time projects; shorten work fulfillment cycles; and, in so doing all of the above, reduce the cost of recruiting, screening, and training the overall work force. The U.S. Bureau of Labor Statistics estimates that almost $1.5 trillion is spent each year by U.S. corporations on contingent labor, with an expected annual growth rate of nearly 10 percent in most service categories including information technology staffing, legal and engineering services, facilities management, security, and others. These figures point to the absolute necessity of almost any company of any size automating its temporary staffing operation. A wide range of consulting and management services companies offer their own particular variety of software and systems programs to help businesses cut costs, save time and resources, and streamline their procurement processes, depending on individual company requirements. These so-called vendor management programs help the organization in procuring and managing human resources (full time as well as temporary), gaining control of service expenses, analyzing the cost of services, and monitoring vendor or supplier performance. Some systems also give resource managers the ability to have and review worker skill profiles, which may include detailed summary of skills, education, past performance, and work experience. Not much is left to chance or manual paperwork: Once contingent workers are aboard, vendor management systems can monitor and approve time reports, accumulate all process and cost information online, generate invoices, and integrate expense data into the company's financial system for settlement.

Latest vendor management systems may also include online recruitment capabilities allowing candidates to know more about the company and its benefits, apply for open positions, and have job openings mailed to them. Hiring managers could have the advantage of searchable candidate data bases, including job postings, resume collection, candidate tracking, and on-line screening, as well as on-line help and training tools.

Software and consultant firms estimate that internal cost savings of up to 30 percent may be realized by companies using their particular vendor management systems, and that costs of processing such as improving the sourcing process, reducing requisition costs, and improving project accounting could account for a savings of up to 20 percent.

Even with latest estimates that 80 to 90 percent of American firms use contingent/temporary workers, and that such workers make up 30 to 40 percent of the U.S. workforce, it is still safe to predict that full-time employees will never be extinct. However, the growing demand for Web-based automated work force procurement tools continues unabated, and the consequences of such a trend might prove an interesting subject for future debate.

e-Learning Initiatives

e-learning has been defined as a technology-based learning system involving a wide range of electronic media, with potential application to educational, industrial, political, or scientific uses. Delivery systems may include the Internet, intranets, extranets, satellite broadcasts, Web TV, and CD-ROMs. At first glance, the definition seems to apply to any aspect of our civilization, and indeed the rapidity of its spread and usage on a global basis gives some weight to that impression. Prior to the current recession, of large organizations (10,000+ employees), 63 percent were implementing or developing e-learning programs focusing mainly on corporate training and professional management. For example, some ten years ago, Bechtel Engineering launched a global approach to learning that includes "Bechtel University," an e-learning platform designed to support all internally developed training programs. Effective e-learning addresses an organization's training requirements as well as its need to use knowledge strategically and may indeed revolutionize how companies manage knowledge in the future. e-learning technology can enable and encourage workers, managers, and executives to learn and acquire new skills within the context of their own jobs and on flexible schedules.

Various state universities have banded together to provide extended learning to students via computer and Internet connection. They offer college courses of any description, and the student may attain a complete college program, degree, or certificate without ever coming on campus. Students may take a variety of courses from different universities in the program while receiving a single billing and single academic record from the student's home campus. Self-paced or moderated courses are available online and are especially valuable to disabled individuals, those with developmental disabilities, and the mentally retarded, all of whom may benefit from extended learning opportunities. Young people, especially, by having access to these convenient learning systems can develop the skills and tools they need to succeed in the new knowledge-based economy.

On the global scene, the European Union (EU) is leading the way to encourage member states to share their experience and to support and coordinate the EU's efforts to accelerate the use of extended learning education and training systems all over Europe.

The e-learning phenomenon represents another of those exciting by-products of the Internet revolution that HR specialists must have knowledge of, research, and recommend implementation if it is to have value for their particular organizations.

THE FUTURE

Considering the vast scope, interest, utility, and popularity of the Internet and World Wide Web that exist today, HR professionals and others must realize that this electronic phenomenon has even still greater potential, and that changes and developments are taking place at breathtaking speed! Recent innovations—such as the rapid explosion of broadband transmission speeds and the advent of netbooks, e-book readers, smart phones, and 3G wireless networks—should convince us that further advancements like these and other capabilities are likely on the drawing boards of hundreds of enterprising companies.

As predicted in the second edition of this book, the one-world and global community concepts are at least one step closer to reality, thanks to the Internet and the Web. HR staff should be as familiar with the Internet and its capabilities as they are, for example, with wage and hour laws. Among other advantages, the ability to post job openings at any hour of the day or night, and to browse through resumes at work or after hours at home via the Internet has changed the way the HR employment function operates. In fact, the power, capabilities, and permanence of the Internet has forever changed the operation of the entire Human Resources department, and you'll never be the same HR person you once were.

WEB SITES FOR HUMAN RESOURCES PROFESSIONALS

The Society for Human Resource Management (SHRM)
(Home Page address and Web site: *http://www.shrm.org*)

There are probably few, if any, practitioners in the personnel/human resources profession today who have not heard of (or do not belong to) the Society for Human Resource Management, more familiarly known as SHRM. Founded in 1948, the society was formerly known as The American Society for Personnel Administration (ASPA), but changed its name to more properly reflect the profession's increasing emphasis on human resources as opposed to personnel.

The Society for Human Resource Management acts as the leading voice of the human resource profession, and represents the interests of more than 250,000 individual members in over 140 countries, and has a network of more than 575 affiliated chapters in the United States, as well as offices in China and India. SHRM offers its members information and education services, conferences and seminars, government and media representation, and publications to support the advancement of human resources professionals as leaders within their own organizations.

SHRM also makes available to members, through its affiliate, the Human Resource Certification Institute, three levels of human resources certification to those individuals who qualify through examination and experience in the HR field, namely, Professional in Human Resources (PHR), Senior Professional in Human Resources (SPHR), and Global Professional in Human Resources (GPHR). Such certifications in the HR profession are becoming increasingly important to practitioners, and employers are more and more interested in finding such certifications on HR applicant resumes.

SHRM Membership Benefits
Membership in the Society for Human Research Management includes a wide variety of no-charge benefits in the areas of professional resources, publications, and research.

Free to Members
Research and Tools

▬ SHRM Online—HR Web site with features such as daily news updates, online bulletin boards, HR job openings, surveys on HR topics, and more.

▬ HR Knowledge Center—Receive assistance with HR issues or questions via e-mail, live help, assistance request form, or by phone.

■ HR Jobs—Search HR job listings with customized job alerts. Placement opportunities are available for a few, online and in print.

■ SHRM White Papers—Collection of articles written primarily by SHRM's special Expertise Panels, focusing on specific areas of HR management.

■ Samples—Sample documents on various HR topics.

■ HR Toolkits—Collection of resources, articles, links, and other resources related to a specific HR topic.

■ Express Requests—Instant information and resources on current issues impacting HR.

■ HR Basics—Database of basic HR information, checklists, and forms, and brief explanations of employment law suitable for the novice HR professional or anyone who needs a refresher.

■ HR Disciplines—Online communities for specialized HR information.

■ Webcasts—Free Webcasts including presentations by noted experts followed by Q&A sessions.

■ Membership Directory—Online database searchable by name, title, company, company size, job function, or location.

■ SHRM Mentor Program—Enables members to share knowledge and learn from fellow members.

■ Volunteer Opportunities Center—Information on volunteer opportunities within SHRM.

■ HR Talk—Forum for sharing information and best practices with SHRM members.

■ Government Affairs/Advocacy—Information on pending and enacted regulations and legislation and member involvement opportunities.

■ HR Voice—Member legislative outreach program.

■ SHRM Podcasts—Hear weekly news broadcast from SHRM that includes the latest HR news plus updates, interviews, and other features.

■ Video Interviews—View interviews with HR practitioners and industry experts discussing a wide variety of "hot" HR topics.

Publications
Publications include *HR Magazine*, *HR Week*, *Workplace Visions* (on emerging workplace issues), *SHRM Legal Report*, *Washington, DC & State Insider*, *Echoes* (for SHRM student members), and *Managing Smart* (for line managers and supervisors).

Research
SHRM Foundation Resources (supporting research and education to promote the HR profession), SHRM Research Activities and Survey

Reports (research on current and emerging workplace issues affecting HR domestically and globally) and SHRM/Rutgers LINE (measures changes in job vacancies, recruiting, new-hire compensation, and employment expectations for upcoming month).

Discounted to Members
Professional Development and Resources
PHR/SPHR and GPHR Certification (through HR Certification Institute), SHRM Learning Systems (for PHR/SPHR and GPHR prep resources), Seminars and Certificate Programs, SHRM e-Learning (over 100 online educational courses), SHRM Compensation Data Center, Customized Benchmarking Service, SHRM Store (discounted books and products), and Local Chapters (over 575 SHRM-affiliated professional local chapters).

Conferences (2010)
Sixty-second Annual Conference and Exhibition, Employment Law and Legislative Conference, Diversity Conference and Exhibition, Strategy Conference, and Staffing Management Conference and Exhibition.

Bureau of National Affairs, Inc. (BNA)
(Home Page address and Web site: *http://www@bna.com*)

The Bureau of National Affairs, Inc., is a leading publisher of print and electronic news analysis and reference products, providing intensive coverage of legal and regulatory developments for professionals in business and government. Headquartered in Washington, DC, since its founding in 1929, BNA is uniquely qualified to understand and interpret the ever-dynamic legislative climate and the forces behind it. BNA offers books, training programs, customized research, surveys, and indexing services. Its products are delivered in periodical, CD-ROM, online, book, video, or reference binder form to its many business subscribers and others.

BNA's product groups include
- New products
- All products
- Corporate law and business
- Employee benefits
- Employment and labor law
- Environment, health, and safety
- Health care
- Human resources
- Intellectual property

■ Litigation
■ Tax and accounting
■ Documents and research

In addition to the above, BNA provides information on workforce strategies, payroll, workers' compensation, EEOC compliance, and many other important and timely topics of interest to HR managers and professionals, in manual, CD, newsletter, report, or book format.

CCH, Inc. (CCH)

(Home Page address and Web site: *http://www.cch.com*)

CCH, Inc., founded in 1913 in its current form, is a leading provider of tax and business law information and software. The company tracks, reports, explains, and analyzes tax and related law, producing approximately 700 publications in print and electronic form for human resources, accounting, legal, banking, securities, insurance, government, and health care professionals. The company, currently headquartered in Riverwoods, Illinois, has always made its home in the Chicago area.

CCH is organized into four business groups, with each group focusing on a defined marketing and subject area:
■ Tax and accounting
■ Legal
■ Health-care compliance
■ Business compliance

Information is provided in a variety of media in order to meet the needs of a diverse customer base, including loose-leaf publications, CD-ROM, Internet, soft- and hardcover books and booklets, newsletters, proprietary online data base, computer disk, audio cassette, Lotus Notes, America Online, Lexis-Nexis, West Law, and CompuServe.

Many CCH products are subscription publications that are updated daily, monthly or annually, its flagship being *The Standard Federal Tax Reporter*.

Federal Government Information Sources

In addition to all of the available commercial resources, including those listed here, HR professionals should also be aware that the Internet provides them with a vast storehouse of information from the federal government. As an added advantage, much of the material may be accessed without cost and, since it resides in the public domain, may be freely used and quoted, so long as users credit the source appropriately. In addition, due to the rapid development and expansion of the World Wide Web, navigating it to obtain the desired information becomes ever easier.

Some of the primary federal government sources of Internet HR information are given below:

United States Department of Labor (DOL)
(Home Page and Web site: *http://www.dol.gov/*)

The home page of the U.S. Department of Labor (DOL) contains a great deal of data on the department itself, including its history and mission, how it is organized, portraits of the secretaries of labor, major statutes, and links to other data sources, including a link for regulatory and statutory information. From there, you can determine the laws and regulations administered by the DOL, text of some of the statutes and executive orders, proposed regulations, and compliance assistance information.

Reporting to the Secretary of Labor are some thirty offices, administrations, or bureaus, including the following, which should be of more than passing interest to HR professionals: Wage and Hour Division, Office of Safety and Health Administration, Women's Bureau, Office of Disability Employment Policy, and Office of Federal Contract Compliance Programs.

Another interesting feature you will find in the DOL Internet data is a reference to the Economics and Statistics Administration (ESA), whose key responsibilities include the compilation of all statistical, economic, and demographic information collected by the federal government. These data are then made available to the public through the bureaus and offices of the Department of Commerce, known collectively as the Economics and Statistics Administration.

The various ESA departments and work groups, include:
- The Bureau of the Census—the nation's fact finder
- The Bureau of Economic Analysis—the nation's accountant, gathering and interpreting voluminous data to draw a complete and consistent picture of the U.S. economy
- STAT-USA—a giant information service providing economic, business, and social/environmental program data produced by more than fifty federal sources
- ESA reports and working papers

The Wage and Hour Division of the DOL's Employment Standards Administration provides compliance assistance materials on the Internet in the form of handy reference guides, as well as Fact Sheets on a wide variety of topics, all under the Fair Labor Standards Act. These subjects, among many others, include:
- Retail industry
- Manufacturing establishments

- Exemption for executives, administrative, professional, and outside sales employees
- Record-keeping requirements
- Overtime pay requirements
- Section H-2A of the Immigration Reform and Control Act
- New businesses under the FLSA
- Family and Medical Leave Act of 1993

The DOL also includes the Center for Faith-Based and Community Initiatives (CFBCI), which seeks to empower faith-based and community organizations (FBCO) as these organizations help their neighbors enter, succeed, and thrive in the workforce. Specifically, the DOL has reshaped its policies and programs to respect, embrace, and empower faith-based and community organizations that act as "social entrepreneurs" in local communities across America and around the world. The work of the CFBCI at the U.S. Department of Labor stems from a simple conviction: Americans can do better for our neighbors in need when we draw upon the unique strengths of every willing partner.

It is part of the DOL's mission to foster a prepared, competitive, safe, and secure workforce through the CFBCI organizations in order to help more individuals overcome barriers to employment, find jobs, and stay employed. These collaborative efforts have produced innovative public–private partnerships that decrease unemployment and recidivism among prisoners; increase access to publicly funded employment resources in low-income communities; help homeless veterans find housing and jobs; withdraw and prevent children from entering exploitive child labor around the world; increase workplace safety outreach to Spanish-speaking workers; and much more.

HR professionals have always been in the forefront of promoting limited equivalents of faith-based initiatives in their respective communities. Now in cooperation with the DOL many more individuals can be reached and much more can be accomplished!

AJE. The Department of Labor sponsors America's Job Exchange (*http://www.americasjobexchange.com*) job site that connects "good people with good jobs." AJE offers the same national labor exchange services that DOL's America's Job Bank (AJB) previously provided (AJB ended operations on July 1, 2007), and will also offer additional services including job spidering and Web services. Site visitors use the same screens and functions as AJB, ensuring a seamless transition between sites. And finally, the Key to Career Success Web site (*http://www.careeronestop.org/MilitaryTransition/*) is sponsored by the DOL as part of the Department's assistance to service members, military families, and employers.

U.S. Bureau of Labor Statistics (BLS)

(Home Page and Web site: *http://stats.bls.gov:80*)

This federal government agency is the source of survey, statistical, and other data frequently used in the human resource function, including:

- Surveys and programs
- BLS information
- Economy at a glance
- Publications
- Research papers
- Regional information
- Feedback
- Keyword search of BLS Web pages

By entering desired searches on subjects such as employee benefits, compensation, turnover, health and safety standards, or whatever HR subject you may be interested in, you follow the links on the screen that guide you sequentially from the general to the specific topic you are seeking. Experienced human resources professionals are already aware of the traditional gold mine of information contained in the Bureau of Labor Statistics. BLS access via the Internet will now make the mining process easier and more productive.

Occupational Safety and Health Administration (OSHA)

(Home Page and Web site: *http://www.osha.gov/*)

One hundred fifty-five million working men and women in the United States, together with their 7.7 million employers, are covered by the Occupational Safety and Health Act of 1970 (OSHA). This law is administered by the U.S. Department of Labor's Occupational Safety and Health Administration in partnership with the federal and state governments, all of whose mission is to save lives, prevent injuries, and protect the health of America's workers. OSHA began fiscal year 2007 with a staff of 2,150, including 1,100 inspectors plus discrimination complaint investigators, engineers, physicians, educators, standards writers, and other technical support staff in area and regional offices throughout the country.

A listing of the various services OSHA offers on its Internet home page include:

- Information about OSHA
- Directories
- Media releases
- Publications

- Programs and services
- Compliance assistance
- Federal register notices
- Frequently asked questions
- Statistics and data
- Standards
- Safety and health Internet sites

Similar to other divisions of the U.S. Department of Labor, OSHA is continually seeking feedback from employee surveys, in meetings with employee and employer groups, and from focus group discussions with workers from many plants and industries around the country, in efforts to upgrade and improve the quality of performance in delivering services.

Academic Information Sources

Various colleges and universities across the nation are also involved in providing management and human resource information to Internet users. As previously mentioned in this chapter, the difficulty in assessing the value of these and other sources is the uncertainty of not knowing whether such entities will continue to be viable and have Web sites in the future; however, shown below are two academic sources that will probably have Internet sites for some time to come.

Cornell University School of Industrial and Labor Relations (ILR)
(Home Page and Web site: *http://www.ilr.cornell.edu/*)

Cornell's ILR's Virtual Library on the Internet displays the following partial subject index that would be of interest to unionized companies, although a number of subjects would apply to the nonunion business, as well.

- Behavior at Work—Psychology; sociology; communication
- Compensation and Fringe Benefits—Compensation management, policies, and theories; wage systems; enterprise, government, and labor union benefit plans
- Current Contracts—Negotiations in progress between specific companies and unions; strikes over contracts; collective agreements reached and evaluated
- Economics and Business—Enterprise, government, and labor union policies; economic conditions; cost of living; productivity statistics
- Education and Training—Enterprise, government, and labor union programs; scholarships; vocational rehabilitation
- Employee Representation—Labor union organizing activities; unionization and representation elections; labor union memberships statistics and trends

■ Human Resource Management—Employment procedures; absenteeism; employment discrimination and fair employment practices; office procedures; retirement policies; placement; performance appraisal

■ Industrial Engineering—Data processing technology; human factors engineering; time and motion studies; production standards; work measurement; data security; manufacturing technology; technology transfer; technological development

■ International Relations and Governments

■ Labor and Industrial History—Development and evolution of workers' movements and labor unions; labor union structure, legal status; industrial development

■ Labor Force and Labor Market—Enterprise, government, and labor union manpower policies; employment and unemployment; labor force statistics

■ Labor-Management Relations—Industrial relations; labor-management cooperation; participative management; antiunionism

■ Negotiation Process and Dispute Settlement—Collective bargaining theory and statistics; labor disputes; strikes over grievances; arbitration, mediation, grievance procedures

■ Research Institutes and Academic Programs

■ Safety and Health—Enterprise, government, and labor union programs; government safety and health standards; hazardous substances and occupations; accident, sickness, and mortality statistics; industrial and transportation security

■ Socioeconomic, Political, and Ethical Issues—Position of enterprise, labor unions, and professional groups; enterprise and labor union community activities; ethical issues and behavior in society

University of Southern California (USC), Department of Government Documents

(Home Page and Web site: *http://libguides.usc.edu/govdocs*)

USC's Government Documents Department is an excellent depository for federal, state of California, and Canadian documents. In particular, the federal government web sites allow human resources surfers to explore many locations that should be of more than casual interest to them. These sites include:

■ Administration on Aging

■ Code of Federal Regulations (CFR)—Allows the viewer to search the complete CFR

■ Environmental Protection Agency

■ Federal Grant Information

■ Government Printing Office

■ Superintendent of Documents Home Page

■ Health and Human Services Department
■ Health Care Financing Administration
■ Labor Department—Including America's Job Bank (listing job opportunities that can be searched by job category) and Bureau of Labor Statistics
■ Library of Congress
■ National Institutes of Health
■ National Performance Review
■ Social Security Administration
■ Supreme Court—Searchable Supreme Court decisions, 1990 to present
■ Veterans Affairs

At other sites, full text is included of the *Congressional Record* for recent sessions of Congress, NASA, and the White House.

The Library of Congress
(Home Page and Web site: *http://www.loc.gov*)

One particular Web site in the above listing merits special attention and mention. The Library of Congress, probably the most voluminous and prestigious library in the world, offers to the Internet citizen expansive data on research and reference data bases and resources; acquisitions, cataloging, preservation, special programs and services, publications, and historical collections—much of which, though not directly related to human resource endeavors, is noteworthy if only for the fact that from our offices at home or work, at any time of the day or night, we have the opportunity to access one of the premier information sources on earth.

FINAL THOUGHTS ON THE INTERNET
The versatility of this medium of global communication seems to be endless. With many new potentials and possibilities still to come, the Internet permits its cybercitizens to:
■ access literally a world of information from a wide variety of companies and institutions, universities, and government agencies, some by subscription and some for free, but all of great value to the human resource practitioner and other professionals;
■ send and receive messages via electronic mail (e-mail), and communicate with other citizens at work, in professional, family, or social groups, or anywhere on earth;
■ join in one of the thousands of electronic discussion groups with persons of similar interest—such as human resources personnel—throughout the world;

▬ view artists' works and tour museums in all the major capitals of the world;

▬ purchase books, cars, or any number of other products and services offered by the hundreds of thousands of advertisers on the Internet;

▬ post job openings on Web sites;

▬ check resumes posted on the Web for that ideal candidate for the management slot you've been trying to fill.

Corporate Intranets and Human Resource Tools

As stated previously in this chapter, the Internet can be thought of as a global worldwide network of networks—a pipeline or superhighway circling the earth and picking up and providing data and information of every conceivable kind from and to anyone who has access to it. But now we have the intranet, a *private* information network within a corporation, rather than on a global scale, designed in general to provide employees with whatever information they may need in order to do their jobs. Current somewhat sophisticated intranets can also include links to customers, vendors, suppliers and whatever else the mind of an IT specialist can conceive. Originally, the most avid advocates of the use and expansion of intranet technologies were the human resources, communications, and sales and marketing departments where performance depends in large measure on the interacting with people and providing them with all necessary documentation as well as any other verbal or written data essential to success.

Examples of useful intranet data for employees from a human resources standpoint might include, though not be limited to, job opportunities, wage and salary ranges, job descriptions, personnel policy manuals, corporate announcements and bulletins on new projects or processes, benefit eligibility data, annual benefit sign-ups online, and changing options or funds in 401(k) programs. Workers, supervisors, managers, and executives with the proper identification codes may have access to intranet information either at work and/or from their own personal computers at home. Intranets are also designed to serve and provide data to any company employee at any work site, no matter how distant or remote.

Much of the data stored on an intranet is often of a proprietary, highly sensitive, and confidential nature and must be closely guarded and maintained with the strictest privacy. Normally, user ID's, passwords, and/or personal identification numbers (PINs), based on the individual's job level in the organization are the means of controlling and guaranteeing the privacy of the data. So-called firewalls are built into the system, and the data are protected via authorized user codes similar to automated teller machines. One especially valuable intranet item might be a leadership section designed to help company managers and supervisors perform their managerial duties more effectively. This part might consist of a library of company policies applicable to managers, as well as various articles and information from management experts on recommended methods of supervising employees.

Intranets may be developed internally by HR professionals working with competent company IT departments or by contracting with software vendors providing turnkey intranet technology packages. Individual company needs, program capabilities, ease of access and navigation, and budgetary limitations as to installation and maintenance costs are all factors, of course, in deciding on the proper system to choose. Intranet programs may be set up using a single common browser thus significantly reducing corporate expenses owing to decreased training and communication costs. In addition, intranet costs per user are much less in comparison with Internet installations based on a two-tiered client-server structure. But the real savings of the intranet involves the many hours saved by human resources and other departments when the intranet obviates the need for handling a myriad of phone calls and repeated questions on such topics as company policies, employee benefits, job descriptions, and wage and salary ranges. And even though a higher level of intranet design and complexity (and expense) may be involved, having employees do their own annual benefit sign-ups, for example, and changing their personal and demographic information online would certainly make an HR specialist's life easier and provide many more needed hours to perform more productive duties. (And be sure a Frequently Asked Questions, FAQs, display is *always* included and updated in your company intranet.)

One of your biggest human resources challenges, however, might be in convincing your workforce that any intranet system is only valuable and worth the effort *if* it is used by the employees. Ongoing communication to new hires as well as current employees of the existence of an intranet (and the importance of using it) could be one of the HR department's most important functions.

Webmasters

Large and small companies use this function to handle the coordination, management, marketing, and all other aspects—technical as well as nontechnical—of the Internet.

As might be expected, the title and function of such a job will vary from company to company, but a key point to be considered is that even though the Webmaster is responsible for the overall Internet operation, including the company's home page and Web sites, we should probably think in terms of function rather than as a full-time job in itself. In most cases, the Webmaster will have other duties and should therefore be the type of individual who thrives on a full plate of job responsibilities.

Employee Abuses of the Internet

As noted in the introduction of other new products or services into the business world, employers are now showing increasing concern about losses in productivity among workers who abuse the Internet by exploring nonbusiness-related topics on the World Wide Web.

While there are software programs available to restrict access to Internet sites, the wise employer simply makes it known to employees that such conduct is unacceptable and will be dealt with and discipline assessed in the same manner as for any other infraction of company rules or regulations.

Employees should also be cautioned about the misuse of e-mail privileges and that the Internet and corporate e-mail systems are not private. In most companies, messages sent by e-mail are usually stored on hard disks or tapes in company historical archives. Even if sender and receiver delete e-mail messages in their mailboxes, such messages can still be saved in company backup files. Legal problems could result for both employee and the company if Internet and e-mail policies are not followed and monitored.

CHAPTER PERSPECTIVE

In this chapter the phenomenal, worldwide communications system known as the Internet was discussed. We examined the origin, history, and development of this revolutionary communications network and its effect on the millions of people all over the world who now make up this incredible scientific achievement. We discussed the hardware and software necessary in order to gain access to the Internet. A definition and explanation of service providers was given, and it was then pointed out how human resources managers and professionals can and should take advantage of the almost limitless knowledge and information that the Internet represents, including e-learning initiatives for all internally developed training programs.

The home page and World Wide Web features of the Internet were explained, and a number of reliable and respected information sources for human resources practitioners on the World Wide Web was described in detail.

The types of human resources/personnel information available from all of these various sources was listed and described in some detail, and the home page or Web site address to access each of them was provided.

Descriptions were also given of restricted company communications systems—intranets—and the advisability of appointing one individual to coordinate and manage an organization's Internet operations (known as a Webmaster) was also discussed. Advice was given to organizations about the proper means of dealing with employees who explore Internet nonbusiness-related topics on company time with resulting losses in productivity.

Disciplinary policies were also discussed in relation to problems of employees misusing e-mail communications at work, together with possible legal liabilities for the company as well as the employees involved.

The new direction of software vendors in turning their attention to the procurement and automation of recruiting and managing temporary employees was discussed in some detail.

The Evolving and Future Role of Human Resources

INTRODUCTION AND MAIN POINTS

This chapter focuses on the expanded role and responsibilities of the human resources function. The strategic, as opposed to the traditional bureaucratic, role of human resources is gaining recognition in the modern business world, as human resources becomes the leader in areas such as manpower planning, diversity programs, community programs, and management training. Company priorities determine how the people department is valued, and whether or not HR executives will represent this important function at Board of Directors meetings.

Human resources is viewed as an excellent background for a CEO position and as a prerequisite for other executive positions. A vital and critical function that reaches into every aspect of the employer-employee relationship, human resources is seen as an area of growth and an excellent career path.

After you read the material in this chapter:

— You will understand how the human resources function is involved in all aspects of the employer-employee relationship.

— You will see that the complexity of the modern world, with its legislation and other new cultural needs, has expanded the role of the human resources function.

— You will recognize the critical need for human resources representation on the Board of Directors.

— You will see human resources as an appropriate background for the CEO and other positions.

— You will understand that human resources is a growing area and a viable career path.

AN EXPANDING ROLE

Much has been said and written in recent years concerning the increasingly important role the human resources or personnel function plays in the infrastructure of the modern business organization. Gone is the "smiling and filing" image (Jac Fitz-enz, *The ROI of Human Capital*) of the personnel department so prevalent some two or three decades ago. (The "picnic, parking and paperwork" department moniker might also fit the personnel function at that time.) But as pointed out in preceding chapters, today's human resources department in any business corporation is very much involved, sometimes in great detail, with practically every phase of an employee's life and service with a business. Should we be doing anything less for the company's most important asset?

The human resources department has the awesome responsibility at all times of dealing with and overseeing this most important, complex, and valuable commodity or resource any company can have—its people. As this key responsibility of this most vital department begins to be more recognized and better understood by top company managements, the *strategic*, as opposed to the stereotypical *bureaucratic* role of human resources is being acknowledged in ever-increasing numbers of company boardrooms and CEO offices within industry and throughout the business community.

If we look at HR's role as a profit center—even if it is sometimes an indirect one—it begins to become even more apparent as human resources departments lead the way in

1) corporate manpower planning.
2) designing and developing present and future work force diversity programs.
3) creating and maintaining a positive company image in training and counseling services for disadvantaged youths, and other local community action programs.
4) successful negotiation and dealings with unions, where applicable.
5) education and training of company supervisors and managers in the proper handling of discrimination and wrongful termination charges in order to protect the company against potential monumental punitive and/or compensatory damages and other awards in jury trials.
6) researching, analyzing, and recommending new employee involvement programs dealing with assessment, empowerment, reengineering, and team-building concepts.

And all of these activities, whether the company is an established Fortune 1000 one or a fledgling five-employee operation, are essential and important to the success of the company now, and to its survival in the future.

Community Consciousness

Just as society's economic and social views of the world are fast changing to a one-world concept, so the successful business organization must understand that it can no longer operate in a vacuum of self-interest and isolation from the problems and concerns of the community in which it is located. Farsighted CEOs rightly communicate to their executives, managers, and operative people that business organizations in the United States operate only with the permission and tolerance of the American public, and that, therefore, business has the obligation to act at all times in a responsible manner to the people it serves, whether in establishing the quality and pricing of its products, complying with federal, state, and local laws and ordinances, maintaining appearance standards, obeying local zoning regulations, having genuine concern for environmental matters, and so forth.

Good Neighbor Policy

More and more U.S. companies are realizing and acting on the premise that just as good residential neighborhoods depend upon the goodwill, cooperation, and sharing of the individual neighbors involved, these same attitudes apply equally as well to a corporate neighbor. In a rather strict sense, the corporation is accepted and permitted to operate in the neighborhood in which its office, plant, building, or other facility is located, and it should reciprocate and recognize its obligation of being a really good neighbor!

While there is no question that being a corporate good neighbor may be equated by some as simply a matter of good business (and who can deny that it is), nevertheless, the increasing involvement of shareholders, the media, environmentalists, and other groups makes it imperative that companies be aware of and constantly strive to improve their corporate as well as public image.

Executives from companies both large and small are permitted and encouraged to volunteer hours, days, or are even loaned out for periods of time to organizations such as United Way, Junior Achievement, Big Brothers and Sisters, and other forms of charitable and public service. In the past, AT&T has made public commitments to provide employees with a paid day off for volunteering or performing a public service. American Express, Xerox, The Gap, and other civic-minded organizations make every effort to teach, train, and work with disadvantaged youth and adults to help prepare them to enter the work force, or to change occupations when downsizing or layoffs result in calamitous family and financial situations.

There are many serious problems in our world that require much thought and attention, but as more and more companies provide for these types of commitments in their operating budgets, the lot of many potential workers will improve, society will benefit, and the reputation of big (as well as small) business cannot help but improve.

Whatever the issue, charitable, civic, or social, the corporation has the obligation to act as a good neighbor in the community in which it operates. The company's human resources staff can and should be instrumental in making sure this good neighbor policy is in operation at all company locations.

PRIORITIES WITHIN A COMPANY

Based on the major obligations and responsibilities of the human resources function, it becomes apparent that because people are the most important asset of any organization, the people department must necessarily command a prominent place in the company leadership hierarchy. As indicated above, this is beginning to happen in some companies, while, in others, top management has no idea what projects or activities the human resources department handles, and, in some cases, it literally does not even know on what floor its people department is located and sometimes make little effort to find out. This is a sad commentary, since it says so much about the value such companies place on their most important asset!

Recognition of the importance of the human resources function in the business community has been gradual and slow, but it is beginning to happen. In the typical large corporation, the marketing, finance, engineering, and production areas still continue to receive priority emphasis and attention, with the exception perhaps being those occasions when, for example, major discrimination or wage and hour problems arise and the human resources head is asked to give a full accounting to top management as to the causes and circumstances of the matter. It is undeniable that these above-named functions are vital to the success of any organization, no matter how large or small, but in many instances, practically the only time full attention is focused on the people aspect of the business is when sales are off, inventories up, or profits down, and the rumors begin to circulate throughout the plant that layoffs and a reduction in force are imminent. Our most important asset now commands attention simply because, as usually happens in difficult times, it once again becomes the most expendable asset.

On the other hand, prior to the current very difficult financial and business recession, there still were companies that guaranteed their people employment after a specified number of years of service. And although production-line workers might suddenly find themselves in the sales department—or sales people on the assembly floor—they all appreciated the fact that they were *still* employed; and they doubtless gave 100 percent effort regardless of the nature of their new job and surroundings to which they were assigned.

THE HUMAN RESOURCES MANAGER, THE BOARD OF DIRECTORS, AND THE CEO

With all of the key responsibilities and duties of the human resources function, it follows with some logic that the head of that department merits a seat on the company or corporate board of directors alongside the representatives of the legal, finance, manufacturing, accounting, and other departments or divisions. There is no one more qualified than the manager, director, or vice president of human resources to best represent the interests of the employees of the enterprise, and to provide information and guidance to the board concerning personnel policies, practices, and procedures. The one area in which confusion often reigns supreme in these meetings is on the very subject of personnel or human resources (in other words, people matters). As a board member, the human resources executive can literally function as a gyroscope to add balance to the proceedings and enable the board to deliberate on important matters on the basis of fact and truth rather than on guesswork and those ever-popular glittering generalities. The overwhelming personalities on the board will continue to quote those impressive-sounding but often erroneous statistics relating to people, employment, and other HR matters of concern, but the capable human resources member who has the real, unvarnished facts, and doesn't hesitate to make the rest of the board aware of them, can be of invaluable assistance in helping the other members distinguish between perception and reality.

In the future, human resources executives will represent the company's most important asset on company boards. Today, union leaders, clergy members, and dissident shareholders are often appointed to the boards of major corporations. Tomorrow, human resource directors or vice presidents will be recognized to be in the best position within a corporation to speak for the men and women of the company. Human resources executives know the most about the opinions and attitudes of the company's employees and about personnel law, company personnel policies, compensation, benefits, diversity, and other employee issues. A board of directors should include representation from each of the major operational elements of the organization, including one of the most important elements, the personnel or human resources function.

In order to fulfill such a role, of course, the human resources executive must be one who

■ demonstrates outstanding leadership and competency;

■ is admired as a genuine people person; and

■ consistently relates to the needs, concerns, problems, and potential of the employees of the enterprise.

While ideal people executives maximize these qualities partially from a sense of social or community responsibility, they are also well aware that, in a very real sense, it's just plain good business practice to do so. If the emphasis is on people, all other advantages follow, and there can be no limit to the company's potential progress and success.

What better candidate for the CEO job than a human resources executive to whom the emphasis on people is simply second nature? Of course, this person must also have a grasp of finance and marketing principles, legal matters, and computer technology, combined with a certain amount of that intangible charisma that every good leader must possess. Insofar as surrounding himself or herself with capable if not outstanding executives, who should have more ability to recruit and select people than the head of human resources? Where better to expect to find that most necessary CEO quality of good interpersonal skills than in this particular executive?

There should be no doubt in anyone's mind that such human resources executives exist today, and that they become more and more qualified for top executive echelon positions as they continue to meet and resolve the same kind of complex people-related problems that modern CEOs must cope with and that increasingly demand more of their time and attention. Aspiring human resources executives must, of course, work diligently to increase their expertise in the many other required aspects of corporate leadership, but as the era of individual and employee rights continues to expand, qualified human resources practitioners will find their corporate ladder of success reaching ever closer to the top level of the organization.

LEARNING ABOUT THE HUMAN RESOURCES PROFESSION

Experienced practitioners in the personnel or human resources field must understand their responsibility to encourage and inform their own staffs, personnel trainees and interns, as well as interested college students and recent graduates, about overall potential of the human resources profession. It should be stressed that a career in human resources can be the beginning of a promising business career, and that it can lead to the top job in the company. They must understand that knowledge of other business disciplines, such as marketing, finance, sales, and manufacturing, are also necessary qualifications for those interested in making it all the way to the top.

As it becomes known that such upward job potential exists in the human resources profession, more highly qualified candidates should be encouraged to consider a career move or change to the human resources field. Regardless of a person's ultimate career choice, experience in human resources can give a good, basic grounding in people relationships, company policies and organization, and a firsthand exposure to the philosophy and culture of the organization. For those whose goals involve supervisory or management responsibilities, there is no better training ground anywhere in the company than in the human resources function.

Although even today applications for the human resources department exceed the number of openings, in the future it will be one of the most popular and sought-after professions. Experience in human resources will be a prerequisite training stop on all executive management career paths. The problem might be, however, that once they experience human resources, aspiring managers and executives might discover that this is really the career they have been seeking.

CHAPTER PERSPECTIVE
This chapter examined how human resources responsibilities have grown and how the role of human resources in the business world has gradually become more important in modern times. HR was viewed as being involved in every stage of an employee's career with a company, including retirement and beyond. As the people department, human resources was seen as the most appropriate representative of a company's most important asset at board of directors meetings. As a discipline, human resources was seen as an excellent background or prerequisite for the CEO, managerial, and other positions. It was also seen as a currently growing employment area and an excellent career path.

Glossary

AAP (Affirmative Action Plan) plan or program originated by an employer to demonstrate support of and compliance with civil rights legislation. Such plans generally indicate the company's current minority population and stipulate its future plans and programs for increasing minority as well as female participation in hiring and promotion. For all practical purposes, government contractors are required to have and comply with affirmative action plans.

ADA (Americans with Disabilities Act) (as amended) 1992 law prohibiting discrimination in employment due to an individual's physical or mental disability; requires reasonable accommodation on the part of the company to assist the disabled person in performing the job.

ADEA (Age Discrimination in Employment Act) act passed in 1967 and amended in 1978 and 1986 that prohibits employers with over twenty employees from discharging or discriminating in any way against their employees who are age 40 or older, because of their age.

Bargaining unit employee unit appropriate for collective bargaining (especially in representation elections) between employers and unions, as determined by the National Labor Relations Board. The commonality of interests among employees is one of the primary criteria in the Board's bargaining unit decisions.

Benchmarking program in which businesses send their employees to visit other firms to discover new ways of running a company and handling its problems.

Blind ad newspaper or magazine advertisement for employment, requesting replies to a post office box number rather than listing the company name, address, or phone number.

BLS (U.S. Bureau of Labor Statistics) federal government agency that is the source of survey, statistical, and other data frequently used in the human resources function, business groups, personnel associations, and a variety of other sources.

Broadbanding a wage system that eliminates multiple salary grades and replaces them with a few in order to encourage more movement among jobs.

Chain of command managerial or supervisory reporting function within any organization or company.

Civil Rights Act, 1964 act that contains Title VII, which, together with Executive Order 11246, forever outlawed discrimination in the United States on the basis of race, color, religion, sex, or national origin. This prohibition against unlawful discrimination applies to all terms and conditions of employment, including hiring, discharge, and promotion.

COBRA (Consolidated Omnibus Budget Reconciliation Act, 1985)(as amended) act that states employers with twenty or more employees are legally bound under COBRA to provide their former employees (as well as the families of these employees) the opportunity to purchase the same health care (medical and dental) group coverage that they had been receiving from their employer and that would normally cease at the time they left the company for any reason, other than gross misconduct.

Direct deposit program that allows employees to authorize their employer to make automatic deposits from their paychecks directly into their checking and/or savings accounts in any financial institution.

Diversity overall process of assimilation, training, promotion, management, and implementation of ever-increasing numbers of minority personnel into the industrial work force. Human resource leaders must consider rapid implementation of the diversity concept a prime target and priority within their own organizations.

Downsizing scaling back of numbers of employees in order for a company to become more efficient and profitable.

Drug-free environment policy determination made and communicated by a company that it will make every reasonable effort (including applicant and employee drug testing) to create and maintain a working environment free from illegal drug use, possession, or sale within its organization.

EEOC (Equal Employment Opportunity Commission) a specific federal body created by the Civil Rights Act of 1964 to oversee and enforce the provisions of this law banning discrimination, especially in the workplace.

e-learning initiatives a technology-based learning system involving a wide range of electronic media with potential application to educational, industrial, political, or scientific uses. Delivery systems may include the Internet, intranet, extranet, satellite broadcasts, Web TV, and CD-ROMs.

Employment-at-will concept maintained by most employers that any employment relationship is *at will*, that it may be terminated by either party—employer or employee—at any time, and that only the president of the company has the right to make any other arrangements to the contrary. Various court cases, decisions, and opinions may be found upholding or rejecting the at-will doctrine.

Empowerment act of giving workers more power and authority to make decisions that affect their own jobs.

EPPA (Employee Polygraph Protection Act, 1988) law that prohibits polygraph testing by employers except under somewhat limited and restricted conditions. Lie detector tests may not be given to job applicants and may be used only when there is clear evidence a theft of money or property has occurred on employer's premises. Some states prohibit polygraph testing altogether.

Ergonomics *Merriam Webster's Collegiate Dictionary*, Eleventh Edition, defines ergonomics (also called "human engineering") as an applied science concerned with designing and arranging things people use so that the people and things interact most efficiently and safely.

ERISA (Employee Retirement Income Security Act, 1974) law administered by U.S. Department of Labor that protects retirees' and employees' rights regarding retirement, health, and welfare plans. Employers are held to rigid accountability standards including provision that all retirement plan assets be held in trust, together with strict fiduciary responsibilities.

ESOP (Employee Stock Ownership Plan) a type of profit-sharing program in which an employer allocates shares of company stock to eligible employees, based on a percentage formula relating to annual company profitability. Employee eligibility is normally based on the individual's length of service, with the actual number of shares awarded each person determined by a ratio of his or her annual wage or salary.

Exemption status classification of each job in an organization to determine whether or not it is exempt from the provisions of the Fair Labor Standards Act, especially the overtime provision of the act. Specific salary and other criteria tests must be applied (normally by company compensation personnel) to determine eligibility for executive, administrative, professional, outside sales, computer-related occupations, and highly compensated employee exemptions.

Fair Credit Reporting Act, 1970 (as amended) employers who require investigative-type consumer reports on current or prospective employees must advise these individuals in writing that information about their character, general reputation, or personal characteristics may be disclosed in such reports.

Fluctuating Workweek provision of the Fair Labor Standards Act that allows companies to set up a weekly paid, nonexempt, guaranteed salary method of compensation without the need to pay time and one-half for overtime hours. If employees' working hours vary such that they can never be sure of specific beginning or ending of daily work shift duties, employees may be classified on Fluctuating Workweek and paid half-time for all overtime hours; however, if employees work any amount of time during the work week, the employer must pay them the weekly salary guarantee.

FMLA (Family and Medical Leave Act, 1993) (as amended) law requiring covered employers to provide up to 12 weeks of unpaid, job-protected leave to eligible employees for certain family and medical reasons. The employer must maintain employees' current health coverage under any existing group health plan during FMLA leave.

Globalization operation of a company or business without regard to international borders. Instead of operating from their home country, companies go where their customers and clients are, and using foreign nationals, they establish manufacturing and service facilities in order to serve those customers.

Health Insurance Portability and Accountability Act of 1996 (HIPAA) law to protect and insure the health coverage of people who switch from one job to another. Generally eliminates restrictions based on health status. First major step toward health care reform in United States.

Home page first or primary screen (page) of a particular organization's total presence on the Internet; used by advertisers, in particular, to display company's logo, mission statement, general company information, and listings of what it offers to viewers.

Human capital one of the major themes of this book is the value of an individual to an organization. The experience, competency, education, and training a company's most valuable asset (i.e., its people) bring to the job all add up to "human capital."

Human engineering see "Ergonomics" buzzword definition. Also applies to "human engineering."

Human resources function that deals with all aspects of a company's employees; usually administered by a human resources (or personnel) department responsible for employment, compensation, benefits, equal employment opportunity, employee counseling, personnel software and hardware systems, retirement matters—and all other phases of employer-employee relationships.

Information superhighway Internet, the World Wide Web, linking together people of all nations through electronic communication.

Internet huge collection of interconnected electronic networks spanning the globe and relying on well-defined communications protocols. An electronic pipeline or information superhighway made up of millions of individual computers (nodes) connected to a network, with data and information of practically every kind flowing through and on it; an outgrowth of military and scientific computing networks developed by Rand Corporation and the Pentagon.

Intranets networks that may be thought of as miniature Internets offering the business organization all the qualities and features of the Internet, but on a corporate rather than global scale.

IRCA (Immigration Reform and Control Act, 1986) (as amended) attempt by Congress to eliminate the illegal practice of employers hiring unauthorized alien workers for their companies. All employers, regardless of size, are subject to the provisions of IRCA.

Job description written description of the duties and responsibilities of a particular job function in an organization or company, prepared by the wage and salary analysts of the human resources department. The job description should begin with an initial summary paragraph indicating the job's general duties and responsibilities, followed by subsequent paragraphs describing in some detail the general duties referred to in the summary paragraph. The job description should relate only to the required duties of the position and never to the qualifications of the current or prospective incumbent. It should be written clearly and succinctly. Seldom recommended to exceed one page in length, it must give a reader unfamiliar with the job a clear understanding of what the job entails.

Job evaluation formal system of analyzing and evaluating jobs based on the duties and responsibilities of the individual job. Job evaluation attempts through a given rating plan to determine the relative weight of the function, and its overall importance to the company. The wage and salary analysts of the human resources department normally have the responsibility of performing the job evaluation process.

Job questionnaire form document used by human resources wage and salary personnel to gather data from job incumbents and/or managers in preparation for job evaluation projects. The questionnaire asks incumbents about day-to-day duties and responsibilities, including type and nature of work performed, frequency and level of contacts, difficulty of the work, decisions made, and so on. The questionnaire is used as a supplement to personal interviews with job incumbents.

LAN (Local Area Network) network of computers linked together in a restricted or local area, most often in a single building or adjacent group of buildings, in a specific department or floor of a building, and so forth.

Lilly Ledbetter Fair Pay Act of 2009 this law addressess the pay equity concept with special emphasis on the timing and filing of a charge of discrimination in an equal-pay lawsuit. This legislation amending the Civil Rights Act of 1964 provides that the 180-day statute of limitations for filing an equal-pay lawsuit regarding pay discrimination resets with each new discriminatory paycheck delivered to the complainant.

Management by Objectives (MBO) top down sequential, formal, and cooperative method of setting and developing organizational goals and their supporting objectives at each level of the organization. MBO addresses key result areas such as profitability, productivity, market share, customer service, satisfaction, employee training, career development and performance, corporate image, conservation of resources, public responsibility, and ethics. MBO's five procedural steps include: identification of key result areas, setting performance standards, creating objective measures of performance, appraising performance, and mutually determining ways to improve performance.

Management by Walking Around (MBWA) theory that managers cannot possibly do an effective job of supervising others unless they leave their office or desk to observe and collect data and impressions by informal visits to work sites and areas.

Merit pay method of compensating employees based on established company standards of performance. More and more companies are now installing merit pay systems and eliminating automatic wage increases based on time on the job or overall seniority.

Modem acronym for *mo*dulator, *dem*odulator, a device connecting a computer to a phone line allowing computers to talk to each other over the phone system, thus providing access to the Internet.

Multiculturalism political or social philosophy promoting cultural diversity. This philosophy is supported by many educators in the United States who favor the teaching of different cultures so that they may be understood and appreciated. This teaching, known as multicultural education, especially relates to the contribution of women, non-Europeans, and people of Hispanic ancestry to our society.

Organization chart graphic representation of jobs or positions within a company, department, or other unit. Chart depicts jobs and job titles, reporting relationships, and the number of current or authorized incumbents on each job; used by wage and salary analysts as an important tool in job evaluation.

OSHA (Occupational Safety and Health Act, 1970) act, also known as the Williams-Steiger Act, which requires virtually every employer in the United States to furnish its employees with a place of employment literally free from any safety hazards likely to cause death or serious injuries to them. The law empowers OSHA representatives to levy fines and assessments on employers who do not maintain an environment of safety and protection at work sites.

Outsourcing practice of hiring vendors or other outside companies to perform work previously done within a given company. Such decisions by corporations to farm out work to other organizations are normally based on cost/value judgments considering both economy and effectiveness.

Payroll cards workers' wages are downloaded onto a plastic card (resembling a credit card) by which they can then make debit-like purchases, make ATM withdrawals, and shop on-line. Eliminates waiting in line to cash paycheck and the need to carry larger amounts of cash. People with no checking accounts find these cards especially convenient.

People principle principle practiced by a company when it shows genuine respect for its employees (whether union or nonunion), and recognizes the dignity of work as well as the dignity of the individual. Employees, even in our modern era of eroding employee loyalty, will still respond favorably to a management that demonstrates sincere concern for their welfare.

Performance appraisal periodic supervisory evaluation of an employee's job performance. Process should include discussion of areas in need of improvement, as well as praise for improvements made. Goal setting, sincere compliments on work well done, and genuine supervisory interest in the employee's comments or complaints, are all essential elements of the performance appraisal.

Piecework rates method of compensating workers based on number of items or parts produced per given time period. Consideration is made for accuracy, complexity, and other factors involved in the production of individual units.

Protected concerted activity Section 9(a) of the National Labor Relations Act that provides that any employee or group of employees has the right to present grievances to the employer whether or not that employee is represented by a labor union.

Reengineering procedure whereby a company reorganizes its work process to more effectively create its product or service for the customer. Reengineering often eliminates layers of jobs.

Representation election election by eligible employees of a company to determine whether a particular labor union will represent the employees of the company, department, or unit involved. The election is conducted by the National Labor Relations Board by secret ballot. A simple majority of those voting determines the winner of the election.

Restructuring process of reorganizing businesses and/or getting rid of unnecessary operations.

Rightsizing eliminating or scaling back unnecessary or outdated jobs to achieve more efficient operations.

Sarbanes-Oxley Act of 2002 act that establishes sweeping reforms to corporate governance law, including guidelines on disclosure obligations, security, and accounting reforms. The law specifically protects employees when they take lawful acts to disclose information or otherwise assist criminal investigators and other authorized parties in a judicial proceeding in detecting and stopping fraud. Act was passed following a number of corporate governance scandals of major U.S. companies.

Search engine electronic Internet information searching device that allows the user to access predetermined multiple networks or categories of information or data, without having to enter individual addresses or locations for each specific item of information desired. Examples of well-known search engines include Google, Yahoo, and Bing.

Sexual harassment "unwelcome sexual advances, requests for sexual favors, and other verbal or physical conduct of a sexual nature constitute sexual harassment when (1) submission to such conduct is made either explicitly or implicitly a term or condition of an individual's employment, (2) submission to or rejection of such conduct by an individual is used as the basis for employment decisions affecting such individual, or (3) such conduct has the purpose or effect of unreasonably interfering with an indi-vidual's work performance or creating an intimidating, hostile, or offensive working environment." (U.S. Equal Employment Opportunity Commission)

SHRM (Society for Human Resource Management) leading association and voice of the human resources profession; offers its 250,000 plus members in over 140 countries information and education services, conferences and seminars, government and media representation, and publications to support the advancement of human resources professionals as leaders within their own organizations.

Substance abuse testing drug testing by employers, the major areas of which include: employment testing of newly-hired job applicants, post-accident testing of employees following industrial accidents, probable-cause testing of employees, based on reasonable suspicion of impaired performance, random testing, which refers to a company policy of unscheduled, unannounced random drug testing of employees within the organization and safety-sensitive position testing of employees in selected high-risk occupations such as vehicle drivers and equipment operators.

Taft-Hartley Law (Labor Management Relations Act, 1947) law passed as a balance to the 1935 National Labor Relations Act giving employees the legal right to join a labor organization, Taft-Hartley essentially gave employees the legal right to not join a union.

Teaming process of organizing teams of employees at all levels of an organization to discuss and make decisions or effective recommendations about how work operations should be organized or structured, work assignments for team members, and other operational matters or problems. Teaming objectives are based on the premise of greater work efficiency.

Telecommuting a relatively new trend in the work force in which workers virtually (virtual office) take their offices (a laptop or desk computer) with them while working at home, at a company store or field location, on the road, at a customer location, or a combination of these. The virtual office then, by definition, is "wherever the worker happens to be performing work for the organization."

Total Quality Management (TQM) attempt by employee teams to find ways of improving their own productivity and the quality of their product or service.

Unemployment insurance laws laws governed and controlled by individual state laws, designed to provide temporary income protection for those workers who find themselves out of work through no fault of their own. Unemployment insurance is paid for by the individual employer to the respective state, based on volume of unemployment claims payments made by the state on behalf of a particular employer.

Uniform Guidelines on Employee Selection Procedures (UGESP) was adopted in 1978 by the EEOC and a group of other federal agencies to meet the need for clarification of federal agency guidelines on employee selection procedures. The guidelines incorporate a single set of principles designed to assist employers, labor organizations, employment agencies, and licensing and certification boards to comply with federal law prohibiting employment discrimination practices.

Uniformed Services Employment and Reemployment Rights Act, 1994 (USERRA) is intended to ensure that persons who serve or who have served in the Armed Forces, Reserves, National Guard, or other "uniformed services" (1) are not disadvantaged in their civilian careers because of their service; (2) are promptly reemployed in their civilian jobs upon their return from duty; and (3) are not discriminated against in employment based on past, present, or future military service.

Validations statistical programs used by employers and outside professional groups designed to serve as reliable predictors of successful job performance. Validation methods are commonly used in determining the value as well as legality of employment tests used in industry.

Vendor management systems and e-procurement the procurement and automation of services, including recruitment, management, and administrative processing of contingent or temporary workers. Such vendor management systems are designed for companies to work with contingent work force suppliers to gear up or gear down worker volume as operational needs change, acquire special talent for one-time projects, and shorten work cycles, thereby reducing the cost of recruiting, screening, and training.

Vesting process whereby an employee is required to remain with a given employer a specific amount of time in order to be eligible to share partially or totally in company contributions to an employee pension, profit-sharing or retirement-savings plan.

Wage and Hour Law (Fair Labor Standards Act) 1938 law (as amended) that is the principal federal law relating to overall employee compensation, including minimum wage, overtime pay requirements, and child labor; the keystone of employee compensation.

Wage surveys tool used by compensation analysts to determine wage and salary rates and ranges offered by other companies in a geographic area. Survey methods include letters, phone calls, and personal visits to companies, local chambers of commerce, libraries, and local businesspeople and merchants' associations.

Wagner Act (National Labor Relations Act, 1935) legislation that essentially gave employees the legal right to join a labor organization of their choice. The law also established the National Labor Relations Board to coordinate and administer the provisions of this first major piece of labor legislation.

WARN (Worker Adjustment and Retraining Notification Act, 1988) law that in general requires employers of 100 or more employees to provide at least 60 days' written advance notice of layoffs and plant closures to affected employees, their union representatives, and local government officials. If employer does not give required notice, it may be held liable for all back pay and benefits for the 60-day notice period.

Web browser a software program used to research a wide variety of Internet resources and to explore the World Wide Web (WWW).

Webmaster individual or function designated by a company or organization to handle the coordination, management, marketing, and all other aspects—technical and nontechnical—of the Internet.

Workers' compensation insurance insurance that covers any injury or illness requiring medical attention that is incurred by an employee, out of or in the course of his or her employment, making the employer generally immune from damage suits arising out of occupational injuries. Every employer is required to carry this insurance for all company employees. Four states (North Dakota, Ohio, Washington State, and Wyoming), together with the U.S. Virgin Islands and Puerto Rico, have their own state-funded workers' compensation programs to which employers must contribute.

WWW (World Wide Web) graphical and interactive area of the Internet; the whole gamut of resources that can be accessed using the various related computer tools provided to the Internet user.

401(k) plans savings plans based upon Section 401(k) of the Internal Revenue Code, which allows eligible employees to contribute a percentage of their salary on a tax-deferred basis into a company-administered investment plan.

Bibliography

Armstrong, Sharon, and Mitchell, Barbara. *The Essential HR Handbook—A Quick and Handy Resource for Any Manager or HR Professional.* Pompton Plains, NJ: Career Press, 2008.

Bardwick, Judith M. *One Foot Out the Door: How to Combat the Psychological Recession That's Alienating Employees and Hurting American Business.* New York: AMACOM, 2008.

Bogardus, Anne M. *PHR/SPHR Professional in Human Resources Certification Study Guide.* 3rd Edition. Hoboken, NJ: Sybex, a division of John Wiley and Sons, Inc., 2009.

Coens, Tom, and Jenkins, Mary. *Abolishing Performance Appraisals: Why They Backfire and What to Do Instead.* San Francisco: Berrett-Kohler Publishers, 2002.

Coffman, Curt, and Gonzalez-Molena, Gabriel. *Follow This Path: How the World's Greatest Organizations Drive Growth by Unleashing Human Potential.* New York: Warner Books, 2002.

Dessler, Gary. *Human Resource Management.* 11th Edition. Englewood Cliffs, NJ: Prentice Hall, 2007.

Fitz-Enz, Jac. *The 8 Practices of Exceptional Companies.* New York: AMACOM, 1997.

___. *How to Measure Human Resource Management.* New York: AMACOM, 2000.

___. *The ROI of Human Capital: Measuring the Economic Value of Employee Performance.* New York: AMACOM, 2000.

Guerin, Lisa, and Delpo, Amy. *Dealing with Problem Employees: A Legal Guide.* 3rd Edition. Berkeley, CA: NOLO, 2007.

Heskett, James L., Sasser, W. Earl, and Schlesinger, Leonard A. *The Value Profit Chain: Treat Employees Like Customers and Customers Like Employees.* Burlington, VT: Burlington Free Press, 2002.

Huselid, Mark A., et al. *The HR Scorecard: Linking People, Strategy, and Performance.* Boston: Harvard Business School Publishing, 2001.

Johnson, Larry, and Phillips, Bob. *Absolute Honesty: Building a Corporate Culture That Values Straight Talk and Rewards Integrity.* New York: AMACOM, 2008.

Mathis, Robert L., and Jackson, John H. *Human Resource Management: Essential Perspectives.* 12th Edition. Mason, OH: Thompson South-Western, 2008.

McKenzie, J. Steven, and Traynor, William J. *Opportunities in Human Resource Management Careers.* Lincolnwood, IL: NTC Publishing Group, 1994.

Messmer, Max. *Human Resources Kit for Dummies.* 2nd Edition. Publisher for Dummies: BK&CD Rom Edition. Hoboken, NJ: John Wiley and Sons, Inc., 1999.

Noe, Raymond A., Gerhart, Barry, Wright, Patrick, and Hollenbeck, John R. *Foundations of Human Resource Management.* 3rd Edition. New York: McGraw-Hill Higher Education, 2008.

Piskurich, George M., Editor. *The AMA Handbook of E-Learning: Effective Design, Implementation and Technology Solutions.* New York: AMACOM, 2003.

Reichheld, Frederick F., and Teal, Thomas. *The Loyalty Effect: The Hidden Force Behind Growth, Profit, and Lasting Value.* Boston: Harvard Business School Publishing, 2001.

Sartain, Libby, and Finney, Martha J. *HR from the Heart: Inspiring Stories and Strategies for Building the People Side of Great Business.* New York: AMACOM, 2003.

Smith, Shawn, and Mazin, Rebecca. *The HR Answer Book: An Indispensable Guide for Managers and Human Resources Professionals.* (In question and answer format.) New York: AMACOM, 2004.

Thomas Jr., R. Roosevelt. *Building on the Promise of Diversity: How We Can Move to the Next Level in Our Workplaces, Our Communities, and Our Society.* New York: AMACOM/AMA, 2005.

Tyson, Shaun. *Essentials of Human Resource Management.* 5th Edition. Oxford, UK: Butterworth-Heinemann, Elsevier, Ltd, 2006.

INDEX